A Literary *Shema*

A Literary *Shema*

Annie Dillard's Judeo-Christian Vision and Voice

Lori A. Kanitz

☙PICKWICK *Publications* • Eugene, Oregon

A LITERARY *SHEMA*
Annie Dillard's Judeo-Christian Vision and Voice

Copyright © 2020 Lori A. Kanitz. All rights reserved. Except for brief quotations in critical publications or reviews, no part of this book may be reproduced in any manner without prior written permission from the publisher. Write: Permissions, Wipf and Stock Publishers, 199 W. 8th Ave., Suite 3, Eugene, OR 97401.

Pickwick Publications
An Imprint of Wipf and Stock Publishers
199 W. 8th Ave., Suite 3
Eugene, OR 97401

www.wipfandstock.com

PAPERBACK ISBN: 978-1-5326-4203-6
HARDCOVER ISBN: 978-1-5326-4204-3
EBOOK ISBN: 978-1-5326-4205-0

Cataloguing-in-Publication data:

Names: Kanitz, Lori A., author.

Title: A literary *Shema* : Annie Dillard's Judeo-Christian vision and voice / by Lori A. Kanitz.

Description: Eugene, OR : Pickwick Publications, 2020 | Includes bibliographical references and index.

Identifiers: ISBN 978-1-5326-4203-6 (paperback) | ISBN 978-1-5326-4204-3 (hardcover) | ISBN 978-1-5326-4205-0 (ebook)

Subjects: LCSH: Dillard, Annie. | Mysticism—Judaism. | Mysticism—Christianity.

Classification: BV5083 .K35 2020 (print) | BV5083 .K35 (ebook)

I would like to thank the Wesleyan University Press for permission to reprint excerpts from "Feast Days," "The Man Who Wishes to Feed on Mahogany," "The Shape of the Air," "Christmas," and "Tickets for a Prayer Wheel," found in *Tickets for a Prayer Wheel*.

I would also like to thank Peter Lang for permission to republish material in chapters 4 and 6 that originally appeared in "Suspended Endings, Theodicean Spaces, and Annie Dillard's Asyndetic Style," in *Last Things: Essays on Ends and Endings* (2015).

Manufactured in the U.S.A.   02/05/20

For Richard

Contents

Preface | ix
Acknowledgments | xv
Abbreviations for Works by Annie Dillard | xvi

CHAPTER 1: Annie Dillard and Jewish Mysticism: A Brief Overview | 1

CHAPTER 2: "Each Day Splintered Down": Hasidic Pansacramentalism and Dillard's Mystical Descents | 27

CHAPTER 3: The Emptying God: Kabbalah, Creation, and Kenosis | 64

CHAPTER 4: *Tsimtsum*, Theodicean Spaces, and Annie Dillard's Asyndetic Style | 84

CHAPTER 5: "It Could Be That We Are Not Seeing Something": Affective Absences and Asyndeton | 114

CHAPTER 6: *Tikkun*: Redemption, Memory, and Mysticism Turned *Ethos* | 138

Conclusion | 179

Bibliography | 183
Index | 191

Preface

I FIRST BECAME ACQUAINTED with Annie Dillard's work decades ago when friends gave me a copy of *Pilgrim at Tinker Creek* as a gift. I did not make it past page eight's description of a frog instantly necrotized by a predator's poison. At the time, I was reeling from my own life's "waste of pain"[1] experienced in several unexpected losses and could not stomach such a close, unflinching gaze at more. Consequently, no one was more surprised than I was when years later I heard myself volunteering to my PhD supervisors Dillard's work as a possible dissertation topic. If it is possible to bear texts grudges, I did so for *Pilgrim*. Dillard's brilliance was undeniable, but something in the tenor of her work seemed to levitate, always suspended between irreconcilable and perhaps unanswerable questions, and I had wanted it to land *somewhere*. Though I could not articulate it as such then, I intuited its suspension of an eschatological end and found the absence dislocating. I have since come to believe this is exactly where the theological power of Dillard's work lies and, moreover, it eventually pointed me to one of her lifelong interests, Jewish mysticism, in which there is no messianic *denouement*, only fervent watchfulness and waiting.

    Still, I hesitated to take it up. Yet, in art as in life, the most challenging subjects often prove to be the most fruitful. As I spent time with her work, Dillard's exquisite language and spiritual moxie began to raise intriguing intellectual and theological questions for me. So, I took up the challenge and made her work mine. I completed the obligatory reading of secondary literature and yet felt something was still missing. I went back to the primary sources, starting again with *Pilgrim at Tinker Creek*. One afternoon, re-reading "The Waters of Separation" in which her apostrophic complaint to God for life's cruelties becomes her own heave offering before the altar, the penny, as they

---

1. PTC, 9.

say, dropped. I had been overlooking the manifold references to Hebrew scripture and Jewish mysticism informing her reasoning about suffering and evil. Then began some old-fashioned counting. Page by page, I re-read every one of her books, listing every allusion to or quotation from Jewish mysticism and the Hebrew scriptures. They filled several notebooks.

Dillard's fascination with Jewish mysticism spans her entire career. In her final, book-length work of literary non-fiction, *For the Time Being* (1999), she openly acknowledges her enduring interest, stating "For twenty-five years, with increasing admiration, I have studied [Isaac Luria and the Baal Shem Tov]: the gloomy Luria because he influenced the exuberant Baal Shem Tov, and the Baal Shem Tov because he and his followers knew God, and a thing or two besides."[2] Her inaugural books, *Pilgrim at Tinker Creek* and *Tickets for a Prayer Wheel* include scores of references. Near the end of *For the Time Being*, Dillard states outright its indebtedness to Hasidism: "It is the Baal Shem Tov [the founder of eighteenth-century Hasidism] . . . who thought most of the best of these thoughts."[3] Yet, nearly all the scholarly literature about Dillard that takes up theological questions reads her work through the lens of Christianity or Christian mysticism alone.

The absence of any investigation into her knowledge of Jewish mystical writers, and, indeed, the absence of any thorough examination of the role of Hebrew scripture in her work, leaves much fertile scholarly ground to be explored. Attention to this aspect of Dillard's work is crucial to avoid a partial, perhaps even inaccurate understanding of her work. In view of this gap in the existing scholarship on Dillard, this book explores ways in which her work has been shaped by Jewish mysticism. At the heart of this analysis is the assertion that Dillard's work cannot be properly understood without examining ways in which she is a *Judeo*-Christian, not merely a Christian, thinker and writer.

Further, it should be emphasized that this analysis is critical not biographical. Its central concern is Dillard's texts, not Dillard's life or extra-literary experiences of God. It seeks to argue for and explain a Judeo-Christian theological and critical framework and the insights such a critical approach can afford. Whether Dillard is or is not a mystic, did or did not experience ecstatic visions or theophanies, and was or is not any longer a Christian, is impossible to prove from the art objects she has meticulously crafted to speak of those experiences. Dillard is an artist and has candidly acknowledged the grueling process she undertakes to craft her work, and she has admitted to taking poetic license to create dense, highly wrought literary texts. The

2. FTB, 22.
3. FTB, 198.

current argument will seek to build its case about those texts primarily *from* those texts and leave biographical questions about Dillard's extra-literary experiences and religious commitments to the side.

The book will follow a tripartite structure shaped by the arc of the argument's movement through the broad categories of creation, evil, and redemption, which are of central concern throughout Dillard's work. It will do so in order to demonstrate how within these three seminal movements typically used to frame a specifically Christian worldview, her work reveals the shaping influence of her life-long interest in Jewish mystical thought, particularly that of Martin Buber, Isaac Luria, and the Baal Shem Tov.

Chapter 1 will provide a more detailed introduction to Dillard's interest in Jewish mysticism, its presence in her work, and a brief overview of the histories and major concepts in Lurianic Kabbalism and eighteenth-century Hasidism that appear in Dillard's work.

Chapter 2, "Each Day Splintered Down: Hasidic Pansacramentalism and Dillard's Mystical Descents," explores a central feature of Dillard's mysticism, namely its embracing of the physical world through a descent into the chaotic mêlée of sensory experience. Using the motif of mystical "descent," the chapter examines how Dillard fuses Christian sacramentalism with images and texts from Jewish mysticism, particularly Martin Buber's Hasidism, to create a panentheistic, or pansacramental view of God's presence in the world. Although the Neoplatonic tradition with which Dillard is frequently linked includes panentheistic elements, the chapter demonstrates that her vision for the sustaining and irrupting presence of God in creation as well as of ecstatic mystical experiences seems far more closely allied with a robust and earthy Hasidic pansacramentalism than with the cool, disembodied Plotinian ascent of the alone to the Alone.

Chapter 3, "The Emptying God: Kabbalah, Creation, and Kenosis," argues that Dillard's artistic and theological witness to God's pansacramental presence leads immediately to questions about the fallenness of creation and evil that arise when one presupposes the classical Western notions of God's omniscience and omnipotence. The chapter explores Dillard's explicit and implicit challenges of those assumptions through her literary synthesis of the Kabbalistic notions of *tsimtsum* and *shevirat ha-kelim* with Christian kenotic theology to create within her literary cosmos a God who elects to be self-limiting.

Chapter 4, "*Tsimtsum*, Theodicean Spaces, and Annie Dillard's Asyndetic Style," then takes up Dillard's consideration of the problem of evil and explores how the kenotic imagery and theology of the Jewish mystical traditions, particularly the concept of *tsimtsum*, allows Dillard to explore questions about evil and suffering within the tension of literary and "theodicean spaces" created by Dillard's refusal to reconcile seemingly contradictory fiduciary claims, arising from discrepancies between existential facts and spiritual truths. The chapter also examines the role of what will be referred to as Dillard's asyndetic style, in both reflecting and creating deliberately unsettling textual gaps and ellipses that locate readers within the silence of theodicean spaces.

Chapter 5, "It Could Be that We Are Not Seeing Something: Affective Absences and Asyndeton," begins the arc of the book's movement toward redemption by taking up the idea that gaps and absences within Dillard's work are not merely theodicean spaces created by the room God concedes to evil within creation but also may be affective absences—white spaces or silences, like the Torahnic white spaces described in Rabbi Levi Isaac of Berditchev's "Tale of the Hidden Teachings." Existing within both literary and lived narratives, these affective absences in Dillard's work define the contours of created things (including the intellectual and physical shape of her own literary artifacts), and they function, paradoxically as fecund, plurivocal silences from within which emerge mystery and meaning.

The sixth and final chapter, "*Tikkun*: Redemption, Memory, and Mysticism Turned *Ethos*," aims to bring the theological arc of creation, evil, and redemption full circle, and in so doing examine Dillard's adoption of the stance and apostrophic voice of a poet-prophet in her literary works' calls to attentiveness, remembrance, and redemptive action. The first section of the chapter will argue that Dillard adopts what Martin Buber, in his essay "Prophecy, Apocalyptic, and the Historical Hour," identifies as a prophetic rather than apocalyptic stance toward the present hour. The chapter's second and third sections will argue that in keeping with a prophetic stance, Dillard's texts quite literally eclipse through textual silence the apocalyptic ending of the Christian gospel story, namely Christ's resurrection and return, and adopt what Buber defines as the prophetic attitude toward the historical hour in which the future can "establish itself ever anew."[4] It will also examine another distinctive feature of Dillard's literary voice, namely the frequency with which she shifts into an apostrophic voice and confronts the reader through second-person direct address. This section will suggest that Dillard's apostrophic voice allows her to create a literary equivalent of the "*Shema*, Israel" and precipitate in readers a potentially ethical and redemptive theological experience. In so doing, it will be argued that Dillard's work is profoundly ethical, yet its ethics are predicated not upon ideology but upon memory and that this is a distinctively Hebraic feature of her work.

4. Buber, *On the Bible*, 173.

Thus, in Dillard's work, as in Hasidism, "mysticism has become *ethos*,"[5] and by converting memory into the metaphors of art, she urges readers through her prophetic voice to imagine "what it is to be someone else."[6]

5. Buber, *Origin and Meaning*, 198–99.
6. Ozick, *Metaphor and Memory*, 279.

Acknowledgments

THIS BOOK BEGAN AS a doctoral thesis at the School of Divinity, St. Mary's College, at the University of St. Andrews in Scotland. I wish to thank once again my PhD supervisors, Gavin Hopps and Trevor Hart, for their support, wise counsel, and encouragement throughout the project. I also owe a huge debt of thanks to the friends whose generosity took many forms. Thank you especially to Denise Young, Toby and Carol Foster, Barbara and Terry Law, Lenore and Ken Mullican, Kellen and Fleta Buckles, Helen Vera, Tom Mohn, and the O'Connor and Payne families. I also wish to acknowledge the generous financial support provided by Oral Roberts University. My former colleagues and dear friends there worked scheduling and budgeting heroics to allow me to complete the doctorate while working full-time. Thank you. I am also grateful to friends and colleagues at Baylor University who encouraged me to turn the project into a book.

Finally, thank you to my parents, sister, and her family for their patience, love, and support. They bore without grumbling shortened or cancelled family visits, two trans-Atlantic moves in eleven months, and the general demands of this project on my time. I dedicate this book to my step-father Richard Lusk. From its beginning, he committed to seeing me through to its completion. Though he never had a day of college education himself, he understood what the project meant and wanted to be a part of it. He did not live to see its completion, but I could not have done it without him.

Abbreviations for Works by Annie Dillard

AAC   *An American Childhood*

FTB   *For the Time Being*

HTF   *Holy the Firm*

LBF   *Living by Fiction*

PTC   *Pilgrim at Tinker Creek*

TST   *Teaching a Stone to Talk*

TPW   *Tickets for a Prayer Wheel*

TWL   *The Writing Life*

CHAPTER 1

Annie Dillard and Jewish Mysticism

A Brief Overview

> "I quit the Catholic Church and Christianity;
> I stay near Christianity and Hasidism."
>
> —ANNIE DILLARD, "OFFICIAL WEBSITE"

Introduction

IN THE VAULTS OF Yale University's Beinecke Library are seventy-eight boxes that hold the *Annie Dillard Papers*, a vast collection, dating from 1955 to 2012, including everything from the note cards Dillard used to write the Pulitzer Prize-winning *Pilgrim at Tinker Creek* to a torn scrap of newspaper on which Dillard has written a phone number, no doubt long since disconnected. Her earliest research journals contain page after page of handwritten notes on Jewish mysticism, Hasidic theology, and Martin Buber's works, including *The Tales of the Hasidim, Between Man and Man, I and Thou,* and *The Origin and Meaning of Hasidism.* Interspersed between definitions of "mitzvot" and research on insects are long quotations from the books of the Hebrew prophets. A marginal note reveals she was reading through the "Old Testament" systematically while doing the research that eventually made its way into *Pilgrim at Tinker Creek.* In the very first of her writing journals, "Book 1—Summer 1970," one finds in Dillard's quick and legible hand, "Been reading theology. Like this fellow Buber. Just read The Dialogue w/ God [sic], a little essay. Marked it all up. Like the way he talks about God." Dillard would return decades later to this same journal and remark in the margin, "Look at that. / (decades later) / (over 30 yrs) . . . I keep finding *Time Being* in here / maybe its [sic] *all* in here."[1]

Indeed, her reading log from two decades later, labeled "Books '95–'02," provides a window into the research that informed *For the Time Being*. Several of Buber's works, such as both volumes of *Tales of the Hasidim* appear, with Dillard's parenthetical note "(again)." One also finds listed Abraham Heschel, Elie Wiesel, Moshe Idel, Gershom Scholem, Lawrence Kushner among many other Jewish authors, as well as studies on Hasidic prayer and Torah commentators. Written in cramped hand below the entry for *Your Word is Fire: Hasidic Masters on Prayer* is Dillard's explanatory note: "I've never listed in here all the zillions of Hasid [sic], etc. books I've read—only the light ones."[2] One can only imagine how long the list might have been had she recorded them all, and one can only regret she did not.

The Dillard papers corroborate the ample evidence from her canon that Dillard's fascination with Jewish mysticism spans her entire career. As noted in the preface, her earliest books contain scores of references to its thinkers and texts, and, in her final book-length work of literary non-fiction,[3] *For the Time Being* (1999), she openly acknowledges her enduring interest, stating "For twenty-five years, with increasing admiration, I have studied [Isaac Luria and the Baal Shem Tov]: the gloomy Luria because he influenced the exuberant Baal Shem Tov, and the Baal Shem Tov because he and his followers knew God, and a thing or two besides."[4] As Dillard herself indicates, Jewish mysticism is not a late-emerging or incidental interest but a pervasive, shaping influence on her thinking and writing that significantly pre-dates 1974, the year her inaugural books, *Pilgrim at Tinker Creek* and *Tickets for a Prayer Wheel*, were published.

A brief overview of the presence of Jewish mystical elements in her work indicates its scope and longevity. Dillard's earliest work of non-fiction, *Pilgrim at Tinker Creek*, reveals that she was even at the outset of her writing career well acquainted with Kabbalistic and Hasidic strains of Jewish mysticism. The book contains nearly twenty references to Martin Buber,

---

1. Dillard, *Annie Dillard Papers*, s.v. "Notebooks/One—Summer 1970."

2. Dillard, *Annie Dillard Papers*, s.v. "Book 43–July 94 to Spring 97." Given that her journals hardly include merely "light" reading on the subject—Moshe Idel's *Hasidism: Between Ecstasy and Magic*, for example—one comes away with a deepened appreciation not only for her intellectual appetite but also for her considerable expertise on the subject.

3. Dillard, *Abundance* was published later, in 2016. However, despite the subtitle, "narrative essays old and new," it includes no new essays. All its selections are from previously published works.

4. FTB, 22.

the Kabbalah, Hasidic tales, and Hasidic doctrine. The framing motif in her most overtly Christian book, *Holy the Firm* (1977), alludes to the Jewish custom of salting newborns spoken of in Ezekiel 16:4 and the covenant of salt between God and Israel described in Leviticus 2:13. Old Testament texts such as Isaiah, the Psalms, and Proverbs also appear, as do concepts from Jewish mysticism, such as *tsimtsum* and *shevirat ha-kelim*. Over half of the essays in *Teaching a Stone to Talk* (1982) contain allusions to Hasidic tales, doctrines, and motifs as well as to Hebrew scriptures.

Moreover, *For the Time Being*, devotes significant and lengthy sections to the Jewish mystic and founder of Hasidism, the Baal Shem Tov, as well as to Jewish rabbis, artists, philosophers, and scholars. Dillard invokes the Talmud, Midrash, Mishnah, and the *Zohar*. She quotes rabbis Isaac Luria, the Baal Shem Tov, Tarfon, Akiva, Pinhas, Dov Baer the Great Maggid, Yehudah Hechasid, Nathan of Nemirov, Nachman of Bratslav, Judah Halevy, Menahem Mendel, Yehuda Aryeh, Menachem Nahum of Chernobyl, Abraham Halevi, Abraham Heschel, Aryeh Kaplan, Lawrence Kushner, as well as Jesus and unnamed rabbis of first, eighteenth, nineteenth, and twentieth centuries. She quotes Maimonides, Martin Buber, Gershom Scholem, and Jewish anthropologist and philosopher Ernest Becker. Her allusions and quotations of Jewish artists or students of the Hasids reveals the vastness of her reading; they range from the Hebrews "of the fifth century BCE who wrote out the stories of Moses, of Abraham, and even of Noah"[5] to Nelly Sachs, Meir Shalev, Israel Joshua [I. J.] Singer, Cynthia Ozick, Edmund Fleg, Marc Chagall, Robert Eisenberg, Lis Harris (author of *Holy Days: The World of a Hasidic Family*) and Joel Goldsmith. The book specifically names as well as repeatedly alludes to the Hasidic and Kabbalistic concepts of *shevirat ha-kelim*, *devekuth*, and *tikkun*. Futhermore, although allusions to the New Testament appear, most point to the Hebrew scriptures. In *For the Time Being* alone, Dillard quotes from or alludes to Genesis, Exodus, Leviticus, Judges, Ezekiel, Isaiah, Zechariah, Nehemiah, Psalms, Jeremiah, and Ezra.[6] Further, the landscape of ancient Palestine and modern Israel feature prominently in many of the narrative sections, with settings ranging from ancient and modern Safed, Bethlehem, and Nazareth, to the Sea of Galilee, the Judean desert, Mt. Tabor, and the Jordan River, places where Jews, Christians, and

---

5. FTB, 60.

6. From the Hebrew Bible alone, one can find in Dillard's work explicit references to at least sixteen significant historical figures and nine books. The list of individuals includes Aaron, Abraham, Amos, David, Elijah, Elisha, Ezekiel, Ezra, Isaiah, Jacob, Jeremiah, Job, Joel, Moses, Nehemiah, and Zechariah. The list of books includes Amos, Ezekiel, Ezra, Isaiah, Jeremiah, Job, Joel, Psalms, and Zechariah. It is worth noting that references to Ezekiel appear most frequently.

Annie Dillard, believe eternity intersected time irrupting in sea, clay, sand, rock, and the human flesh of Jesus Christ.

In addition, the names of individuals whether real or fictitious found in many of the narrative threads in *For the Time Being* are Jewish, such as the obstetric nurse Pat Eisberg, and a missing Lubavitcher Hasid girl, Suri Feldman. Most significantly, in the book's final sections when Dillard wrestles with the ethical dimensions of suffering, she quotes or paraphrases almost exclusively Jewish thinkers: Edmund Fleg, Lawrence Kushner, Aryeh Kaplan, the Baal Shem Tov, Abraham Joshua Heschel, Martin Buber, and Rabbi Tarfon.

Admittedly, Dillard's non-fiction reflects her vast reading within many religious and intellectual traditions—Buddhism, Islam, Judaism, Christianity, Transcendentalism, and Romanticism—to name but a few. Dillard has even described herself as "spiritually promiscuous,"[7] and, clearly, she blends the symbolism and narratives of various religious and philosophical systems to suit her artistic and theological purposes. Within a single sentence one may find a phrase from the Hebrew prophets, an allusion to Eskimo myth and an Emersonian quotation. To complicate matters further, multiple connections exist historically, geographically, intellectually, and theologically between the bodies of thought and religious traditions she favors. Jesuit priest Pierre Teilhard de Chardin's pansacramental concept of the "Mass of the world," for example, has rich resonances with Buber's Hasidic pansacramentalism, and Dillard draws extensively from each. Likewise, the influence of Neoplatonism can be found both in nineteenth-century American Transcendentalism and process theology, each of which Dillard has studied and from which she borrows. Consequently, making any claim about Dillard's work proves challenging simply because of the constant temptation to add endless qualifiers and book-length footnotes to trace threads of thought back through the ages. B. Jill Carroll, in *The Savage Side: Reclaiming Violent Models of God*, articulates well the complexity of Dillard's writing and the difficulty of trying to categorize either her body of work or the external influences shaping it:

> Dillard's philosophical or theological method may appear differently at various moments in her work. Some passages may ring more Heraclitian than Emersonian, more Whiteheadian than Platonic; . . . The fact is that *all* these are present in her work to the extent that their perspective supports her endeavor to read the raw, natural world as a text and determine what, if anything, can be said about deity, or the powers that "brood and

---

7. Smith, *Annie Dillard*, 15.

light" in the universe, powers over which people have little or no control.[8]

Despite the complexity, two elements appear both central to and persistent throughout her work. The first is Dillard's life-long interest in Christianity. In a 1978 interview with Phillip Yancey, she explains that she has considered herself a Christian since her teens, with only a brief lapse in her senior year of high school, a "rebellion [that] lasted a month."[9] In a 1981 interview with Karla Hammond, Dillard states: "I am a Presbyterian. . . . I am comfortable in any of the Christian Churches."[10] In the late 1980s she quietly converted to Catholicism. As she explains to Colleen Smith, "My conversion was no big deal. . . . I just said, 'You know, I'd like to join this Church.' I didn't know if they'd take me; I'd been married and divorced twice. . . . I've always liked lining up with Catholics; they're a motley crew."[11] In a 1999 interview, Maureen Abood notes Dillard's ecumenical approach to God in her books and asks, "And yet you remain a Christian, a Catholic," to which Dillard replies, "That's right."[12] Most recently, she has stated, "I quit the Catholic Church and Christianity; I stay near Christianity and Hasidism."[13]

The second persistent feature, as the brief overview above indicates, is Dillard's long-standing interest in Jewish mysticism. The consistency and longevity of Dillard's interest in the subject seems to suggest that it is one of the chief literary and spiritual instruments with which she explores "the rim of knowledge where language falters; . . . all those areas of human experience, feeling, and thought about which we care so much and know so little."[14] It is not merely one among many of the religious traditions she periodically mines to suit her artistic purposes. Nor are its mystical traditions subsumed by Christianity and its mystical traditions. The Hebrew scriptures and Jewish mysticism shape her Christian understanding of creation, evil, and redemption and contribute to her work's distinctive prophetic voice. She is a *Judeo*-Christian thinker and writer.

Curiously, in spite of the overwhelming evidence of Jewish thought and mysticism in Dillard's work, and its growing rather than diminishing presence over the course of her career, only glancing references to this dimension of her writing appear in reviews and academic studies of her work. Two early

8. Carroll, *Savage Side*, 13.
9. Yancey, "Face Aflame," 14.
10. Hammond, "Drawing the Curtains," 35.
11. Smith, "Annie Dillard," 11.
12. Abood, "Natural Wonders," 31.
13. Dillard, "Official Website."
14. LBF, 170.

reviews of *Pilgrim at Tinker Creek* mention a connection to Martin Buber. Lawrence Cunningham's 1975 review, "Revisiting Tinker Creek" notes that the book embodies what Rabbi Abraham Heschel calls "'radical amazement'; i.e., that vivid awareness of the newness and freshness of creation," and he observes that portions of Dillard's book are reminiscent of Martin Buber's 1957 afterword to *I and Thou*.[15] Yet his comments overlook the fact that both Heschel and Buber as well as Buber's Hasidic tales are actually quoted in the book and are formative influences on Dillard's understanding of the presence of God in creation. Letha Dawn Scanzoni's January 1983 review of *Teaching a Stone to Talk* (1982) begins by quoting Buber's explanation of the dialogical relationship between humans and nature from *I and Thou*, but the review stops short of making any connection between Buber's thought and Dillard's, in spite of the fact that Dillard had been reading Buber for over a decade by then.[16] Some critics note the presence in Dillard's work of the Hebrew scriptures or Jewish mysticism but see them as contingent or as merely one discourse among many, overlooking her diligent study of them as well as their pervasive and shaping influence.[17] Strangely, although Dillard states outright in *For the Time Being* "It is the Baal Shem Tov . . . who thought most of the best of [the book's] thoughts," publicity materials and reviews scarcely mention the presence of Jewish thought, let alone Jewish mysticism.[18] Farrell in "Annie Dillard Demands We Look Life in the Eye" twice quotes Martin Buber, drawing analogies between his ideas and hers in *For the Time Being* without mentioning Dillard's more general indebtedness to Buber's philosophy and works on Hasidism.[19] Feldman, in "If I Could Tell You," remarks that "in many ways, Dillard's book reminds me of Torah study" but does not note the remarkable number of references *to* the Torah in the book.[20] The authors of the four scholarly books on Dillard—Linda Smith, Sandra Humble Johnson, Sue Yore,[21] and Colleen Warren—make passing mention

15. Cunningham, "Revisiting Tinker Creek," 768.

16. Scanzoni, "Review," 23.

17. See, for example, McFadden-Gerber, "I in Nature," 3–5; Elshtain, "Review," 541; Kelleher, "In the Face of Brutality," 58; Rosenthal, "God's Eye View," 28–30; Heffern, "Real Miracle," 37–40; Lavery, "Noticer," 255–270; Goldman, "Sacrifices to the Hidden God," 195–213.

18. FTB, 198.

19. Farrell, "Annie Dillard Demands," 29–31.

20. Feldman, "If I Could Tell You," 34–39.

21. Yore, *Mystic Way*, compares Dillard to Buber but seems to be unaware that Dillard had been reading Martin Buber since 1970 and frequently cites his work. Yore notes that Dillard's description of an encounter with a weasel "is illustrative of Buber's concept of an 'I-Thou' relationship as opposed to an 'I-It,' one that relates to the meeting of two equals rather than an objective gaze that seeks to dominate" (Yore, *Mystic Way*,

of Hasidic or Kabbalistic allusions but focus their analyses elsewhere, and none acknowledge the considerable influence Buber's philosophy and works on Hasidism have had on the corpus of Dillard's poetry and literary nonfiction.[22] The single exception is B. Jill Carroll's superb study, *The Savage Side: Reclaiming Violent Models of God*, which undertakes a rigorous philosophical analysis of Dillard's work in light of Jewish philosopher Emmanuel Levinas. Carroll argues convincingly against what she views an erroneous turn in contemporary theological and philosophical discussions about God and nature, namely their domestication of both. Yet Carroll's focus on philosophical constructs leaves the evidence within Dillard's texts of Jewish mystical thought still largely unexamined. Other critics disregard entirely the shaping influence of Jewish mysticism and the Hebrew scripture, often misreading her texts as a result.

Broadly speaking, most scholarly work focuses on one of five dimensions of Dillard's work: the presence of Catholic elements; her place within the tradition of American naturalists such as Emerson and Thoreau; her use of scientific theories; the presence of myth and ritual in her approach to nature; its literary techniques, such as narrative collage; and her Christian spirituality, including her interest in Christian mysticism. The scholarly focus on this latter element, to the exclusion of Jewish mysticism, results perhaps from the influence of the author's own claims. In 1975, shortly after the publication of *Pilgrim at Tinker Creek*, Annie Dillard wrote to Eleanor Wymard, "Art is my interest, mysticism my message, Christian mysticism."[23] Dillard has read and obviously been influenced by mystics within the Western Christian tradition. She alludes to, and evidently admires, Plotinus, Pseudo-Dionysius, Meister Eckhart, John of Ruysbroeck, Julian of Norwich, and many others within the Western, largely Neoplatonic Christian mystical tradition. Furthermore, she self-consciously places her own work within its lineage. In the 1999 interview with Maureen Abood, Dillard explains:

> It would be appropriate to say that my writing fits very squarely in the Christian mystical tradition dating from Plotinus. And that's simply a rational category. It's a statement of literary criticism. It's not making any claims that I'm getting revelations right and left and writing them down as fast as I can. It's just saying

---

250). Yore uses Dillard's description to make a point about ways of relating to nature, not to make an observation about the possible influence of Buber on Dillard.

22. This is the genre term Dillard coins to describe works that include *Pilgrim at Tinker Creek, Holy the Firm, Teaching a Stone to Talk,* and *For the Time Being.*

23. Wymard, "New Existential Voice," 496.

there is a long mystical tradition in Christianity, and my work is solidly in it.[24]

However, her literary non-fiction reveals an equally influential and manifest tradition—that of Hebrew scripture and Jewish mysticism, particularly Lurianic Kabbalism and Hasidism. Within the same interview, Dillard acknowledges (nearly thirty years after first researching Jewish mysticism) that she is still fascinated by Hasidic thought, stating, "I find the Hasids particularly rich in insight."[25]

The absence of any investigation into her knowledge of Jewish mystical writers, and, indeed, the absence of any thorough examination of the role of Hebrew scripture in her work, leaves much fertile scholarly ground to be explored. Attention to this aspect of Dillard's work is crucial in order to avoid a superficial, partial, perhaps even inaccurate understanding of her work. In view of this gap in the existing scholarship on Dillard, this book will explore ways in which her writing and spirituality have been shaped by Jewish mysticism.

At the heart of its argument is the assertion that Dillard's work cannot be properly understood without examining ways in which she is a *Judeo-Christian*, not merely a Christian, thinker and writer. The analysis seeks not to overturn Dillard's authorial claims that her work fits squarely within the Neoplatonic Christian mystical tradition but to add to and thereby qualify them. As the following discussion will explain, early Kabbalistic thought borrowed heavily from Neoplatonism's philosophical categories. Consequently, one cannot draw clean lines demarcating where the influence of one tradition stops and another begins in her work. Yet, as the ensuing discussion will maintain, there are features distinctive to Jewish mystical thought, especially Buber's Hasidism, and examining Dillard's work in light of them can be enormously illuminating to features of Dillard's work that are often perplexing or simply overlooked if they are examined solely from Christian perspectives. A Judeo-Christian, rather than solely Christian, analytical approach potentially resolves problems critics have noted, such as her work's failure to bear the hallmarks of Christian mysticism, its seemingly unorthodox view of the existence of evil in creation, as well as the conspicuous absence of textual references to Christ's resurrection to make suffering meaningful, despite her theological preoccupation with the problems of suffering, evil, and death.

In each of these areas her art appeals not only to Christian doctrine but also with surprising frequency to Jewish mysticism and to Hebrew

---

24. Abood, "Natural Wonders," 32.
25. Abood, "Natural Wonders," 31.

scripture for its literary and theological material. To understand the distinctive role of Jewish mysticism in Dillard's thought and work to be explored in chapters that follow, it is necessary at the outset to provide a brief overview of the two streams found most often in her work, Lurianic Kabbalism and eighteenth-century Hasidism.

Historical Overview

The Jewish and Christian mystical traditions do, of course, share many features, in part because they share geographies, histories, and texts. It is perhaps not surprising, therefore, that as with any literary, intellectual, or spiritual movement developing within roughly the same time and place, Jewish and Western Christian (namely, Neoplatonic) mystical traditions occupy common ground. Gershom Scholem openly acknowledges the influences of Neoplatonism, particularly in early Kabbalistic thought.[26] There are, however, important differences which are enormously helpful in explaining anomalies in Dillard's work that emerge when trying to analyze its central concerns from within a Christian framework alone. Of course, any generalization of these vast historical, cultural, and theological movements is unavoidably problematic. The history of Jewish mysticism, like any phenomenon spanning thousands of years, is rich and complicated, made so not only by time and geography but by the interpretive interests and primary sources of the scholars who write about them. As Joseph Dan points out, the history of Kabbalah according to Kabbalists is quite different from the "Kabbalah" explicated by historical scholars. Kabbalists understand it as an ever-evolving and deepening revelation of one truth; there is nothing new, only newly unearthed revelations of a single, eternal Truth formulated within one tradition. It is therefore, in their view, an essentially conservative enterprise.[27] The historical scholar, however, sees distinct differences emerging from Kabbalistic schools (Provence, Girona, Safed, for example), its many personalities (Moses de Leon and

---

26. Scholem explains, "The speculative expositions of kabbalistic [sic] teaching largely depended on the ideas of neoplatonic [sic] and Aristotelian philosophy, as they were known in the Middle Ages, and were couched in the terminology customary to these fields" (Scholem, *On the Kabbalah*, 87).

27. Dan, *Kabbalah*, 5–8. See also Idel, *Hasidism*. He notes that Kabbalists, with the exception of Isaac Luria, weren't particularly concerned with creating "comprehensive systematic consistency" and, therefore, Kabbala's seeming eclecticism is the result, in part, of the manifold philosophical streams from which it drew, "Neoplatonism, hermeticism, Aristotelianism," etc. (Idel, *Hasidism*, 50).

Isaac Luria, to name but a few), and its major epochs (e.g., medieval and sixteenth century), each adding something new.

The same difficulty emerges when generalizing about the history of eighteenth-century European Hasidism. As Moshe Idel notes, while Martin Buber saw eighteenth-century European Hasidism as *"sui generis"* and focused on its phenomenological aspects, Gershom Scholem saw it as a more recent expression of a larger and continuous historical trend. Scholem focused, therefore, on its historical and theological elements.[28] Abraham Heschel, like Buber, felt Hasidism expressed essential Judaism but understood its vitality to inhere in its rich spiritual resources for lived experience rather than in its more esoteric, mystical elements.[29] These scholars' interests, not surprisingly, led them to focus on different bodies of Hasidic literature. While Buber drew mainly from Hasidic legends and tales, which recount the lived experiences of the *tzaddiks* ("righteous ones") and the communities they led, Scholem examined the sermons and theoretical texts produced by Hasidic masters. Heschel drew from both the legends and the more theological forms.[30]

In short, there is no such thing as "the" Kabbalah, or "Hasidism" for that matter, if what one means by these terms are single, homogenous movements or bodies of thought. Within these vast literary and spiritual movements are countless figures, texts, and sub-groups each with its particular outlook. Thus, in generalizing, one risks obscuring important differences, for example, in Kabblistic schools, differences between one Hasidic *tzaddik* and another, or between one scholar of Jewish mysticism and another. Nevertheless, generalizations about the origins and definitions of concepts at the heart of Kabbalistic and Hasidic thought are both possible and necessary for understanding ways they inform Dillard's work. As Scholem points out, one can identify "a common range of symbols and ideas" accepted by adherents as being within the Jewish mystical system, even if its various interpreters disagreed about exactly what those symbols meant.[31] Thus, the following is not an exhaustive account, but one that seeks to explain merely the main features of Kabbalistic and Hasidic thought appearing in Dillard's work, particularly those features that are seemingly at odds with the Christian Neoplatonic mystical tradition. Doing so will require focusing on common denominators found in the work of some of its most notable scholars

---

28. Idel, *Hasidism*, 2–5.
29. Idel, *Hasidism*, 6.
30. Idel, *Hasidism*, 5–6.
31. Scholem, *Kabbalah*, 87.

rather than on those elements about which they disagreed as they sought to explain Jewish mysticism's development.

Kabbalism

Because Kabbalism came to influence not only Judaism at large but Hasidim in particular, an overview must begin with it. First, it is helpful to note that "Kabbalah" simply means "received tradition" in Hebrew.[32] Only in the middle ages did it acquire the connotation of esoteric knowledge received by a select few with which it is often now associated.[33] The Kabbalah in this latter sense emerged around the same time as Christianity and developed what came to be its distinctive motifs and doctrines in the fertile cross currents of Hellenistic, Jewish, and Christian thought. As Scholem maintains, Kabbalism "has its sources in the esoteric and theosophical currents existing among the Jews of Palestine and Egypt in the era which saw the birth of Christianity. These currents are linked with the history of Hellenistic and syncretistic religion at the close of antiquity. Scholars disagree on the measure of the influence exerted by such trends."[34] As the Kabbalistic schools developed, Neoplatonism was without question one of those shaping influences. Scholem notes that the early Kabbalists in Provence "worked in a highly charged religious and cultural environment" that brought them into contact with Neoplatonic "theories of the Logos and the Divine Will, of emanations and of the soul," theories that provided generative symbols and categories for Jewish mysticism.[35] Consequently, some Kabbalistic symbols (e.g., emanations proceeding from the Godhead at creation) no doubt echo those of their Neoplatonic neighbors.[36]

Second, it is important to note that the history of Kabbalistic thought falls roughly into two major periods each with its own fairly consistent range of symbols. The first period dates from the birth of Christianity to Moses Cordovero in sixteenth-century Safed, Palestine. Following this is the Lurianic Kabbalistic period, derived from the philosophical system of Rabbi Isaac Luria Ashkenazi of Safed (1534–1572) and spanning from

---

32. Dan, *Kabbalah*, 5.
33. Dan, *Kabbalah*, 5.
34 Scholem, *Kabbalah*, 8.
35. Scholem, *Kabbalah*, 44.
36. This example also illustrates another important difference between Neoplatonism and Kabbalah. In Kabbalistic thought, the emanations of the *sefirot* occurred within God, whereas Plotinus conceives of them emanating outside God's being. Both Scholem and Bloom note this as a crucial difference. See Scholem, *Kabbalah*, 96–105; Bloom, *Kabbalah and Criticism*, 9.

seventeenth-century Safed to the present.[37] Dillard draws primarily from cosmology of the latter, Lurianic Kabbalism. In addition, two general impulses emerge within Kabbalistic thought, the mystical and the philosophical. The philosophical impulse was "an attempt to give a more or less defined ideational meaning to the symbols" developed within the movement.[38] It is widely acknowledged that this philosophical effort used the terminology of Neoplatonism and Aristotelian philosophy of the Middle Ages. Scholem asserts, "the cosmology of the Kabbalah is borrowed from them and is not at all original."[39] However, what *is* original, argues Scholem, is its binding of heavenly realities to earthly ones, namely the historical experience of the Jews.[40] As a system, it "attempted to penetrate and even to describe the mystery of the world as a reflection of the mysteries of divine life."[41] The images and symbols developed within it were, therefore, "of a very special kind, in which the spiritual experience of the mystics was almost inextricably intertwined with the historical experience of the Jewish people."[42] In short, its theosophical symbols bind two worlds—the spiritual and the physical—in a way that is foreign, Scholem maintains, to other religious mystical traditions. "Small wonder," he concludes, "that [Kabbalah] seems strange to students of Christian mysticism, since it does not fit into the categories of 'mysticism' with which they are familiar."[43]

Scholem is referring, of course, to the prevailing view in Western Christian mysticism that the soul's spiritual ascent toward God does not unite two worlds but separates them. In the Neoplatonic tradition, one leaves behind the material world and its mediating structures, including language, as one moves toward a unitive moment in God. Thus, although Buber and Scholem both acknowledge that one hears echoes of gnosticism in Luria's Neoplatonic cosmology,[44] in Kabbalism's practice, it anchored heaven to earth by uniting its cosmological symbols and myths with lived reality—the history and plight of the Jewish people. Interestingly, Dillard notes this very point in her research journal for *For the Time Being*, "Book 43—July 94 to Spring 97."

37. Scholem, *Kabbalah*, 87.
38. Scholem, *Kabbalah*, 87.
39. Scholem, *Kabbalah*, 87.
40. Scholem, *Kabbalah*, 88.
41. Scholem, *On the Kabbalah*, 1–2.
42. Scholem, *On the Kabbalah*, 2.
43. Scholem, *On the Kabbalah*, 2.
44. Moshe Idel takes issue with Buber and Scholem's assumptions about Kabbalism's underlying gnostic structures, calling it "one of the most cardinal (and in my opinion the most problematic) hypotheses related to Jewish mysticism ever formulated by Jewish scholarship" (Idel, *Hasidism*, 7).

She writes, "In old Judaism, there is no mind—or soul—body split. derived [sic], as did reincarnation, from Greeks."[45] Heschel puts it this way:

> Stirred by a yearning after the unattainable, [the Kabbalists] want to make the distant near, the abstract concrete, to transform the soul into a vessel for the transcendent, to grasp with the senses what is hidden from the mind, to express in symbols what the tongue cannot speak. . . . What our senses perceive is but the jutting edge of what is deeply hidden. Extending over into the invisible, the things of this world stand in a secret contact with that which no eye has ever perceived. Everything certifies to the sublime. . . . *There is no particular that is detached from universal meaning.*[46]

As we shall see in chapter 2, this binding of two worlds rather than separating them, of discovering the universal in the particular, is a significant difference between Jewish and Christian Neoplatonic mysticism that is crucial for understanding Dillard's pansacramentalism and the language of mystical descent she so frequently employs.

Hasidism

The impact of Lurianic Kabbalism can hardly be overstated. It transformed all of Jewish thought and culture "along kabbalistic [sic] lines."[47] The philosophical system of Rabbi Isaac Luria Ashkenazi of Safed became so widely known and accepted that it became "the basis for virtually every school of thought in Judaism from around 1700 until well into the nineteenth century,"[48] including the eighteenth-century Hasidic movement that renewed, and some would say revolutionized, Judaism.

Though the earliest forms of Hasidism emerged in medieval Germany, it was eighteenth-century Hasidism,[49] that transformed eastern European Jewish communities, and ultimately Judaism at large, with startling rapidity.[50] The movement began, legend has it, with Rabbi Israel ben Eliezer of

---

45. Dillard, *Annie Dillard Papers*, s.v. "Book 43–July 94" (183).
46. Heschel, *Mystical Element*, 4–5 (emphasis mine).
47. Dan, *Teachings of Hasidism*, 6.
48. Dan, *Teachings of Hasidism*, 6–7.
49. Gershom Scholem maintains that the Hasidism that emerged later—the "Polish and Ukrainian Hasidism of the eighteenth and nineteenth centuries"—had very little to do with its earlier, medieval forms. See Scholem, *Major Trends*, 324.
50. There are numerous theories about the degree to which it did or did not break with Kabbalism and earlier forms of Hasidism. For an excellent overview of this and

Mezbizh, known as the Baal Shem Tov (or Besht), "Master of the Good Name."[51] Few autobiographical details of his life are certain: "Controversies, confusion of places and dates, paradoxes, the Baal Shem's legend abounds with them," explains Elie Wiesel.[52] It is generally accepted that he was born around 1700 in a small village, Okop, in present day Poland. He died in 1760.[53] Marked by a peculiar intimacy with God from a young age, the Besht did not begin his public ministry until 1736 at the age of thirty-six. Poor, itinerant, and unlearned but possessed of a contagious and fiery joy, he left no one he encountered unchanged. Wiesel remembers his Hasidic grandfather telling him, "'In the Besht's universe, no one felt left out.'"[54] Drawn particularly to the outcast and dejected, the Besht perceived the divine spark even in the local thieves and town drunks and thus showed them mercy.[55] "To pull another out of the mud, man must step into the mud himself," he said.[56] He was not afraid to get his hands dirty, literally or metaphorically. He and his wife mined the Carpathian Mountains by hand, "selling lime in the villages."[57] His legendary capacity to bring heaven to earth, or more accurately, to reveal God's presence *in* earth, became the hallmark of this new movement.

If, according to Scholem, the distinguishing feature of Kabbalism is the "interweaving of two realms [heaven and earth], which in most other religious mysticism have remained separate,"[58] Hasidism universalized this mystical impulse by moving it from the secret chambers of the learned few to the streets, crowning the humblest peasant and simplest soul with the capacity to encounter God's Shekinah glory in the shabbiness of daily life. The movement, "broadly speaking represents an attempt to make the world of Kabbalism, through a certain transformation or re-interpretation, accessible to the masses."[59] As Buber notes, at a juncture in Jewish history when Kabbalism had ossified, there arose in the "dark, despised East, among

---

of the differences between Buber and Scholem's views, see Idel, *Hasidism*. Idel even questions the degree to which Lurianic Kabbalism influenced Hasidism, arguing convincingly that there are many features of Hasidic thought and practice that simply do not appear in Luria's work. See Idel, *Hasidism*, 45–54.

51. Potok, Foreword, ix
52. Wiesel, *Souls on Fire*, 10.
53. Scholem, *Major Trends*, 324; Dan, *Teachings of Hasidism*, 1.
54. Wiesel, *Souls on Fire*, 19.
55. Wiesel, *Souls on Fire*, 20–30.
56. Wiesel, *Souls on Fire*, 20.
57. Wiesel, *Souls on Fire*, 13.
58. Scholem, *On the Kabbalah*, 2.
59. Scholem, *Major Trends*, 327–28.

simple, unlearned villagers," a volcanic movement that made "mysticism the possession of the people."[60]

Interpreters of Hasidism disagree about its nature as an historical phenomenon—whether its emergence should be understood as a continuation of previous messianic movements; as a proximate movement catalyzed by the dissemination of Lurianic thought and Shabbateanism, a devastating crisis among Eastern European Jews precipitated by the charismatic leader Shabbetai Zevi's false messianic claims; or as a spiritual upheaval akin to a revolution in thought and practice.[61] However, in terms of its central concepts, it is generally agreed that Hasidism, whether a revival or revolution, resulted in a significant reworking of long-standing and widely accepted concepts derived from "the theoretical Kabbalah of the Middle Ages [expressed in the *Zohar*] and the Lurian [sic] Kabbalah of sixteenth-century Safed."[62]

Central Concepts—Creation, Evil, Redemption

Both Luria's cosmology—and subsequently Hasidic interpretations of it—had such a widespread and lasting significance, in part, because its symbols and doctrines seemed to answer two pressing existential questions: "Why is there an exile?" and "What is the meaning, or function, of the

---

60. Buber, *Legend of the Baal Shem Tov*, 12.

61. See Moshe Idel's historical analysis of these various perspectives—particularly those of Buber, Scholem, and Heschel—in his introduction to *Hasidism: Between Ecstasy and Magic* (Idel, 1–30). A particularly compelling voice for Hasidism as renewal is Chaim Potok. In his foreword to Buber's *Tales of the Hasidim*, he describes the eighteenth-century Hasidic movement as "an explosive act of creation: a response by a single person to the cry of the masses" (Potok, Foreword, ix). Decades of oppression and poverty, external pressures and internal suffering, had caused Polish Jewry to turn "in upon itself and became so restrictive and hermetic as to drain it of the possibility of creative spontaneity. The Jewish community lay in a torpor of congealed ritualism; and its most esteemed activity, the learning of Torah, became abstruse, elitist, and far removed from the grim reality and miseries of everyday existence" (Potok, Foreword, ix). Prayer had become an esoteric exercise, partly as a result of Lurianic Kabbalism's "proliferation of an extraordinarily complex theology and a tenuous type of practice." Further, Torah study was only for the learned. How, then, asks Potok, "does one come to God when one is a shoemaker, a wagon driver, a water carrier; when one must work day and night and has little time for study?" (Potok, Foreword, ix). The Hasidism of the Baal Shem Tov provided an answer. He taught that *all* of life was Torah study, and that one could encounter the holy sparks of God's Shekinah in the herbs of the fields, the tools of one's trade, the laughter of children, the love of one's neighbor.

62. Friedman, *Martin Buber*, 17.

commandments in the Torah?"[63] The Lurianic doctrines of *tsimtsum* ("withdrawal"), *shevirat ha-kelim* ("breaking of the vessels"), *tikkun* ("mending" or "restoration") and *devekuth* ("devotion" or "fervent clinging" to God), in particular, offered potent answers, especially when democratized by the Hasidic movement. Because these concepts and their attendant symbols appear frequently in Dillard's journals and in her literary canon, a brief explanation of each is necessary.

Tsimtsum

Luria's creation cosmology attempts to resolve a familiar theological dilemma: if the eternal, non-mortal, and immaterial God is all that existed in the beginning, how could a temporal, mortal, and material world, come into being, *ex nihilo*? In short, if God's eternal, all-consuming light was both the only thing and everything, "where" could a finite world have been made? The Lurianic idea of *tsimtsum* (meaning "withdrawal" or "retreat") attempts to provide an answer.[64] Luria posited that all things were in fact created within God, but in a void made when he chose to withdraw or contract part of himself in order to make space within which creation could come into being.[65] Luria thus explains the paradox of God's creating *ex nihilo* by proposing that God did indeed create everything from nothing—from the nothing, or the void "made" from his self-imposed exile within his own being, the first and necessary preliminary act of creation. Scholem is worth quoting at length here, since he articulates well the extraordinary power of Luria's cosmology and ways it differs from Neoplatonic notions of emanation:

> According to Luria, God was compelled to make room for the world by, as it were, abandoning a region within Himself, a kind of mystical primordial space from which He withdrew in order to return to it in the action of creation and revelation. The first act of *En-Sof*, the Infinite Being, is therefore not a step outside but a step inside, a movement of recoil, of falling back upon oneself, of withdrawing into oneself. Instead of emanation we have the opposite, contraction. The God who revealed himself in firm contours was superseded by one who descended deeper into the recesses of His own Being, who concentrated Himself into Himself, and had done so from the very beginning

---

63. Dan, *Teachings of Hasidism*, 10, 24.
64. Scholem, *Major Trends*, 260.
65. Dan, *Teachings of Hasidism*, 11; Scholem, *Major Trends*, 260–61.

of creation.... The first act of all is not an act of revelation but one of limitation.[66]

Luria's idea became enormously influential for many reasons, not the least of which was its power to provide a despairing and exiled people with a potent symbol. As Scholem explains, *tsimtsum* suggests God "banish[ed] Himself from His totality into profound seclusion. Regarded this way, the idea of *Tsimtsum* [sic] is the deepest symbol of Exile that could be thought of."[67] Franz Rosenzweig explains, "God himself separates from himself... he suffers with [Israel's] suffering, he migrates with it into the misery of foreign lands, he wanders with its wanderings."[68] Thus, exile comes to be seen not as an existential anomaly but as an ontological reality intrinsic to God himself.[69]

In Luria's dialectical concept of creation, this first act of withdrawal is followed by a second and opposite act, God's emanation in which he "sends out a ray of His light and begin[s] his revelation, or rather his unfolding as God the Creator, in the primordial space of His own creation."[70] The first movement of *tsimtsum*, God's retreat, Luria suggests is cathartic, separating out a latent potential for evil from within the Godhead and leaving it suspended in the residue of divine light that remained in the primordial void. Just as perfume or oil leaves residue in a jar even when it is emptied, the Kabbalists reasoned, so too, in the initial movement of *tsimtsum*, a residue of God's light remained in the primordial void and with it the seeds of evil.[71] In the second movement of God's creative act, a ray of light (*sefirot*) proceeds from the Godhead, "brings order into chaos and sets the cosmic process in motion, by separating the hidden elements and moulding [sic] them into a new form."[72] Every following act of creation follows this dynamic motion of contraction and emanation in which the rays of divine light enter the void. As Scholem explains, "just as the human organism exists through the double process of inhaling and exhaling and the one cannot be conceived without the other, so also the whole of Creation constitutes a gigantic process of divine inhalation and exhalation."[73] Thus, Luria's dialectical motion afforded not only a plausible explanation of creation *ex nihilo*

66. Scholem, *Major Trends*, 261.
67. Scholem, *Major Trends*, 261.
68. Rosenzweig, *Star of Redemption*, 432.
69. Dan, *Teachings of Hasidism*, 11; Scholem, *Major Trends*, 261.
70. Scholem, *Major Trends*, 261.
71. Scholem, *Major Trends*, 263–64.
72. Scholem, *Major Trends*, 263.
73. Scholem, *Major Trends*, 263.

but also a possible explanation for the existence of evil. Seeds of evil lay dormant in the void created by God's withdrawal, and yet they could only exist because some residue of God's life lent them the power to be. As we shall see in subsequent chapters, Dillard frequently borrows the imagery of *tsimtsum*, most notably in motifs of voids or absences, to portray evil, suffering, and the "icy dab of non-being"[74] in all that exists.

Finally, it is also important to note that Luria's concept of *tsimtsum* guarded against pantheism—what many argue is suggested by the Kabbalistic and Hasidic concept of emanation.[75] Because, in Luria's view, the material world has its own discrete existence and is animated by the remnants of God's Shekinah held within all things, they are not one with God or forms of God. Scholem explains: "Not only is there a residue of divine manifestation in every being, but under the aspect of *Tsimtsum* [sic] it also acquires a reality of its own which guards it against the danger of dissolution into the non-individual being of the divine 'all-in-all.' Luria himself was the living example of an outspoken theistic mystic. He gave the Zohar, for all its intrinsic pantheism, a strictly theistic interpretation."[76]

The Hasidic view of *tsimtsum* reflected not so much a new doctrine as a shift in focus that imbued the concepts with "an emotional content" and made their focus individual piety and communal life rather than esoteric knowledge for a select few.[77] Friedman explains:

> [*Tsimtsum* is given] a metaphorical rather than a literal interpretation which enables it to coexist with the strongest possible emphasis on the immanence of God, of God's Glory, in all things. The world is in the closest possible connection with God, and nature is in fact nothing but the garment of God. God clothed Himself in the world in order to lead man step by step to the place where he can see God behind the appearances of external things and can cleave to Him in all his actions.[78]

Additionally, Hasidism retained *tsimtsum*'s notion that creation was made by emanations of divine light proceeding from God. However, it reinterpreted the initial movement of withdrawal not as an internal catharsis hinting at a cosmic struggle within God but rather as God's loving choice to diminish the power of his light in order to render it visible to created worlds and

---

74. PTC, 91.
75. Scholem, *Major Trends*, 262.
76. Scholem, *Major Trends*, 262.
77. Friedman, *Martin Buber*, 20–21.
78. Friedman, *Martin Buber*, 20.

beings, in keeping with their "limited absorbing capacities."[79] Paradoxically, "[God] rendered His light visible, or revealed it, by limiting it. Thus, while from God's standpoint the zimzum [sic] was a withdrawal of divine light, from man's it was a revelation, or flowing out (not in), of divine light."[80] Consequently, in the Hasidic view, the potent symbol of exile remains—the Shekinah of God is indeed exiled within creation—yet the material world is no longer merely a dark, imprisoning shell but is infused with and animated by a holiness that is both "present and perceptible" at all times, to those who have eyes to see beyond its outer garment.[81]

Yet, even with this emphasis on the indwelling presence of God in the world, for the Hasidim as for the Lurianic Kabbalists, God's presence in creation is not pantheism but *panentheism*,[82] or what Buber would call "pansacramentalism." Buber asserts, "The world is an irradiation of God, but as it is endowed with an independence of existence and striving, it is apt, always and everywhere, to form a crust around itself. Thus, a divine spark lives in every thing [sic] and every being, but each spark is enclosed by an isolating shell. Only man can liberate it."[83] Furthermore, because Hasidism shifted the motivation of *tsimtsum* from God's self-limiting act to his loving condescension to the frailty of his creatures, cloaking, as it were, the blinding light of his being in material form so that they could behold him, Hasidism thus moved the ethical center of creation from limitation to love. Friedman explains:

> For the Hasidism the world was created out of love and is to be brought to perfection through love. Love is central in God's relation to man and is more important than fear of God, justice, or righteousness. The fear of God is only a door to the love of God.... Love is not only a feeling; it is the godly in existence. Nor can one love God unless he loves his fellow man, for God is immanent in man as in all of His creation.[84]

---

79. Dan, *Teachings of Hasidism*, 18.

80. Dan, *Teachings of Hasidism*, 18.

81. Scholem, *Major Trends*, 348. Scholem points out that, at least in the early period of the Hasidic movement, the Hasidim viewed *tsimtsum* as a symbol of one's natural self (a being with a holy spark trapped in a fallen shell) rather than as an actual event in cosmic history within the Godhead; for "a ray of God's essence is present *and perceptible* [emphasis mine] everywhere and at every moment" (Scholem, *Major Trends*, 348).

82. Friedman, *Martin Buber*, 20; Buber, *Hasidism and Modern Man*, 126.

83. Buber, *Hasidism and Modern Man*, 126.

84. Friedman, *Martin Buber*, 22.

It is perhaps worth noting here that this shift makes *tsimtsum* amenable to Christian kenotic theologies, particularly those centered on the Christic hymn in Philippians 2. In it, Christ is described as having chosen to be self-limiting, to have "emptied" (*ekenōsen*) himself, and become a servant as God incarnate. The connections between *tsimtsum* and kenosis were not lost on Dillard and, as will be discussed in forthcoming chapters, they provided her with theological and poetic tools for exploring the limits of God's omni-attributes while still affirming his presence in creation.

Shevirat ha-Kelim

A second essential part of Luria's cosmic myth is the *shevirat ha-kelim*, or the "breaking of the vessels" that occurred in the second movement of *tsimtsum*, when God's light went forth into the void to create all things.[85] Since material things require finite forms, they had to be separated and contained somehow within physical containers, or "bowls."[86] According to Luria, when the infinite power of God's light went forth, however, these forms shattered, and pieces of the vessels with "fragments of divine light (termed *nizonot*, or 'sparks') clinging to them, fell downward, while the remaining lights ascended back toward the Ein Sof [sic]."[87] Scholem interprets Luria's concept of *shevirat ha-kelim* as cathartic, separating the latent potential for evil within the Shefiroth from them, making evil a by-product of the "life process of the Shefiroth."[88] Scholem observes that "taken as a whole, [the shattering of the bowls] is the cause of that inner deficiency which is inherent in everything that exists and which persists as long as the damage is not mended."[89]

While Luria's theosophy developed, according to Scholem, along gnostic lines, focusing on the imprisoning dark shells,[90] the Baal Shem Tov and his disciples reasoned "that if there are sparks in the shells, then the shells themselves may contain the possibility of sanctity: the material world may well be a manifestation of the divine. Food, a melody, a sunset—all tell us of the presence of the sacred in the everyday world."[91] Human artifacts also contain the holy sparks. Thus, the Baal Shem Tov could say: "one should

---

85. Dan, *Teachings of Hasidism*, 11.
86. Scholem, *Major Trends*, 265–66.
87. Dan, *Teachings of Hasidism*, 12.
88. Scholem *Major Trends* 266–67; Dan, *Teachings of Hasidism*, 12.
89. Scholem, *Major Trends*, 268.
90. Scholem, *Major Trends*, 260, 267–68.
91. Potok, Foreword, xi.

have mercy on all his tools and all his possessions for the sake of the sparks that are in them."[92]

Tikkun and Devekuth

Though the presence of the holy sparks affirms the immanence of God, both in Lurianic Kabbalism and in Hasidism, *shevirat ha-kelim* also signals an ontological brokenness, or fragmentation at the heart of the cosmos, in fact, in the very being of God. As noted earlier, because God's light and power were shattered, he, too, wanders the earth in exile, separated from the unified Godhead, the En Sof, which is the "hidden God, the innermost Being of Divinity [that] has neither qualities nor attributes."[93] Thus, according to Lurianic Kabbalism, it is the role of every person, starting with Adam, to aid in the process of *tikkun*, or the "mending" of all that was broken in the primordial catastrophe of the *shevirat ha-kelim*.[94] The *telos* of creation is redemption, or the completion of *tikkun*. And though Luria asserted that in the heavenly realms, God's light has nearly completed *tikkun*, "certain concluding actions have been reserved for man."[95] Redemption's completion, therefore, depends on humans. Scholem observes that herein lies the connection between spiritual and earthly redemption: humans "must struggle with and overcome not only the historic exile of the Jewish people but also the mystic exile of the *Shekinah*."[96] Consequently, "every event and every domain of existence faces at once inwardly *and outwardly*."[97] Dan notes that in the Lurianic concept of *tikkun*, "the life of each individual [is] a reflection or an enactment, writ small, of the situation in the cosmos as a whole."[98] Even the unlearned and lowly, therefore, can participate in a grand dialectical movement of cosmic significance; for, he who participates in *tikkun* starts at the end of all things (the shattered glory of God) and ends at the beginning of all things (God himself) by bringing the exiled holy sparks back to their primordial unity in the En Sof.[99]

---

92. Buber, *Hasidism and Modern Man*, 188.
93. Scholem, *Major Trends*, 207.
94. Scholem, *Kabbalah*, 142–43.
95. Scholem, *Kabbalah*, 142.
96. Scholem, *Kabbalah*, 143.
97. Scholem, *Major Trends*, 274 (emphasis mine).
98. Dan, *Teachings of Hasidism*, 13.
99. Scholem, *Major Trends*, 274–75.

For the Hasids as well, it was believed that one can, not metaphorically but in fact, participate in the redemption of the world.[100] Each human soul, it was believed, has a special connection with the sparks that are "rooted near its own place of origin in the divine world," and releasing the divine sparks with which one has an intimate connection is as much a part of one's own redemption as it is of the world's.[101] Martin Buber explains:

> Man's service of the sparks takes place in everyday life; men can accomplish it even with the most profane bodily action that brings him into contact with things and beings, for even the most profane action can be done in holiness, and he who does it in holiness raises the sparks. In the clothes that you wear, in the tools that you use, in the food that you eat, in the domestic animal that toils for you, in all are hidden sparks that are anxious for redemption, and if you have to do with the things and beings with carefulness, with good will, and faithfulness, you redeem them. God gives you the clothes and food that belong to the roots of your soul in order that you may redeem the sparks in them.[102]

As Buber's explanation suggests, the Hasidic rendering of *tikkun* also transformed Luria's "gloomy" (to use Dillard's word)[103] view of the material world into a holy and exuberant joy in the life of the senses.[104] Rather than to be denied, one's senses were the gateway to the glory of God. Buber asserts, "[Hasidism is] anti-ascetic. No mortification of the urges is needed, for all natural life can be hallowed."[105] In fact, for the Hasid, cultivating joy is seen as a holy obligation, for it both affirms the presence of God in all things, and it requires one to exercise a holy vision that penetrates the outward appearances of things to see their true, inner nature.[106] To the Hasid, "only joy can drive out the 'alien thoughts' and *qelipot* [imprisoning material forms] that distract man from the love of God. Conversely, despair is worse than even sin; for it leads one to believe oneself in the power of sin and hence to give in to it."[107]

---

100. Dan, *Teachings of Hasidism*, 22–25.
101. Dan, *Teachings of Hasidism*, 23.
102. Buber, *Origin and Meaning*, 84.
103. FTB, 22.
104. Friedman, *Martin Buber*, 21–22.
105. Buber, *Hasidism and Modern Man*, 32.
106. Friedman, *Martin Buber*, 22.
107. Friedman, *Martin Buber*, 22.

Furthermore, though Hasidism never renounced Judaism's messianic hopes, its understanding of *tikkun* shifted their emphasis from redemptive hope placed solely or even primarily in a future, messianic age to redemptive hope for the present moment. Through love of God and love of neighbor, one could redeem the things at hand.[108] Thus, it made the humblest chore one of *avodah*, or worship, and infused every action with ethical significance that ultimately gave its mysticism a social dimension. As Friedman observes, because every action and interaction could be approached with holy intentions in prayer, there was no longer "any division between religion and ethics—between the direct relation to God and one's relations to one's fellows, nor is its ethics limited to any prescribed and peculiar action."[109]

In addition, the Hasidic idea that one worships God in all one's actions by performing them with *devekuth*, or fervent cleaving to God, transformed attitudes toward the Torah. Though *devekuth* in Lurianic Kabbalism denoted mystical union with God achieved primarily through mystical prayer bordering on magic,[110] the Hasidic movement redefined it as fervent, inner attentiveness to God in one's daily tasks. As Dan explains, "medieval thinkers had regarded devekuth [sic] as a supreme ecstatic state reserved for a tiny spiritual elite, and even for them not to be achieved without God's help. Hasidism, however, made devekuth [sic] into a minimal requirement . . . attainable by all Hasidim at least while praying and preferably while engaged in other activities as well."[111] This shift not only democratized prayer but took it outdoors, so to speak, to the carpenter's shop, the plowman's fields, the blacksmith's anvil. Its untutored enthusiasm that literally spilled out into the streets had the perhaps unintended effect of demoting the privileged place of Torah study, bringing the Hasidim into conflict with traditional leadership.[112] Thus, though reverence for Torah study and Judaism's historical traditions remained, particularly within its leadership, Hasidism affirmed God's self-revelation well outside of these modes and emphasized personal responsibility for cultivating spiritual disciplines that allowed one to cleave to God in every moment. For those who had eyes to see, God's presence leapt from every blade of grass, every rock, every tree, every hammer of the anvil. For the Hasid, "The Torah is a priceless gift of God, when it is used to conquer the evil impulse and to transform the inner life of man, but not when it is made an end in itself—a

---

108. Friedman, *Martin Buber*, 19.
109. Friedman, *Martin Buber*, 19.
110. Scholem, *Major Trends*, 277–78.
111. Dan, *Teachings of Hasidism*, 23.
112. Dan, *Teachings of Hasidism*, 24.

joyless burden or an occasion for intellectual subtlety."[113] This shift brought renewed emphasis on each individual's responsibility to seek God in life, not merely in the Torah, and to redeem it. As Friedman explains, "The revelation of God to the fathers of Israel must be confirmed and renewed in the inner life of every believer,"[114] for the ultimate purpose of *tikkun*. Indeed, for the Hasidism *tikkun* signaled not merely the redemption of one's soul but redemption of the entire universe.

Though shortly after its flowering, Hasidism's initial ethos of its being a "people's movement" ossified around the structure of Hasidic courts lead by *tzaddikim*, or righteous men, these central mystical ideas of *devekuth* and *tikkun* retained their uniquely Hasidic social and thereby ethical dimensions. At the center of the Hasidic community was the paradox that those mystics who "had attained their spiritual aim—who, in Kabbalistic parlance, had discovered the secret of true *Devekuth* [sic]—turned to the people with their mystical knowledge" and "instead of cherishing as a mystery the most personal of all experiences, undertook to teach its secret to all men of good will."[115] Idel explains:

> the "righteous men," the *ẓaddiqim*, did not conceive of ecstasy as their ultimate goal; rather, they had an additional spiritual aim: the *drawing down* of divine effluence for the benefit of the community. This . . . shows that mysticism and leadership are part of a more coherent way of life, one that incorporates the sublime experience of the *perfecti* into a large ideal, and that strives to contribute to the more ordinary well-being of the *ẓaddiq*'s adherents.[116]

As Hasidism evolved and communities formed around revered and beloved *tzaddiks*, these leaders came to be understood as possessing unique mystical powers to protect and intercede on behalf of their followers. Thus, their mysticism was far from individual, private, and esoteric but was always connected by the deepest of spiritual and social bonds to their followers who saw in them spiritual exemplars. Scholem explains:

> The believer no longer needed the Kabbalah; he turned its mysteries into reality by fastening upon certain traits which the saint, or Zaddik, whose example he strove to follow, had placed in the center of his relation to God. Everyone, thus the doctrine

---

113. Friedman, *Martin Buber*, 21.
114. Friedman, *Martin Buber*, 21.
115. Scholem, *Major Trends*, 342.
116. Idel, *Hasidism*, 1 (emphasis mine).

ran, must try to become the embodiment of a certain ethical quality. Attributes like piety, service, love, devotion, humility, clemency, trust, even greatness and domination, became in this way enormously real and socially effective.[117]

In short, "*personality* takes the place of *doctrine*; what is lost in rationality by this change is gained in efficacy."[118] Part of that efficacy is its ethical dimension. As Martin Buber asserts in *The Origin and Meaning of Hasidism*, "In Hasidism—and in it alone, so far as I can see, in the history of the human spirit—mysticism has become ethos.... Here the mystical soul cannot become real if it is not one with the moral."[119] Scholem concurs. Quoting Buber's now-famous line, "'mysticism has become ethos,'" he adds "the opinions particular to the exalted individual [the *tzaddik*] were less important than his character, and mere learning, knowledge of the Torah, no longer occupies the most important place in the scale of religious values. ... It is no longer his knowledge but his life, which lends a religious value to his personality."[120]

Conclusion

The Baal Shem Tov adopted the Kabbalistic symbols and concepts that gave expression to and formed "the foundations of his immediate experience."[121] Though these ideas were not at all new, they were transformed. No longer cloistered in esoteric schools or cloaked in arcane practice, Kabbalistic theurgy became quotidian mystery. "What has really become important," Scholem asserts, "is the direction, the mysticism of the personal life. Hasidism is practical mysticism at its highest. Almost all the Kabbalistic ideas are now placed in relation to values peculiar to the individual life, and those which are not remain empty and ineffective."[122] In Buber's words, "No leap from the everyday into the miraculous is required.... Around each man—enclosed within the wide sphere of his activity—is laid a natural circle of things which, before all, he is called to set free."[123]

---

117. Scholem, *Major Trends*, 342.
118. Scholem, *Major Trends*, 344.
119. Buber, *Origin and Meaning*, 198–99.
120. Scholem, *Major Trends*, 344.
121. Scholem, *Major Trends*, 335.
122. Scholem, *Major Trends*, 341.
123. Buber, *Hasidism and Modern Man*, 104.

In the chapters that follow, each of these major concepts—*tsimtsum*, *shevirat ha-kelim*, and *tikkun* and *devekuth*[124]—will be explored in Dillard's work. They illuminate Dillard's unique understanding of God's pansacramental presence in creation, the nature of evil and suffering, and possibilities for redemption as the artist wrestles with her world through words and challenges her readers to do the same.

---

124. Because Lurianic Kabbalism is primarily what Dillard studied and borrows from, when Kabbalistic thought is referenced from this chapter onward, it refers to Lurianic Kabbalism.

CHAPTER 2

"Each Day Splintered Down"

Hasidic Pansacramentalism and Dillard's Mystical Descents

"Purity does not lie in a separation from the universe
... but in a deeper penetration of it."

—Teilhard de Chardin, in *For the Time Being*

Introduction

DILLARD'S CLAIMS THAT THE focus of her work is mysticism and that it "fits very squarely in the Christian mystical tradition dating from Plotinus"[1] have caused much scholarly attention to be devoted to examining her solely from within the Christian historical stream. When working from the texts themselves, classifying her in this way has proven problematic. Her literary accounts of mystical experiences, while at times sharing similarities with this long mystical tradition, make a number of sharp departures from it.[2] Dana Wilde acknowledges the challenge. In "Annie Dillard's 'A Field of Silence:' The Contemplative Tradition in the Modern Age," she observes that Dillard's essay "A Field of Silence" seems a clear enough literary rendering of a mystical experience to warrant categorizing her work as within the "contemplative literary tradition"; yet "its distinctly modern depiction, or

---

1. Abood, "Natural Wonders," 32.

2. For a thorough examination of Dillard's work as mystical yet *post*modern, see Yore, *Mystic Way in Postmodernity*.

re-creation, of the classic mystical experience makes it a really troubling work in the context of contemplative literature."[3] In "Mystical Experience in Annie Dillard's 'Total Eclipse' and 'Lenses,'" Wilde admits that "most of the accompanying aspects of the mystical experience" cannot be found. "No reference is made to a particular sense of reality or objectivity; to feelings of joy, blessedness or peace; to a sense of holiness or divinity; nor to any of the experience's being ineffable."[4]

Although Wilde's comments are limited to only a few of Dillard's nonfiction essays, they hold true for most of Dillard's accounts of divine encounters in her other non-fiction works. Margaret Loewen Reimer, in "The Dialectical Vision of Annie Dillard's *Pilgrim at Tinker Creek*," observes that the narrator seems to invert theological categories and stances, including the traditional role of the mystic. Loewen Reimer writes:

> The mystic, for example, desires to move from the material world to the spiritual, from the particular to the universal, from the self to God. The mystic strives to leave self, to become "empty" in order to experience the divine. Dillard, who casts herself in the role of the mystic, also strives to become "transfixed and empty" . . . but her attention is always focused on the most minute detail, the most particular of objects.[5]

Though Dillard's narratives do describe encounters with the divine, as Loewen Reimer notes, they occur by her becoming "lost in the 'lower' world instead of the 'higher.'"[6] This becomes problematic when one attempts to classify her work as "solidly" within the Neoplatonic[7] Christian mystical tradition.

A possible explanation for this seemingly anomalous inversion of categories, and its concomitant language of descent, is that it reflects not only her fascination with Christian mysticism but also her life-long interest in Jewish mysticism and the Hebrew Bible. As noted in chapter 1, Dillard begins *For the Time Being*, the last, non-fiction book of her career, by telling readers that "for twenty-five years, with increasing admiration, I have studied the gloomy Luria because he influenced the exuberant Baal Shem Tov, and the Baal Shem Tov because he and his followers knew God, and a thing or two besides."[8] No

---

3. Wilde, "Annie Dillard's 'Field of Silence,'" 31–45.
4. Wilde, "Mystical Experience," 48–83.
5. Reimer, "Dialectical Vision," 188.
6. Reimer, "Dialectical Vision," 189.
7. When the term "Neoplatonic" is used in this discussion, it refers to the system of thought Plotinus developed from Platonism. For an excellent introduction, see the chapter on "Plotinus," in Louth, *Origins*, 36–51.
8. FTB, 22.

doubt, her long-standing interest arises from her affinity for mystical modes that affirm the presence of God *in* creation, not just transcendent of it, one of the hallmarks of Jewish mysticism that distinguishes it from the Western Neoplatonic mystical traditions.[9]

In fact, Dillard is aware of and draws attention expressly to this distinguishing feature in the Jewish mystical traditions. In *For the Time Being*, she celebrates the fact that "Jewish spiritual life takes place in the thick of, and sanctifies, the multiple world of created things" and that Luria, despite his fervor and Kabblism's gnostic tendencies, "did not despise the body: the body may be 'turbid,' but its flesh shares in the joys to come. Luria warned his disciples against living in lonely places, or even visiting them."[10] Though the focus of this chapter will be primarily Dillard's interest in and affinities with Hasidic pansacramentalism, this distinctive intertwining of the earthly and heavenly realms was, as noted in chapter 1, a hallmark of Kabbalistic thought as well, and helps explain why Dillard finds the symbols of Lurianic Kabbalism amenable to her efforts to express transcendent presence in creation's particulars.

It perhaps bears repeating that Kabbalistic and Hasidic thought are not by any means the only theological influences found in Dillard's work. As discussed in chapter 1, her canon exhibits a wide range of reading and borrows freely from numerous religious traditions to create rich and theologically complex texts. However, in her use of all these traditions, she gravitates toward a view of the physical world and an apprehension of God that differs significantly in some of its major features from Western Christian mysticism, particularly in unitive experiences, typically understood as the supreme moment of mystical experience in which an individual's soul becomes one with God. Whereas most mystical discourse in Western Christianity about the mystical ascent follows the Plotinian model of purgation, illumination, and union, Dillard seems to favor instead a mysticism[11] of the

---

9. See explanation of this distinctive feature—particularly Gershom Scholem's analysis of it—in chapter 1. Kabbalistic, and later Hasidic thought, wed heaven to earth by linking the spiritual world to the historical experiences of the Jews.

10. FTB, 52.

11. Using the term "mysticism" raises questions about taxonomy. How does one classify the experiences Dillard describes? The scholarly literature on Dillard uses various terms, most typically "epiphany," "revelation," and "the sublime." Since Dillard uses the term "mysticism" to describe her interests and experiences, it will be used throughout the book. Bernard McGinn's definition of mysticism in *Foundations of Mysticism* provides a suitable working definition that is broad enough to encompass both Dillard's experiences as a Christian and her rendering of those experiences in the language of other mystical traditions, specifically that of Hasidism. McGinn defines "'the mystical element in Christianity" as "that part of its belief and practices that concerns the

senses that is closely aligned with what Martin Buber calls Hasidism's "embracing" of the world[12] and its pansacramental view of God in it.

Pansacramentalism

Hasidic pansacramentalism is perhaps best defined in Martin Buber's essay, "Symbolic and Sacramental Existence," found in *The Origin and Meaning of Hasidism*:

> For Hasidic pansacramentalism the holy in things is not, as for the primitive, a power which one takes possession of, a force which one can master, but it is laid in the things as sparks and awaits the liberation and fulfillment of the man who gives himself completely. The man of sacramental existence is no magician; he does not merely stake himself in it, he really and simply gives himself; he exercises no power but a service, *the* service. ... To the question what (in the sacramental sense) is important, the answer is given: 'What one is engaged in at the moment.' ... But the actual . . . shows itself as what cannot be anticipated, what is withdrawn from foresight.[13]

As explained in chapter 1, this view emerged from the Hasidic reworking of Lurianic Kabbalism's concepts of *shevirat ha-kelim* and *tikkun*. Hasidism transformed Luria's tendencies toward gnostic dualism into exuberant joy in the life of the senses, making all of life holy and set apart for God.[14] This embracing, rather than rejection, of the material realm and the senses (and the unanticipated, often shattering, ways the holy emerges in it) is one of the most noticeable features of Dillard's depictions of her encounters with holiness, and it suggests deep affinities with the Hasidic masters. Further,

---

preparation for, the consciousness of, and the reaction to what can be described as the immediate or direct presence of God" (McGinn, *Foundations of Mysticism*, xvii). In addition, because the features of these experiences vary in Dillard's work as widely as those found in the Hebrew Bible, Martin Buber's term "encounter" will be used to signify that these experiences exist in relationship to God and are as unique as God's dealings with individuals (Buber, *On the Bible*, 1). See also Buber, *Pointing the Way*. These two terms seem fitting in light of Dillard's synthesis of Jewish and Christian mystical traditions.

12. The word "embraceable" is Hugo Bergman's translation of Buber's word "erfaßbar" used in *Pointing the Way*. Bergman adds that Buber connects it to the Hebrew word "to know" which means "to embrace lovingly" (Bergman, "Martin Buber and Mysticism," 299). See Buber, *Pointing the Way*, 29; Bergman, "Martin Buber and Mysticism," 297–318.

13. Buber, *Origin and Meaning*, 170–71.

14. Friedman, *Martin Buber*, 21–22.

Dillard's texts consistently employ the language of a mystical *descent* rather than *ascent* and thus differ quite markedly from the language of mystical ascent typical in the Neoplatonic mystical tradition.[15] In fact, the metaphor of descent is so rare in Western Christian mysticism that, when it appears, scholars find its provenance difficult to trace.[16]

Of course, Christian mysticism is not monolithic. Within its history are vastly different personalities and accounts of mystical experiences as well as variations in the role of senses and in attitudes toward the physical world. Moreover, Christianity has a "descending God" in the incarnation of Jesus Christ. Yet mystical experiences in the Christian tradition, no matter how varied, tend to be described as occurring in heightened states of inwardness or in mystical ascents of the soul away from sensory experiences and the physical world. That Christian mysticism has its roots firmly and deeply planted in Platonism is well established. Andrew Louth in *The Origins of the Christian Mystical Tradition* notes that "Christian mystical theology found [in Platonic thought] very amenable material, so much so that one of the great living authorities on Hellenistic religion, Père A.-J. Festugière, can say: 'When the Fathers "think" their mysticism they platonize. There is nothing original in the edifice.'"[17] Similarly, Evelyn Underhill concludes, "From the thirteenth century onwards, the majority of the medieval mystics show knowledge and appreciation of those Plotinian ideas which reached them—though in an attenuated form—through St. Augustine, Dionysius, and Richard of St. Victor. Even the Fransciscan and Christo-centric enthusiasm of such contemplatives as Jacopone da Todi and Angela of Foglio was affected by [Neoplatonism]."[18]

Consequently, the point is not to controvert the argument for the connections between Dillard and Western Christian mysticism. The connections are undoubtedly there. Rather, the present discussion seeks to focus attention on the Jewish mystical traditions that Dillard is equally if not more consistently vocal about but which, strangely, have been overlooked. Through the fusion of Christian and Jewish mystical traditions, Dillard creates a pansacramental view of creation, animated by the presence of a

---

15. For a helpful discussion about the language of mystical descent in esoteric mystical sources, see Stroumsa, *Hidden Wisdom*, 169–84. He cites as a case in point the inexplicable shift in Merkabah mysticism somewhere in its development from the metaphor of ascent to descent to the Merkabah (Stroumsa, *Hidden Wisdom*, 170). Scholem has no explanation; his discussion about this shift can be found in Scholem, *Major Trends*, 46–47.

16. Stroumsa, *Hidden Wisdom*, 170.

17. Louth, *Origins*, xiii.

18. Underhill, *Essentials of Mysticism*, 137.

descending God who is found, as the chapter's epigraph expresses, not by escaping the world but through a deeper penetration of it.

The limits of time and space prevent a comprehensive analysis of all instances of Dillard's motifs of mystical descent. Thus, this chapter will examine in chronological order passages from three of Dillard's major works of literary non-fiction. In them, Dillard synthesizes Christian and Jewish mystical traditions to create powerful affirmations of the material world as the locus of God's holiness and redemptive activity that seem more closely aligned with Hasidism's earthy, pansacramental vision than with the cool, intellectual flight of the alone to the Alone typical of Western Christian mysticism.

Descending into the Scandal of Particularity:
Pilgrim at Tinker Creek

Hasidism, particularly as interpreted by Martin Buber, has very few if any traces of the gnosticism of the *Zohar*, the lodestar of Kabbalistic thought, or of Luria's cosmogony. Both suggest that matter exists only where God has withdrawn his presence and that the senses perceive only the *qelipot*, or shells of darkness, that trap the exiled Shekinah of God. Buber has certainly been challenged on this point by scholars such as Scholem and Schatz-Uffenheimer who argue that Hasidism retains the gnostic dualism of the later Kabbalah.[19] However, even if the criticisms of Buber's interpretation of Hasidism are valid, Annie Dillard nevertheless seems to align herself more closely to Buber's interpretation of the tales, legends, and sayings of Hasidism than to his critics.' Furthermore, the sources Dillard gravitates toward for her understanding of Hasidism are primarily Martin Buber and Abraham Heschel, both of whom affirm Hasidism's hallowing of the material world. Moreover, Dillard is fully aware of the gnostic leanings of Luria's Kabbalah, identifying them outright in *Pilgrim at Tinker Creek* and *For the Time Being*. But it is not a view with which she most frequently aligns herself, either intellectually or artistically from her first book[20] to her last.[21]

---

19. See Scholem, "Martin Buber's Interpretation of Hasidism," 227–50; Schatz-Uffenheimer, "Man's Relation," 403–34.

20. Her first book of poetry, *Tickets for a Prayer Wheel*, was published the same year as *Pilgrim* (1974), and also, as subsequent chapters will demonstrate, it borrows imagery from Lurianic Kabbalism to express the fecundity of absence and from Hasidism to convey the pansacramental presence of God in creation.

21. Dillard expresses admiration for Luria's Kabbalist creation story, which "however baroque, accounts boldly for both moral evil and natural calamity" (FTB, 50). The shattering of the vessels, means, according to Dillard that "we see only the demonic shells of things. It is literally sensible to deny that God exists. In fact, God is hidden,

Early in *Pilgrim at Tinker Creek*, Dillard employs imagery from Jewish mysticism to establish what has become a settled preference in all her works for a pansacramental rather than Neoplatonic view of the material world. In chapter 2, "Seeing," Dillard recounts her discovery of Marius von Senden's book *Space and Sight*, which documents cases of individuals who, blinded by cataracts since birth, gain their sight through surgery. Before the brain learns to make sense of new stimuli coming through the eye, the newly sighted perceive the world as one-dimensional color patches and have no concept of distance, depth perception, or sense that objects have hard edges that define them from their surroundings. Shadows appear to be merely dark smudges. In short, the newly-sighted possess a unified visual field of pure stimulus. Von Senden's stories cause Dillard to lament how reason, understanding, and self-consciousness prevent her from seeing, as they do, the world as it is, rather than a world where reason has separated subject and object through distance and shadows.[22] For weeks afterwards, she practices eliminating spaces between objects, blurring the lines between subject and object, so as to leave "not one unfilled spot. All day long I walked among shifting color-patches that parted before me like the Red Sea."[23] She is unable to sustain such seeing for long, however. "Form," she observes, "is condemned to an eternal danse macabre with meaning."[24] For one cannot "unpeach the peaches" to make again "the world unraveled from reason."[25] The sighted live now "in a world of shadows that shape and distance color, a world where space makes a kind of terrible sense."[26] In fact, throughout the chapter, Dillard plays with multiple motifs illustrating ways space makes sight possible—for example in her explanation that when one sees fog, one cannot actually see "the fog itself," but only "tatters of clearness through a pervading obscurity."[27]

---

exiled, in the sparks of divine light the shells entrap" (FTB, 50). Yet, despite Dillard's admiration for the intellectual elegance of Luria's gnostic-like theology of evil, she finds equally if not more appealing Luria's affirmation of the physical world and life of the senses. As explained above, Dillard notes, "Jewish spiritual life takes place in the thick of, and sanctifies, the multiple world of created things. Devout Jews then and now have big families. [Luria] did not despise the body; the body may be 'turbid,' but its flesh shares in the joys to come. Luria warned his disciples against living in lonely places, or even visiting them" (FTB, 52).

22. PTC, 31.
23. PTC, 31.
24. PTC, 32.
25. PTC, 32.
26. PTC, 32.
27. PTC, 21. For a full discussion of how absences are, in Dillard's view, also potentially fertile spaces of meaning, see chapter 5.

Of course, Dillard's meditations on seeing and space are about spiritual vision as well as physical sight. Her summative question makes this clear: "What gnosticism is this," she asks, "and what physics?"[28] Dillard's question taken together with the immediately preceding phrase, "a world where space makes a kind of terrible sense," seems to allude to gnostical aspects peculiar to Luria's Kabbalistic notion of *tsimtsum*, not merely to gnosticism in general. For she is clearly not decrying a body/spirit dualism in which the material world is debased. Rather she objects to the paradoxical physical and spiritual facts that for things to be seen at all, they must have space to exist, which is Luria's proposition exactly. In the first primordial phase of *tsimtsum*, God contracted himself to make a void, or space within himself, to enable the material world to be created *ex nihilo*. Subsequently, each time God sent forth his all-powerful, creative light in *tsimtsum*'s second movement, the "vessels," or *qelipot*, made to give discrete forms to created things shattered, resulting in a cosmic catastrophe referred to as *shevirat ha-kelim*, "the shattering of the vessels." Thus, in Luria's view, space itself is the necessary condition for discrete objects to exist, and yet, in coming into being, they both receive animating life from the fragments, or "shards" of God's Shekinah and are simultaneously held imprisoned within their physical forms, enduring a tragic exile from God. It is a logic which "makes a kind of terrible sense." The word "terrible" and the context make clear that Dillard regrets this tragic "danse macabre" of form and meaning, of space and sight. She longs, rather, for a primordial, pre-rational sight that existed before space made objects possible and thereby perceptible.

The connection to Jewish mysticism is made explicit when Dillard recounts in the same paragraph one of Buber's tales of the Hasidim to describe one's loss of pure vision as the brain does its gnostical work. In the story, young Rabbi Mendel boasts to his teacher, Rabbi Elimelekh, that at night and at dawn he sees the angels who roll away the light before the darkness and the darkness before the light. The great Rabbi replies, "Yes, in my youth I saw that too. Later on you don't see these things anymore."[29] Rabbi Elimelekh's reply, although both wise and needed to temper Rabbi Mendel's arrogance and youthful enthusiasm, echoes Dillard's melancholy that with

---

28. PTC, 32.

29. PTC, 32. Dillard chooses to use this tale again in *For the Time Being*, published twenty-five years after *Pilgrim at Tinker Creek*: "'Later on,' a Hasid master said, 'you don't see these things anymore'" (FTB, 168). Its context in this later book is a discussion of the hiddenness of God. Brief and glorious mystical encounters, Dillard asserts, are rare: "Such experiences are gifts to beginners" (FTB, 168).

age, reason overcomes the imagination, preventing one from seeing the natural world inhabited by the supernatural.[30]

Naming is reason's necessary accomplice, reifying the brain's capacity to separate subject from object. Dillard observes, "Seeing is of course very much a matter of verbalization. Unless I call my attention to what passes before my eyes, I simply won't see it. . . . I have to say the words, describe what I'm seeing."[31] Yet, words, too, create distance, making linguistic objects out of sense perceptions, seemingly reinforcing the gnostical separation of form and meaning. If only she could only return to "Eden before Adam gave names," she posits, then "the scales would drop from my eyes; I'd see trees like men walking; I'd run down the road against all orders, hallooing and leaping."[32] In other words, if she could lose the delimiting perception that space and naming affords, she could become the recipient of a more faithful and miraculous vision of the world, as the allusions to Saul's conversion on the road to Damascus (after which the blinding scales fell from his eyes) and Jesus's healing of the blind man in Mark 8:24 suggest. Regaining such sight, however, requires spiritual work—a deliberate unraveling of one's perception of the world from reason, an upending of normal sight. For in both biblical stories, the incursion of the holy inverted all natural laws. Her clever inversion of the healed man's words (in Mark 8:24 he says, "I see men as trees, walking," but Dillard says "I'd see trees like men walking") underscores the point that spiritual vision requires a complete inversion of normal perception, a deliberate undoing of the brain's gnostic-like separation of objects from their surrounding space. In Dillard's view, such an untenable dualism of presence and absence allows her to name things and literally objectify the world, affording her the ability to perceive things but also not see them as they really are.

---

30. The tale's meaning is slightly ambiguous; it seems that Rabbi Mendel's way of seeing is exactly what Dillard aspires to achieve. Consequently, Dillard's use of a tale in which a character who sees this way is rebuked by his superior seems slightly puzzling. This makes it tempting to read the tale another way. Elimelekh's reply could be interpreted to mean that with age, one does not lose but gains proper sight. His wisdom allows him no longer to see light separated from dark and dark from light. Darkness and light are one, both suffused with holy Being. In short, he has gained a kind of vision that eliminates the "shadows" which distinguish subject from object. However, many of Rabbi Menahem Mendel of Rymanov's tales have a similarly self-effacing tone; several of his stories recount mistakes of his youth or instances in which his perception was wrong. The initial reading provided here is therefore the more convincing one. See Buber, *Tales of the Hasidim*.

31. PTC, 33.

32. PTC, 33.

Dillard's claim "I'd see trees like men walking" as well as her lament for the separation naming creates connects the passage unmistakably to Buber's *I and Thou*. In *I and Thou*, Part One, Buber asserts:

> once the sentence "I see the tree" has been pronounced in such a way that it no longer relates a relation between a human I and a tree You but the perception of the tree object by the human consciousness, it has erected the crucial barrier between subject and object; the basic word I-It, the word of separation has been spoken.
>
> —Then our melancholy lot took shape in primal history?
>
> —Indeed, it developed—insofar as man's conscious life developed in primal history.[33]

For Dillard as for Buber, human consciousness—signified most powerfully by one's capacity to name, to speak "the word of separation"—exiles her from seeing truly fellow creatures and creation, and, ultimately, God. Naming reduces the mystery of a dialogical I-Thou relationship to the mastery of an I-It relationship. The sharply-focused edges between matter and space created by rational sight become "the crucial barrier" defining one thing from another, separating subject from object. In terms of Luria's Kabbalah, this is the exile at the heart of cosmological history, when God chose to withdraw himself, or contract his presence, to create a void in which to make worlds, and it is this exile of objectification that Dillard strives to overcome. Undoing the gnostic-like separation is ultimately a spiritual endeavor. Its work blurs the lines between spirit and matter, subject and object, space and things, shapes and their shadows, to unify the world into a one-dimensional perceptual field in which objects and light are once again an "I" and a "Thou" to each other. Near the chapter's end, Rabbi Mendel's lost vision comes to Dillard, unbidden, while she straddles a sycamore over Tinker Creek:

> So I blurred my eyes and gazed toward the brim of my hat and saw a new world. I saw the pale white circles roll up, roll up, like the world's great turning, mute and perfect, and I saw the linear flashes, gleaming silver like stars being born at random down a rolling scroll of time. Something broke and something opened.[34]

---

33. Buber, *I and Thou*, 74–75.

34. PTC, 34.

"EACH DAY SPLINTERED DOWN" 37

This "new world" is a pansacramental one, where "blurred" (that is, spiritual) vision closes the gnostic gap between subject and object, leaving "not one unfilled spot," so that Dillard sees in each particular thing a cosmos made and re-made by eternal light. This pansacramental vision draws to a climax in the chapter's final paragraph when Dillard recounts that after searching "for years," she was at last granted a vision of the "tree with the lights in it": "I saw the backyard cedar where the mourning doves roost charged and transfigured, each cell buzzing with flame. I stood on the grass with the lights in it, grass that was holy fire, utterly focused and utterly dreamed. It was less like seeing than like being for the first time seen, knocked breathless by a powerful glance."[35]

The imagery in both passages is highly suggestive of Kabbalistic creation imagery, particularly as Buber interprets it, and, perhaps most importantly, uses the language of descent rather than ascent. When Dillard looks up, she sees eternal light rolling *down* the scroll of time. As Dillard walks, not in some heightened, mystical state but "thinking of nothing at all," she sees the "tree with the lights in it"[36] and the grass at her feet ablaze with the holy fire. These images clearly echo the Hasidic notion of *shevirat ha-kelim*—God's exiled Shekinah, the holy sparks, inhabiting all created things. To return to Buber's definition of pansacramentalism, God's presence is "laid in the things as sparks and awaits the liberation and fulfillment of the man who gives himself completely."[37]

Moreover, Dillard's lament for "a world where space makes a kind of terrible sense"[38] seems also to suggest limits to certain features of apophatic, or negative, theology, whose best-known exponent, Pseudo-Dionysius, was heavily influenced by the Neoplatonism of Proclus.[39] Since the chapter "Seeing" occurs in the first half of *Pilgrim at Tinker Creek*, which embodies the *via positiva*, it is perhaps not surprising that it explores ways of seeing that open her to the fullness and pleasures of cataphatic theology and hint at the limits of apophatic theology. Yet even in the second half of *Pilgrim*, centered on the *via negativa*'s methods of waiting, self-emptying, and silence, Dillard's experiences never entail the renunciation of the physical world or of the senses. Because Dillard is committed to artistic and spiritual integrity, the silence of the *via negativa* is often the most theologically honest response

---

35. PTC, 36.
36. PTC, 36.
37. Buber, *Origin and Meaning*, 170–71.
38. PTC, 32.
39. Louth, *Origins*, 159.

to life's cruelties and pain.[40] Thus, Dillard does often find the theology of the *via negativa* "more congenial" to her purposes.[41]

But unlike Neoplatonists, such as Plotinus and Pseudo-Dionysius, she does not turn her eyes away from the world to let go. The pilgrim in Plotinus's ascent does, however: "As the soul ascends to the One, it enters more deeply into itself: to find the One is to find itself. . . . Ascent to the One is a process of withdrawal into oneself."[42] By contrast, Dillard always insists, as she explains in the afterword to *Pilgrim at Tinker Creek*, that despite the use of first person, her perspective is persistently that of "a hand-held camera directed *outwards*" rather than inward.[43] Plotinus's description of the role of the senses in the soul's ascent to the One helps to clarify further the differences between Dillard's and Neoplatonic discourse about the physical senses. In the sixth tractate of *The Enneads* Plotinus determines that "To the vision of these [transcendent things] we must mount, *leaving sense to its own low place*."[44] Therefore, when asked what is the way of the mystical ascent, Plotinus responds by explaining the lower world must be left behind:

> 8. But what must we do? How lies the path? How come to vision of the inaccessible Beauty, dwelling as if in consecrated precincts, apart from the common ways where all may see, even the profane?
>
> He that has the strength, let him arise and withdraw into himself, foregoing all that is known by the eyes, turning away for ever [sic] from the material beauty that once made his joy. When he perceives those shapes of grace that show in body, let him not pursue: he must know them for copies, vestiges, shadows, and hasten away towards That [sic] they tell of. . . .
>
> What then is our course, what the manner of our flight? This is not a journey for the feet; the feet bring us only from land

---

40. See Dillard's interviews in Burnett, "Interview"; Abood, "Natural Wonders." She observes to Burnett, "Even to talk about God in the first place for me takes a whole lot of sincerity and it's hard even to begin, and once I do I am of course committed to being absolutely honest, which is very, very difficult" (Burnett, "Interview," 90). To Abood, she explains, "If the writer knows how grim it can get, and then the writer is nevertheless a believer, the belief is a lot more convincing" (Abood, "Natural Wonders," 30).

41. PTC, 279.

42. Louth, *Origins*, 39.

43. PTC, 282 (emphasis mine). Comments in a 1978 interview with Philip Yancey further clarify Dillard's outward focus: "As a writer, I am less a creator than an audience to the artistic vision. In *Holy the Firm* I even inserted a disclaimer. I said, 'No one has ever lived well.' I do not live well. I merely point to the vision" (Yancey, "Face Aflame," 16).

44. Plotinus, *Enneads*, 42 (emphasis mine).

to land; nor need you think of coach or ship to carry you away; all this order of things you must set aside and refuse to see: you must close the eyes and call instead upon another vision which is to be waked within you, a vision, the birth-right of all, which few turn to use.[45]

Plotinus's call to "set aside" the things of this world, to "refuse to see" them, to "close your eyes" in order to behold an inner, truer vision simply cannot be found in Dillard's work. She speaks admiringly of the spiritual discipline of cultivating inner silence, but these practices sharpen her sensory perceptions rather than dim them. In chapter 11 of *Pilgrim at Tinker Creek*, she identifies waiting as the *via negativa*'s way of stalking God.[46] However, she is waiting to see glory unfold materially, in front of and outside of herself, rather than inside her mind or spirit. As she describes waiting in silence to see fish or muskrats, she muses: "The great hurrah about wild animals is that they exist at all, and the greater hurrah is the actual moment of seeing them. . . . They show me by their very wariness what a prize it is simply to *open my eyes and behold*."[47] Later in the same chapter, she includes another of Buber's Hasidic tales, emphasizing the heightening of visual perception:

> Martin Buber quotes an old Hasid master who said, "When you walk across the fields with your mind pure and holy, then from all the stones, and all growing things, and all animals, the sparks of their soul come out and cling to you, and then they are purified and become a holy fire in you." This is one way of describing the energy that comes, using the specialized Kabbalistic vocabulary of Hasidism.[48]

Though Dillard may practice the *via negativa*, doing so vivifies rather than diminishes her perception of created things, enabling her to see "the sparks of their soul[s]" coming out to "cling" to her.

Indeed, her desire for contact with mystery through sensory experiences becomes almost macabre in the following chapter, "Nightwatch." While reading about locusts, she learns of a man who, attacked by locusts while asleep, has to be rescued by friends; when he emerges from beneath their "clicking coat of mail," his wrists and neck are covered in blood.[49] Instead of finding this disturbing, she is fascinated by it, and in

---

45. Plotinus, *Enneads*, 45–46.
46. PTC, 186.
47. PTC, 195 (emphasis mine).
48. PTC, 200–201.
49. PTC, 211.

the remainder of the chapter, the locusts come to symbolize a thrilling assault of the senses and spirit by mystery. Toward the chapter's end, she alludes to the biblical stories of Jacob at Bethel and Peniel[50] and asks, "Had this place always been so, and I had not known it? . . . Why didn't I wrestle the grasshopper on my shoulder and pin him down until he called my name?"[51] By substituting grasshoppers for the mysterious angelic figure who wrestles Jacob, she suggests that both in the particulars of the world and in the vivid physical sensations they produce, mystery emerges with which she longs to engage. "This is what I had come for," she declares, "just this . . . the assault of *real* things."[52]

Furthermore, the movement of holiness is downward. The subsequent paragraphs allude to Jacob's dream of angels ascending and descending from heaven as she exultantly describes the ascent and descent of all she sees—grasshoppers, thistledown, a goldfinch, herself—suggesting that these particular things are, like angels, harbingers of a holiness that simultaneously terrifies and thrills.[53] Importantly, she seems to stress that it is the descent that matters. She describes the spectacle of a juggler's balls and notes, "The ascending arc is the hard part, but our eyes are on the smooth and curving fall. Each falling ball seems to trail beauty as its afterimage."[54] In the next paragraph, in response to the sleeping wonders of goldfinch and wasps, she exclaims, "Everybody grab a handle: we're spinning headlong down."[55]

In her meditation on Genesis 3's account of the fall, she rejects its claim that the world is cursed because of Adam's sin. If it is, she exults, "then the fall was happy indeed."[56] She then makes a startling conclusion: "Creation itself was the fall, a burst into the thorny beauty of the real."[57] Dillard's creation theology departs sharply here from the Genesis account,[58] and the departure seems to signal a shift to a different narrative, namely Luria's creation story in which "creation itself" was indeed the fall. In Luria's account, the shattering of the holy vessels simultaneously made both the material world and

---

50. See Genesis 28:16; 32:24. Jacob awakes from a dream in which he sees angels ascending and descending a ladder to heaven and exclaims, "Surely the Lord is in this place—and I did not know it!" (Gen 28:16).

51. PTC, 223.

52. PTC, 215 (emphasis mine).

53. PTC, 223.

54. PTC, 223.

55. PTC, 223.

56. PTC, 218.

57. PTC, 218–19.

58. For a full treatment of this seemingly anomalous passage as it relates to Dillard's understanding of evil and suffering, see chapter 3.

evil possible. In one cosmic catastrophe "the real" was made both beautiful and "thorny." Dillard asserts, however, that, for the creature, the fall is an exhilarating coming into being, and she glories in her own descent. She writes, "I am puffed clay, blown up and set down. That I fall like Adam is not surprising: . . . The surprise is how good the wind feels on my face as I fall."[59] Consequently, even in the midst of the *via negativa*, Dillard exults in the descent into corporeality and in the sensory stimuli such a fall affords.

The motif of descent continues through the chapter's closing paragraphs. Dillard concludes, "I didn't know, I never have known, what spirit it is that *descends* into my lungs and flaps near my heart like an eagle rising. I named it full-of-wonder, highest good, voices."[60] Again, the mystical encounter is catalyzed by God's descent, not her soul's ascent. Additionally, this spirit inhabits and makes more alive, more real, her corporeal self, not less. It is an animating, vivifying presence, and as such is highly suggestive of the Hasidic notion of the holy sparks that fell downward and indwell creation.

It may be helpful at this point to return once again to Buber's definition of pansacramentalism: "the holy in things . . . is laid in the things as sparks and awaits the liberation and fulfillment of the man who gives himself completely."[61] Buber's phrase "is laid in things" and Dillard's descents speak of the downward motion of a holiness that animates concrete particulars and is therefore to be found in them. The chapter's final paragraph provides highly evocative imagery that reinforces the connection between the senses, descending holiness, and mystical ecstasy:

> And what if those grasshoppers had been locusts *descending*, I thought, and what if I stood awake in a swarm? I cannot ask for more than to be so wholly acted upon, flown at, and lighted on in throngs, probed, knocked, even bitten. A little blood from the wrists and throat is the price I would willingly pay for that pressure of clacking weights on my shoulders, for the scent of deserts, groundfire in my ears—for being so in the clustering thick of things, rapt and enwrapped in the rising and falling real world.[62]

---

59. PTC, 223.
60. PTC, 224 (emphasis mine).
61. Buber, *Origin and Meaning*, 170–71.
62. PTC, 224 (emphasis mine). The imagery could arguably be an implicit allusion to the stigmata, the wounds of Christ received in rare moments of ecstatic mystical experiences, since Dillard imagines the ecstasy of locusts descending and inflicting wounds upon her. Reading the passage this way does link her to the medieval Christian mystical tradition of passion mysticism, and yet it also reinforces her artistic assertion that holiness manifests itself in the body and in the physical realm.

Dillard uses the language of ecstatic rapture here, but it is the "real world" in which she finds herself enraptured. The phrase "clustering the thick of things" expresses in both "thick" and "things" a sort of sensory fatness that is anything but a flight from the finite and corporeal to the thinness of pure spirit and abstraction. In fact, it is difficult to imagine a more aggressive and potent engagement of the senses than the one depicted here; Dillard smells, hears, and feels the voracious insects as they devour her own body.[63] Even in the cataphatic theology of Pseudo-Dionysius, creation serves primarily utilitarian purposes in aiding the soul through praise in its ascent to God, but ultimately, both apophatic and cataphatic theologies "point beyond themselves to the way of negation."[64] In contrast, Dillard's ecstasy results not from ascending to celestial atmospheres but from falling "like Adam" into corporeality and feeling the wind in her face as she plummets.[65] In another telling example, Dillard calls Tinker Creek "a curious, tugged version of the great chain of being,"[66] and states "it descends to me" bringing to her a "distillation of *the* spirit" on the lighted surface of the water; "it comes, mediated, *only* on the skin of the real and present creek."[67] Though Dillard alludes to the Neoplatonic idea of the great chain of being, she qualifies it, saying that this is a "curious tugged version" that "descends" and is mediated through rather than apart from creation. Thus both Dillard's *via negativa* and *via positiva* in *Pilgrim at Tinker Creek* advocate a way of experiencing the divine that seems to resist the Neoplatonic impulse to jettison the world in its ascent to the One and, instead, it embraces the world with eyes, ears, and hands wide open to receive the sacred, even through the jaws of locusts.

---

63. Mark McIntosh notes, in *Mystical Theology*, that not all early Christian mysticism excludes the life of the body. He argues that, for example, in the mystical theology of Maximus the Confessor, "God shines forth, as in Christ, precisely through the perfections of human existence—and these have ever included the perceptivity of our bodies (note that Maximus does not exclude our material being), the linguisticality of our minds and the sensitivity of our feelings. Mystical theology in this view is not the activity of speechless disembodied automatons but of real human beings who find that their whole humanity 'takes place' more intensely and vitally than ever" (McIntosh, *Mystical Theology*, 61–62). Likewise, he argues that in the passion mysticism of later medieval Christianity "bodiliness is not . . . a possessively grasped creatureliness that obfuscates the divine reality, but is rather a *medium of communication*, and quite literally of communion" (McIntosh, *Mystical Theology*, 78–79). While this is true, the language of these mystics describes an interiority and merging of the self with God in ways that are quite different from Dillard's mystical consciousness.

64. Louth, *Origins*, 167.

65. PTC, 223.

66. PTC, 102.

67. PTC, 102 (emphasis mine).

In chapter 6 of *Pilgrim at Tinker Creek* Dillard reprises her account of the "tree with the lights in it," a backyard tree transfigured before her eyes, each cell buzzing with eternal light, offering further analysis of the experience.[68] Here, too, Dillard's vision never obscures the physical tree, nor does it transport her from the particular to the universal, from outward to inward vision. Her commentary about the experience is perhaps the clearest articulation of mystical descent in her work:

> I had thought, because I had seen the tree with the lights in it, that the great door, by definition, opens on eternity. . . . Now that I have experienced the present purely through my senses—I discover that, although the door to the tree with the lights in it was opened *from* eternity, as it were, and shone on that tree eternal lights, it nevertheless opened on the real and present cedar. It opened on time: Where else? That Christ's incarnation occurred improbably, ridiculously, at such-and-such a time, into such-and-such a place, is referred to—with great sincerity even among believers—as "the scandal of particularity." Well, the "scandal of particularity" is the only world that I, in particular, know. What use has eternity for light? We're all up to our necks in this particular scandal. . . . I never saw a tree that was no tree in particular. I never met a man, not the greatest theologian, who filled infinity, or even whose hand, say, was undifferentiated, fingerless, like a griddle cake, and not lobed and split just so with the incursions of time.[69]

While Neoplatonic mystical experience, as described by Plotinus, Eckhart, and others with whom Dillard is often linked, employs the language of ascent as the soul moves ever upward (or inward) toward the Absolute as it frees itself from the grip of the sensual world, here, Dillard emphasizes by italicizing "*from* eternity" exactly the opposite—eternity opens up (descends, as it were) on time, on "a real and present cedar tree."[70] The holy irrupts through the skin of time and space; the door swings earth-ward, not heaven-ward. Most importantly, this revelatory moment occurs not by leaving her senses but by experiencing the present "*purely* through [her] senses."[71] Moreover, by repeating "I never" and by asking rhetorically "Where else?" would eternity show up but in time, she argues forcefully that *only* in the particulars of this world can humans glimpse eternity.

68. PTC, 36.
69. PTC, 81.
70. PTC, 81.
71. PTC, 81 (emphasis mine).

There is an uncanny similarity between Dillard's rhetorical question "What use has eternity for light?" and one that Martin Buber asks in "Symbolic and Sacramental Existence." Identifying key distinctions between the Kabbalah and Hasidism, Buber argues that Hasidism protests against the Kabbalah's "schematization" and "magicizing of the mystery."[72] "The Kabbala," Buber argues, "employing a combination of gnostic and Neo-Platonic schemata, fashioned a Talmudic teaching into a monstrous prodigy."[73] He maintains that, like all forms of gnosis, the Kabbalah creates elaborate doctrines to reconcile the contradiction of "the corroding essence of the world" with the "being of God."[74] In Buber's estimation, this is nothing more than "seeing through the contradiction of being and removing itself from it."[75] The Kabbalah's name-and-letter magical methods are the other side of the same coin. Gnosis sees through the contradiction. Magic provides the *means* to see through the contradiction.[76] Hasidism, however, "is faithful to endure the contradiction and thus to redeem the contradiction itself."[77] Buber acknowledges that Hasidism has retained, at its periphery, vestiges of Kabbalistic practice, but at its heart, he asserts, is an entirely new emphasis—the striving to "overcome the separation between the holy and profane" and to "overcome the emphasis on fixed procedures of intention from out of the fullness of the living act."[78] In a great crescendo to his argument, Buber exclaims, "What concern of ours, if they exist, are the upper worlds! Our concern is 'in this lower world of corporeality, to let the hidden life of God shine forth.'"[79]

In these two rhetorical questions—Dillard's "What use has eternity for light?" and Buber's "What concern of ours, if they exist, are the upper worlds!"—both authors make nearly identical, emphatic declarations that the physical world ("where else?") is where God chooses to reveal himself. As Scholem observes, "To the Hasid" *tsimtsum* means that "a ray of God's essence is present and perceptible everywhere and at every moment."[80] It may, at any time, irrupt through chloroplasts and bark to become perceptible in a particular cedar tree, at a particular time. Both Dillard and Buber appear

---

72. Buber, *Origin and Meaning*, 179.
73. Buber, *Origin and Meaning*, 176.
74. Buber, *Origin and Meaning*, 178, 173.
75. Buber, *Origin and Meaning*, 178.
76. Buber, *Origin and Meaning*, 180.
77. Buber, *Origin and Meaning*, 178.
78. Buber, *Origin and Meaning*, 180.
79. Buber, *Origin and Meaning*, 181.
80. Scholem, *Major Trends*, 348.

therefore to suggest that the eternal is not transcendent but coterminous with the physical world, just on the other side of time's thin membrane, just inside the imprisoning shells.

The implicit and explicit links in Dillard's work to Jewish mysticism that emerge in its robust pansacramentalism would seem to argue against reading her solely as a Christian mystic within the Neoplatonic tradition. As noted above, the fundamental differences between *Pilgrim at Tinker Creek*'s vision of mystical descent and the early voices of Neoplatonism, such as Plotinus and Pseudo-Dionysius, appear to be significant. These differences are underscored when contrasting Dillard with comprehensive surveys of Christian mysticism such as Evelyn Underhill's *Mysticism*. According to Underhill, one of four defining criteria of "true mysticism" is that "its aims are wholly transcendental and spiritual. It is in no way concerned with adding to, exploring, re-arranging, or improving anything in the visible universe. The mystic brushes aside that universe."[81]

Although Underhill argues that such mysticism is no "harsh dualism, no turning from a bad material world to a good spiritual world, her language belies a perhaps subtle but very real dualism. She speaks of the mystic's "vision of the Universe" as one in which an individual ascends "from sense to soul, from soul to spirit,"[82] indicating a progression from the lower world of the senses to the higher realm of the spirit. The privileging of spirit over matter is especially clear when she asserts that the mystic's conception of God will be symbolic and "his experience, if genuine, will far transcend the symbols he employs" and that "[the mystic] lives by an immediate knowledge ... achieved in those hours of *direct, unmediated intercourse with the Transcendent* when, as he says, he was 'in union with God.'"[83] Underhill's language seems to leave little doubt that she sees the physical realm, including symbol and sacrament, as an unfortunate and inferior way-station to be transcended.

Dillard's absolute claim that "[*the* spirit] comes, mediated,[84] only on the skin of the real and present creek" could hardly make the point more clearly that for her, mystical experience is mediated and therefore contrasts entirely with Underhill's claim of "direct, unmediated intercourse" with the

---

81. Underhill, *Mysticism*, 81.
82. Underhill, *Essentials of Mysticism*, 9.
83. Underhill, *Essentials of Mysticism*, 25 (emphasis mine).
84. For a brief discussion of the language of "mediation," see "Excursus on Mediation" at the end of this chapter.

divine.[85] John Baillie, whose thinking is heavily indebted to Buber, expresses well the pansacramental view in *Our Knowledge of God*:

> It seems plain that the consciousness of God is never given save in conjunction with the consciousness of things. We do not know God through the world, but we know Him with the world; and in knowing Him with the world, we know Him as its ground. Just as in the sacrament of Holy Communion the Real Presence of Christ is given . . . "in, with and under" the bread and wine, so in a wider sense the whole corporeal world may become sacramental to us of the presence of the Triune God.[86]

Tellingly, not a single account of an ecstatic moment or brush with the divine in any of Dillard's works involves a flight from the physical to the transcendent realm. Even the rare theophanies, such as her vision of Christ's baptism in *Holy the Firm* do not obscure the local landscape and are lush with physical, sensory detail.

Holiness Splintered into a Vessel: *Holy the Firm*

Holy the Firm, published in 1977, is perhaps Dillard's most identifiably Christian book. Only sixty-five pages long, it is divided into three sections corresponding to three days, November 18, 19, and 20, of Dillard's life in a cottage on Puget Sound and follows roughly the pattern of creation, fall, and redemption.[87] For several reasons, including its tripartite structure, allusions to Julian of Norwich, and theophany of Christ being baptized, it could perhaps more than any of her other books be produced as evidence that her work fits "squarely in the Christian mystical tradition dating from Plotinus."[88] Yet upon closer examination, *Holy the Firm* presents a complex and theologically potent blend of Christian and Jewish mysticism. Dillard fuses Christian elements, particularly the sacrament of the Eucharist, with Hasidic pansacramentalism to explore yet again the "scandal of particularity" and the role of the senses in perceiving the holiness that resides within, not above, creation. In doing so, she is arguably some distance from the Neoplatonic Christian mystical tradition even in her most explicitly Christian book.

---

85. PTC, 102; Underhill, *Essentials of Mysticism*, 25
86. Baillie, *Our Knowledge of God*, 178–79.
87. Yancey, "Face Aflame," 16; Burnett, "Interview," 88.
88. Abood, "Natural Wonders," 32.

In the book's third and final section, Dillard has volunteered to purchase communion wine at a local store. After "forgetting [herself], thank God," while joking with the owner's two-year old son, she begins walking uphill with the California red in a knapsack on her back, her "right hand forgetting [her]" left.[89] In that moment of self-forgetfulness, a mystical event begins. She writes:

> Here is a bottle of wine with a label, Christ with a cork. I bear holiness splintered into a vessel, very God of very God, the sempiternal silence personal and brooding, bright on the back of my ribs. I start up the hill. The world is changing. . . . It is starting to utter its infinite particulars, each overlapping and lone, like a hundred hills of hounds all giving tongue.[90]

The phrase "holiness splintered into a vessel" is derived directly from Jewish mysticism, the *shevirat ha-kelim*, or the "breaking of the vessels" at creation in which "fragments of divine light (*nizonot*, or 'sparks') . . . fell downward, while the remaining lights ascended back toward the Ein Sof."[91] The imagery unites perhaps the most potent of Christian sacramental symbols, Christ's blood, with images from Jewish mysticism which also signify God's immediate, incarnate presence—the holy sparks of his Shekinah, present in every created thing. Further, the imagery and parallelism in the paragraph's first sentences ("wine with a label" and "Christ with a cork") invite a transposition of terms which emphasizes both the humanity and historicity of Christ as well as the mystery of the Eucharist. The California red becomes Christ with a label, the "King of the Jews," who is "splintered into a vessel," a human body, and "splintered" on a cross. Yet he is also wholly other, a "brooding" and "sempiternal" God who is both present and silent.[92] The passage affirms Christ's corporeality and the mystery of the Presence, and makes clear Dillard's belief in the sacramental nature of the "infinite particulars" of the world. It simultaneously foreshadows the ecstatic moment to come that reveals Christ as Immanuel present in the very cells of all that exists.

Bearing the incarnate Christ on her back she begins to experience an unfolding vision of the world transformed, "its infinite particulars" charged with energy and light.[93] The life within "blackberry brambles, white snowberries, red rose hips," becomes visible like "banked fires"; mountains are "raw nerves, sensible and exultant; the trees, the grass, and the asphalt below

---

89. HTF, 64.
90. HTF, 64–65.
91. Dan, *Teachings of Hasidism*, 12.
92. HTF, 66.
93. HTF, 65.

[her] are living petals of the mind, each sharp and invisible, held in a greeting or glance full perfectly formed."[94] Then exultant and awed, she states:

> Through all my clothing, through the pack on my back, and through the bottle's glass I feel the wine. Walking faster and faster, weightless, I feel the wine. It sheds light in slats through my rib cage, and fills the buttressed vaults of my ribs with light pooled and buoyant.[95]

Noteworthy is the repetition of "I feel." Even though Dillard is literally and figuratively moving toward an ecstatic moment, her senses are not dulled or abandoned, but heightened. As the material world becomes charged with light and holiness, her physical senses are so keenly awakened that she can feel the sloshing wine on her back and its ruby-colored light pool in the sanctuary of her rib cage. Moreover, she feels it descending through each material layer (bottle, pack, clothing) to touch nerve endings in her skin.

As she reaches the crest of the hill and the apex of the spiritual vision, she sees the bay before her "transfigured" and the Puget Sound "islands on fire."[96] Then a unitive moment begins:

> Everything, everything, is whole, a parcel of everything else. I myself am falling down, slowly, or slowly lifting up. On the bay's stone shore are people among whom I float, real people, gathering of an afternoon, in the cells of whose skin stream thin colored waters in pieces which give back the general flame.[97]

The imagery of descent echoes Christ's descent into flesh and the phrase "falling down," though equivocal, connotes that the mystical movement is downward as well as perhaps upward. Though Neoplatonism conceives of the soul's search for God as an ascent, Louth notes that the incarnation speaks of God's "*descent* into the world that he might give to man the possibility of a communion with God that is not open to him by nature"; it is here that, historically, Christian mysticism struggles within its Platonic framework.[98] Interestingly, stepping outside this Platonic framework and into a Hasidic one to examine Dillard's text reveals that the imagery of the cells giving back "the general flame" seems very much like Hasidic descriptions of the "sparks" in the souls of created things "com[ing] out and cling[ing]

---

94. HTF, 65.
95. HTF, 65.
96. HTF, 66.
97. HTF, 66.
98. Louth, *Origins*, xiv.

to you" and becoming "a holy fire in you."⁹⁹ Once again, Dillard appears to fuse incarnational theology with Hasidic imagery to create a richly pansacramental view rather than a Neoplatonic vision.

Dillard extends the sacramental motif to include the entire landscape, emphasizing the physicality of everything around her: she floats among "real people," who have gathered at a particular time, on a rock solid shore. Though the bay is "transfigured," it is *figured*. The water, though suffused with holiness, still wets the rocks and reflects the "unraveling sky."¹⁰⁰ In Dillard's vision, then, the corporeal can and does give back the "general flame."¹⁰¹ The scene culminates in Dillard's seeing Christ baptized by John in the bay before her. As the vision unfolds, Christ and the world merge into a blaze of holiness: "For outside it is bright. The surface of things outside the drops [on Christ's back] has fused. Christ himself and the others, the brown warm wind, and hair, sky, the beach, the shattered water—all this has fused. It is the one glare of holiness; it is bare and unspeakable."¹⁰²

This seems clearly to be a mystical, unitive experience but with a crucial difference from those within a Neoplatonic Christian mystical tradition. Dillard's *soul* is not fused with Christ; the *physical world* and Christ are fused, in a vision Dillard beholds external to herself. This is precisely the understanding of the unitive experience found in Hasidism. Martin Buber explains that, for the Hasidim, "*Yihud, unio*, means not the unification of a soul with God, but unification of God with his glory that dwells in the world."¹⁰³ He goes on to observe that this may properly be called "mysticism" because "it preserves the immediacy of the relation, guards the concreteness of the absolute and demands the involvement of the whole being."¹⁰⁴ Furthermore, Buber asserts:

> nowhere [in the Baal Shem Tov's teaching], in contrast to all ascetic teaching that strives to surmount reality, is it intimated that the indwelling principle would draw itself out of the world; rather the unification of the separated means just the unification of God with the world, which continues to exist as world, only that it is now, just as world, redeemed.¹⁰⁵

99. PTC, 200–201.
100. HTF, 66.
101. HTF, 66.
102. HTF, 67.
103. Buber, *Hasidism and Modern Man*, 180.
104. Buber, *Hasidism and Modern Man*, 181.
105. Buber, *Origin and Meaning*, 85. Schatz-Uffenheimer and Scholem challenge Buber precisely on this point, arguing that in Hasidism the "teaching of the uplifting of the sparks through human activity does in fact mean that there is an element in reality

Although there are examples within Hasidic literature of ecstatic experiences in which one leaves behind consciousness of this realm to achieve ecstatic union with God, these are relatively rare.[106] Gershom Scholem notes that even more rare are accounts in which

> ecstasy signifies actual union with God, in which the human individuality abandons itself to the rapture of complete submersion in the divine stream. Even in this ecstatic frame of mind, the Jewish mystic almost invariably retains a sense of the distance between the Creator and His creature. The latter is joined to the former, and the point where the two meet is of the greatest interest to the mystic, but he does not regard it as constituting anything so extravagant as identity of Creator and creature.[107]

As noted in chapter 1, the term generally used in Jewish mystical literature for "unio mystica" is *devekuth*.[108] "Devekuth," Scholem explains, "can be ecstasy, but its meaning is far more comprehensive."[109] It signifies a "perpetual being-with-God, an intimate union and conformity of the human and the divine will."[110] Yet this intimacy, no matter how exalted or blissful, does not eliminate the "proper sense of distance, or, if you will, incommensurateness" between God and humanity.[111]

Dillard's vision in *Holy the Firm* seems to describe exactly this. The world continues to exist as world—the people, the "warm brown wind, sky, the beach, the shattered water" all remain, only now Christ and the world have fused into "the one glare of holiness."[112] God has united himself to the world, "just as world," and transfigured it. Perhaps most importantly, in Dillard's account as in Hasidism, the ontological gap between herself, Christ, and the "glare of holiness" never closes. Neither the material world nor she

---

with which man can and should establish a positive connection, but the exposure or realization of this element simultaneously *annihilates* reality, insofar as 'reality' signifies, as it does for Buber, the here and now" (Scholem, "Martin Buber's Interpretation," 240). The holy joy of Hasidism, Scholem argues, is not a joy in life "as it is" but a joy in the "perpetual life of God" abstracted from the here and now. See Scholem, "Martin Buber's Interpretation," 227–50; Schatz-Uffenheimer, "Man's Relation," 403–34. Even if Buber's interpretation is flawed, he is Dillard's most frequently cited source for her knowledge of Hasidism, and Buber's interpretation and Dillard's text are consonant.

106. Scholem, *Major Trends*, 122–23; Mendes-Flohr, Introduction, xxiii.
107. Scholem, *Major Trends*, 122–23.
108. Scholem, *Major Trends*, 123.
109. Scholem, *Major Trends*, 123.
110. Scholem, *Major Trends*, 123–24.
111. Scholem, *Major Trends*, 123.
112. HTF, 67.

becomes of one substance with holiness. In fact, the particulars of the world become more particularly themselves as her vision reveals "holiness splintered into" each vessel; she is able to see the life-fire in blackberry bramble stems and blood platelets in the veins of beach-goers, all giving "back the general flame."[113] The particulars are not described as being swallowed up in the universal or left behind as is typical of Neoplatonic discourse about unitive experiences with the One. Rather, holiness is hidden in creation, and the two remain distinct. Just as Buber describes, Dillard's experience "preserves the immediacy of the relation, guards the concreteness of the absolute and demands the involvement of the whole being."[114]

Dillard seems to anticipate that her description of this mystical event will precipitate questions about whether God is emanent or immanent, since immediately following she begins a discourse on the subject. Emanence she defines as "the ascetic's metaphysic" in which the world is far from God.[115] At the opposite end of her spectrum is immanence, which she defines as "scarcely different from pantheism."[116] Emanence she rejects, for it saves men's souls but leaves the world "flat and patently unredeemed," making all creatures and creation other than man "irrelevant and nonparticipant" as well as "illusory, absurd, accidental."[117] Immanence she also rejects, for it makes Christ redundant, since "all things are one."[118]

Rather she returns to a question she raised in Part II of the book: does God touch anything in the universe? And if so, how? The questions arise after a neighbor's young daughter is badly burned in a plane crash on the island. The event leads her to ask if creation has any meaning and whether matter is somewhere, somehow connected to God:

> Faith would be, in short, that God has any willful connection with time whatsoever, and with us. For I know it as a given that God is all good. And I take it also as given that whatever he touches has meaning, if only in his mysterious terms, the which I readily grant. The question is, then, whether God touches anything. Is anything firm or is time on the loose? . . . Is there no link at the base of things?[119]

---

113. HTF, 66.
114. Buber, *Hasidism and Modern Man*, 181.
115. HTF, 69.
116. HTF, 69.
117. HTF, 70.
118. HTF, 70.
119. HTF, 47–48.

If not, she must conclude that "the accidental universe spins mute, obedient only to its own gross terms, meaningless, out of mind, and alone."[120]

In the book's third and final section, she answers this question with the idea of "Holy the Firm," a created substance, the fundamental essence of all material, which Esoteric Christianity says can be found in the "waxy deepness of planets, but never on the surface of planets where men could discern it; and it is in touch with the Absolute, at base. In touch with the Absolute! At base."[121] As the final, repeated exclamatory phrase indicates, the connection between God and creatures is "at base"—in other words, within the solidity of the material world. The pun suggested by "base"—meaning both at the lowest point and in the sordidness of life—implies that God does touch even the grossest of elements and thereby infuses it with meaning. Dillard repeats the idea of baseness a few lines later when she asks, "Does something that touched something that touched Holy the Firm in touch with the Absolute at base seep into ground water, into grain; are islands rooted in it, and trees? Of course."[122] She concludes that since God touches everything, "Matter and spirit are of a piece but distinguishable; God has a stake guaranteed in all the world. And the universe is real and not a dream, not a manufacture of the senses; subject may know object."[123]

The motif of Holy the Firm articulates a view of God's presence in the physical world remarkably close to Hasidic panentheism. Dillard speaks knowledgeably of Hasidic panentheism in *For the Time Being*: "Luria despaired of the husk, the shard without; the Baal Shem Tov delighted in the spark, the God within. This is not pantheism but pan-entheism: The one transcendent God made the universe, and his presence kindles inside every speck of it. Each clot of clay conceals a coal."[124] Later she quotes Rabbi Menachem Nahum of Chernobyl's view of God presence in creation, describing it as panentheistic:

> "All being itself is derived from God and the presence of the Creator is in each created thing." This double notion is pan-entheism—a word to which I add a hyphen to emphasize its difference from pantheism. Pan-entheism, according to David Tracy, theologian at the University of Chicago, is the private view of most Christian intellectuals today.[125]

---

120. HTF, 48.
121. HTF, 69.
122. HTF, 69.
123. HTF, 71.
124. FTB, 137.
125. FTB, 176.

No doubt Dillard includes herself in the category of contemporary intellectuals who espouse a panentheistic view. To review briefly, Martin Buber was aware that Hasidic panentheism could be easily misunderstood as pantheism, so he takes care in his discussions of Hasidism to draw clear lines of demarcation between them:

> Hasidism is no pantheism. It teaches the absolute transcendence of God, but as combined with his conditioned immanence. The world is an irradiation of God, but as it is endowed with an independence of existence and striving, it is apt, always and everywhere, to form a crust around itself. Thus, a divine spark lives in every thing and every being, but each spark is enclosed by an isolating shell. Only man can liberate it.[126]

Likewise, Maurice Friedman explains in *Martin Buber: The Life of Dialogue* that "the Hasidic emphasis on the immanence of God is not to be regarded as pantheism, but as panentheism.... Man has a part in the Shekinah which enables him to be a co-worker with God in the perfection of the world toward redemption. Thus the stress of Hasidism is on the actual consummation of religious life" in the manifestation of the inward life of God in one's outward actions.[127]

Holy the Firm repeatedly employs imagery that embodies the role of Hasidic panentheism in the life of worship and redemption. The book begins by describing each day as a god and with Dillard rejoicing: "I praise each day splintered down, splintered down and wrapped in time like a husk, a husk of many colors spreading, at dawn fast over the mountains split."[128] With characteristic syncretism, Dillard blends nineteenth-century American Transcendentalism with Hasidism's joyous description of the world as an "irradiation of God." The words "splintered down," repeated twice and modifying "day," allude to the splintering of God's Shekinah, which as Buber explains has left holy sparks enclosed in an isolating shell, or in Dillard's words, holiness "wrapped in time like a husk." The allusion to Joseph's coat of many colors ("a husk of many colors") seems to strengthen a Hebraic interpretation of the lines.

---

126. Buber, *Hasidism and Modern Man*, 126–27. Even within Lurianic Kabbalism, from which Hasidism springs, the concept of the holy sparks is not pantheistic. Scholem explains that there is a "residue of divine manifestation in every being, but under the aspect of *Tsimtsum* it also acquires a reality of its own which guards it against the danger of dissolution into the non-individual being of the divine 'all-in-all.' Luria himself was the living example of an outspoken theistic mystic. He gave the Zohar, for all its intrinsic pantheism, a strictly theistic interpretation" (Scholem, *Major Trends*, 262).

127. Friedman, *Martin Buber*, 20.

128. HTF, 11.

The Hasidic understanding of redemption finds expression in the final section of *Holy the Firm*. After concluding that God indeed touches everything at base and that matter and spirit are "of a piece but distinguishable," Dillard begins speaking directly to the reader in the imperative mood:

> Hold hands and crack the whip, and yank the Absolute out of there and into the light, God pale and astounded, spraying a spiral of salts and earths, God footloose and flung. And cry down the line to his passing white ear, "Old Sir! Do you hold space from buckling by a finger in its hole? O Old! Where is your other hand?" His right hand is clenching, calm, round the exploding left hand of Holy the Firm.[129]

Though the idea of "Holy the Firm" comes from Esoteric Christianity, the passage's images and tone seem consonant with much of Hasidic pansacramentalism as articulated by Buber. Its levity, including the allusion to the playground game of "crack the whip," suggests that, as the Hasids maintain, unearthing God from within the concealing husks of time and creation can be one of holy joy.[130] She addresses God playfully as "Old Sir!" and then more familiarly as just "O Old!" asking "Where is your other hand?"[131] Moreover, Dillard's description of God as "emerging" from eons of subterranean hiding is highly suggestive of the Lurianic notion of the holy sparks being hidden within the crusts of matter. God is made "footloose" and "flung" by the effort of humans to unearth the holy. Hence, Dillard enlists the help of the reader by shifting into the imperative mood and commanding the reader to "yank the Absolute out of there" with holy joy and fervor. Dillard's recourse to the imperative mood seems entirely fitting given the ethical obligation one has in Hasidism to liberate the Shekinah from the crusts of the earth in order to redeem the world. In Buber's words, "only man can liberate [the holy

---

129. HTF, 71.

130. The Hasids were known for their exuberant joy that even led them to turn cartwheels in the public squares. Scholem notes that "the clearest reflection of this enthusiasm is to be found in the Hasidic prayer which strikes one as an almost complete antithesis of the form of mystical prayer which was developed at about the same time in Jerusalem by the Sefardic Kabbalists of Beth-El. The latter is all restraint, the former all movement" (Scholem, *Major Trends* 335). Friedman observes that in Hasidic thought "only joy can drive out the 'alien thoughts' and [the shells of darkness] that distract man from the love of God" (Friedman, *Martin Buber*, 22). This is why for the Hasid "despair is worse than even sin; for it leads one to believe oneself in the power of sin and hence to give in to it" (Friedman, *Martin Buber*, 22).

131. HTF, 71.

sparks]."¹³² Consequently, Dillard could be seen as justified in commanding the audience to take up its holy duty, to "hold hands" and "yank."

This effort of mending through prayer and art what has been broken completes for both Dillard and the Hasid a circle begun at the foundations of the world. Dillard, thinking out loud about the implications of Holy the Firm, suggests that "if Holy the Firm is 'underneath salts' . . . and since Holy the Firm is in touch with the Absolute at base, then the circle is unbroken. And it is. . . . Time and space are in touch with the Absolute at base. Eternity sockets twice into time and space curves, bound and bound by idea."¹³³ Her reasoning and imagery parallel that of Hasidism in compelling ways. In the concept of *tikkun*, "the life of the individual [is] a reflection or an enactment, writ small, of the situation in the cosmos as a whole."¹³⁴ In a grand dialectical movement, the individual who participates in *tikkun* starts with the brokenness of all things at creation and ends at the beginning of all things, the exiled holy sparks returned to primordial unity in the En Sof.¹³⁵ For Dillard, art is the material means of participating in this dialectical movement that reunites exiled and earth-bound holiness to its home in "eternity."¹³⁶ Through it, the circle is unbroken.

Dillard's synthesis of motifs from esoteric Christianity, orthodox Christianity, and Hasidism admittedly results in a sort of artistic syncretism. Yet Hasidic pansacramentalism informs the whole of the book. As it unfolds, a mysticism of the senses and a view of God's presence in the world emerges that seems remarkably consistent with Buber's Hasidism in its view of the conditioned immanence of a transcendent God, for "matter and spirit are of a piece but distinguishable"¹³⁷; in its understanding the world as an irradiation of God, so that "at base" the Absolute touches everything;¹³⁸ and in its ethical affirmation that "only man can liberate" God's Shekinah from beneath its crust of "salts and earths" to unify it with eternity's "general flame."¹³⁹

---

132. Buber, *Hasidism and Modern Man*, 127.
133. HTF, 70–71.
134. Dan, *Teachings of Hasidism*, 13.
135. Scholem, *Major Trends*, 274–75.
136. HTF, 72.
137. HTF, 71.
138. HTF, 69.
139. Buber, *Hasidism and Modern Man*, 127; HTF, 71, 66.

The Glory Emerges from Its Debasement:
For the Time Being

To illustrate the consistency and span of Dillard's mystical descents, we turn finally to Dillard's last, book-length work of non-fiction, *For the Time Being*, published in 1999. Despite its structural unity (the book has seven chapters, each with ten sections identically named throughout the book) and startling vividness, it is perhaps the most narratively fragmented and spare of her career. She warns the reader in the opening author's note, "Its form is unusual, its scenes are remote, its focus wide, and its tone austere."[140] As explained in chapter 1, it also includes more Jewish elements than any of her other books. *For the Time Being* devotes significant and lengthy sections to the founder of Hasidism, the Baal Shem Tov, includes excerpts from the Talmud, Midrash, the Mishnah, and the *Zohar*, and borrows heavily from books of the Hebrew Bible, including Genesis, Exodus, Leviticus, Judges, Ezekiel, Isaiah, Zechariah, Nehemiah, Psalms, Jeremiah, and Ezra. Dillard quotes over twenty rabbis dating from the first to the present century as well as the work of Maimonides, Martin Buber, Gershom Scholem, and Jewish anthropologist and philosopher Ernest Becker. She alludes to and quotes Jewish artists and scholars ranging from Chagall to Robert Eisenberg. The landscapes of ancient Palestine and modern Israel feature prominently in many of the narrative sections, and the names of individuals featured in recurring story lines are often Jewish, for example, obstetric nurse Pat Eisberg. The book's final chapter synthesizes almost exclusively Jewish voices spanning thousands of years and includes those of Rabbi Tarfon, the Baal Shem Tov, Martin Buber, Abraham Heschel, Edmund Fleg, Lawrence Kushner, and Aryeh Kaplan. Through these final voices, Dillard appeals explicitly to the notion of *tikkun*, the holy duty each person has to redeem the world's intrinsic and inexplicable cruelties, depicted with excruciating vividness throughout the book.

It seems no coincidence that as Dillard fervently explores humanity's exile from God expressed most perplexingly in unjust suffering she should turn more frequently than ever before to Jewish sources. In them, particularly in the Baal Shem Tov, Dillard finds as Martin Buber did "a realistic and active mysticism, i.e., a mysticism for which the world is not an illusion, from which man must turn away in order to reach true being."[141] In this final book, Dillard doggedly refuses to turn away from the world in all its brokenness, and yet she

---

140. FTB, ix.
141. Buber, *Hasidism and Modern Man*, 180.

also refuses to despair, for as Rabbi Nachman of Bratslav asserts, "Every day . . . the glory is ready to emerge from its debasement."[142]

An illustrative example is found in chapter 3's section "Israel," where one finds, yet again, a quite literal descent into an explosion of sensory experiences that paradoxically results in a mystical vision. The section recounts Dillard's trip as part of a tourist group to "one of the queerest spots on earth—I hope," the Church of the Nativity in Bethlehem.[143] The section includes two main narratives juxtaposed: Dillard's descent into the grotto to see where Christ was born and an account from ancient Jewish Merkabah mysticism of an ascent to the throne of heaven. By interweaving these two narratives, she pointedly contrasts her descent amidst a jostling mass of ordinary "people of every color in every costume" with an ascent to heaven recounted by a fourth-century Merkabah mystic.[144]

The narrative begins with a vivid description of Dillard's descent down endless stone steps into an airless cave where a silver star marks the alleged place of Christ's birth. Her tone is just short of disgust as she recounts awkwardly maneuvering to avoid the "arches of brocade hangings" and "gaudy hanging lamps" while competing for oxygen with dozens of other tourists breathing the smoky, oily air.[145] When her turn comes to touch the star, she prostrates herself and fingers the waxy hole at its center. Completely unmoved, she concludes that "Any patch of ground anywhere smacks more of God's presence on earth, to me, than did this marble grotto."[146]

The narrative breaks off suddenly, and without transition Dillard inserts a saying of Rabbi Nachman of Bratslav whose words signal that all is not as it seems: "Every day . . . the glory is ready to emerge from its debasement."[147] Rabbi Nachman, the great-grandson of the Baal Shem Tov, aroused hostility and suspicion within his own community for many reasons—his volatile temperament, precociousness, individualism, arrogance, tendency to associate with "bad company."[148] The content of his tales especially provoked fellow Hasidic masters. Wiesel explains:

> That a Rebbe should waste his time and that of his faithful inventing fables, well, one could accept that. But that his tales should speak not of saints or miracle Rebbes but of princes and

142. FTB, 80.
143. FTB, 77.
144. FTB, 80.
145. FTB, 77–79.
146. FTB, 79.
147. FTB, 80.
148. Buber, *Tales of the Hasidim*, 338; Wiesel, *Souls on Fire*, 176–77.

shepherds, of anonymous beggars and horsemen, of sages and messengers—not even Jewish ones at that—could only dismay them. If only he had spared their feelings by inserting a few more conventional Hasidic legends here and there, praising the powers of the Tzaddik and the faith of the followers, the rest would have aroused less resentment.[149]

Dillard's choice of Rabbi Nachman seems particularly apposite, given that the narrative sequence contrasts her frustration with sweaty tourists and jammed parking lots (and her firm conviction that any place else on the planet would have been more conducive to holiness than the grotto) with the Merkabah account. It thus early on seems to suggest parallels between her own misguided assumptions about where holiness is to be found with where it actually will show up. Like Rabbi Nachman's hearers, she perhaps has an idolatrous "taste for the sublime" that is about to be upended.[150] Significantly, Nachman confided to his scribe and disciple, Nathan, "If one is to believe what people say, stories are written to put them to sleep; I tell mine to wake them up."[151] This is in fact the way his sentence functions within Dillard's narrative; it begins to awaken the reader to the faint stirrings of mystery in the grotto. Immediately following Nachman's saying, Dillard's tone softens, and she notices that in the hot and stifling cave, "high above [her] back, layer after layer of stone away, people were singing."[152] Out of a rag-tag pack of tourists comes a "melody faint and pure."[153]

Further, Nachman's words foreshadow the revelatory moment to come. The narrative again shifts without transition to the discourse on Merkabah, or "throne" mysticism, the most ancient of Jewish mystical traditions dating from at least the first century BC, whose focus is the chariot-throne in Ezekiel 1.[154] The narrative provides luxurious descriptions of the various strata of heaven the soul encounters in its mystical ascent to God until it reaches, above the seven heavens and the seven layers between them and a "layer of wings as thick as the heavens and layers combined, "the Holy One, blessed be He."[155] The sudden juxtaposition of the cool purity and otherworldliness of throne mysticism with Dillard's visceral description of the hot and smoky grotto

---

149. Wiesel, *Souls on Fire*, 188–89.

150. TST, 30. In Dillard, "Expedition to the Pole," Dillard exposes her own spiritual failings, admitting, "A taste for the sublime is a greed like any other, after all."

151. Wiesel, *Souls on Fire*, 179.

152. FTB, 80.

153. FTB, 80.

154. Scholem, *Major Trends*, 40–44.

155. FTB, 81.

heightens the contrast between what seem antithetical worlds. Angel's wings are contrasted with tourists' sweaty limbs; the soul's ascent through heavenly waters, stars, and moons with Dillard's jostling descent on stone steps; the pristine heavenly chambers of snow and hail with the gaudy brocades, tassles, and smoking censers in the crowded shrine.[156] The text begs the question, how can the holy exist in the sensory melee Dillard inhabits?

Dillard tries to convince herself she should be impressed, but the story of the incarnation, "was worn out for now, the paradox and scandal of any incarnation's occurring in a stable."[157] The narrative breaks off again. This time the interruption comes from Rabbi Menahem Mendel, who brought Hasidism to Palestine in the eighteenth century: "He said, 'This is what I attained in the Land of Israel. When I see a bundle of straw lying in the street, it seems to me a sign of the presence of God, that it lies there lengthwise, and not crosswise.'"[158]

The recognizable features of annunciation language ("This is what I attained") lead readers to expect a profound disclosure, yet what follows seems disappointingly mundane. Straw lying in the street, even if it is in Jerusalem, seems unlikely to reveal the divine. Yet this is precisely what it does, for those who have eyes to recognize the "scandal of any incarnation."[159] The rabbi sees how remarkable, miraculous in fact, it is that a particular something rather than nothing exists and that it exists just so—lengthwise and not crosswise. This is the real evidence of God's presence. Mendel's saying, the central image of which is straw, connects his revelation to Dillard's location, the legendary site of the stable in Bethlehem, where the Christ was born.

Abruptly, Dillard states in the next sentence, "I could not keep away from it."[160] She recounts rushing back to the church, and descending the steps "to kneel," "to prostrate myself," "to rub" the star again.[161] The physicality of her actions ("kneel," "prostrate," "rub") underscore the point that the holy is mediated through the body; Rabbi Menahem Mendel's words seem to have revived for Dillard the worn out story of God's taking on the form of a man. Her stammering conclusion signifies the power of the revelation that she, like Mendel, obtained in Israel: "I felt like Harry Reasoner at the Great Wall of China in 1972, who, pressed on live coverage for a

---

156. FTB, 80.
157. FTB, 81.
158. FTB, 82.
159. FTB, 81.
160. FTB, 82.
161. FTB, 82.

response, came up with, 'It's ... uh ... it's one of the two or three darnedest things I ever saw.'"[162]

As seems characteristic with Dillard, the ineffable moment has been precipitated by physical, sensory experiences, and she keeps company with all the biblical writers who often stammered in response to their encounters with the divine. Buber explains:

> The saying of the talmudic [sic] sages to the effect that the Torah speaks the language of men hides a deeper seriousness than is commonly assumed. We must construe it to mean that what is unutterable *can* only be uttered, as it is here expressed, in the language of men. . . . Man cannot but stammer when he lines up what he knows of the universe . . . [with] 'works' from the divine workshop. But this stammering of his was the only means of doing justice to the task of stating the mystery of how time springs from eternity.[163]

The topic of stammering and Dillard's asyndetic style will be discussed fully in chapter 5. For now, it is sufficient to say that Dillard's stammer arises from the revelation that Rabbi Nachman was right. Indeed, "Every day . . . the glory is ready to emerge from its debasement."[164]

This panentheistic vision is expressed succinctly by French Jesuit priest and paleontologist Pierre Teilhard de Chardin, whom Dillard quotes near the end of *For the Time Being*: "'Purity does not lie in a separation from the universe,' he wrote, 'but in a deeper penetration of it.'"[165] This has been Dillard's conviction from her earliest work through her last and seems to place her some distance from the language of ascent that features so prominently in the discourse of the Neoplatonic Christian mystical tradition. Given this distance, it is perhaps not surprising that Dillard's literary non-fiction consistently appeals to the pansacramentalism of Buber's Hasidism to give voice to her vision that holiness is hidden within the infinite particulars of creation and apprehension of it is mediated through, rather than apart from, the senses.

The next chapter will consider how this very conviction raises theological questions about the relationship of God to creation with regard to the problem of evil. Dillard's artistic and theological witness to God's sacramental presence in the world leads immediately to difficult questions arising from classical Western notions of divine attributes such as God's

---

162. FTB, 82.
163. Buber, *On the Bible*, 11.
164. FTB, 80.
165. FTB, 184.

omniscience and omnipotence. It is to these questions that the next chapter will turn as the analysis moves from the present chapter's discussion of God's relationship to creation, to the questions of evil and suffering.

Excursus on Mediation

The language of "mediation" here raises questions about the conjunction between Buber and Dillard on the issue of immediacy. The point to be emphasized is that there are two distinct, though interrelated, historical and philosophical streams in Buber's life and thought in tension and yet distinct from one from another—Buber's work on Hasidism and Buber's dialogical philosophy. The current argument seeks to establish primarily the connections between Hasidic thought as Buber interprets it and Dillard's pansacramental view. Dillard has long been an admirer and student of Buber's work on Hasidism and her thinking is heavily indebted to it. Buber, as an interpreter of Hasidism, argues passionately for its robust pansacramentalism, a panentheistic view that recognizes the holy spark in all that exists and whose redemptive ethos hallows all of life. As Buber understands (and embraces) Hasidism, it expresses fully the Jewish mystical notion of God's Shekinah existing *within* (literally wrapped) in creation—in other words, in mediated encounters with God. See Buber's narrative account of his "conversion" to Hasidism in *Hasidism and Modern Man*. Buber explains, that though he had visited Hasidic villages during childhood with his grandfather, his dramatic encounter with Hasidism occurred when he was twenty-six and opened the testament of the Baal Shem Tov, *Zevaat Ribesh*: "Overpowered in an instant, I experienced the Hasidic soul" (Buber, *Hasidism and Modern Man*, 59), and over the next five years he became increasingly aware of an "inborn binding with Hasidic truth" and of a "summons to proclaim it to the world" (Buber, *Hasidism and Modern Man*, 59, 62).

Buber's work on Hasidism predates and informs *I and Thou*; it was through his work on Hasidism that he arrived at the concept of dialogical relation expressed in *I and Thou*. However, Buber insists dogmatically in *I and Thou* on *im*-mediacy, or non-mediated relations with God that "exist" neither *in* a human self nor *above*, or transcendent, of a human self but in the mysterious realm where the I and *Thou* meet as the I "goes out" to the *Thou* in response to being addressed by it. To speak of "experiencing" God for Buber is to reduce the *Thou* to an It. Yet, one clearly sees the influence of Buber's work on Hasidism in *I and Thou*, and there is sufficient ambiguity and contradiction in the language of immediacy in *I and Thou* to raise questions about his assertions. For example, though Buber insists that "the relation to the *Thou* is direct" not mediated, he also asserts that in moments of presentness or encounter, the eternal *Thou* "invades creation and the knowledge of man, beams of [its] power stream into the ordered world and dissolve it again and again" (Buber, *I and Thou*, 31). Similarly, he describes this indwelling in panentheistic terms, stating "It has no density, for everything in it penetrates everything else" (Buber, *I and Thou*, 32). These and countless other claims like them in *I and Thou* seem informed by Hasidic pansacramentalism. A particularly telling example is Buber's assertion that "Every particular *Thou* is a glimpse through to the eternal Thou; by means of every particular *Thou* the primary word addresses the eternal *Thou*. Through this mediation of the *Thou* of all beings fulfillment . . . of relations comes to them: the inborn *Thou* is realised in each relation and consummated in none" (Buber, *I and Thou*, 75). The focus on concrete particulars that are the "means" of "mediation" of the *Thou* reveals the internal tensions between Buber's Hasidic pansacramentalism in which the indwelling *Thou* hallows all of life and dialogical philosophy which insists on non-mediated relation.

Aside from theological questions are linguistic and cognitive ones. The "I" that responds to the *Thou* is an inescapably bodied self whose perceptions, whether spiritual, physical, or psychological, "happen" in time and space, thus are inevitably mediated. Buber admits in *I and Thou* that each *Thou* is "fated" to become an It, and "continually to re-enter into the condition of things" (Buber, *I and Thou*, 17) and seeks to address the difficulties in his Postscript to the 1958 edition of *I and Thou*. His examples and language only further complicate the issue. To clarify how genuine meeting can happen with an inanimate object, he provides a personal example of being addressed by the impressive mass of a Doric column in a church wall in Syracuse (Buber, *I and Thou*, 135). This seems clearly to describe an encounter mediated through Buber's senses—eyes, body, location—and cognition. In the closing paragraphs, he states "God's speech to men penetrates what happens in the world around us, biographical and historical, and make it for you and me into instruction, message, demand" (Buber, *I and Thou*, 136). This sentence could just as easily have come from Buber's works on Hasidism, and it expresses, at least from the human side, a mediated, pansacramental presence of the eternal *Thou*.

Buber's critics on the point of immediacy are many. A full discussion of its philosophical complexity and difficulties far exceeds the scope of the present discussion. For an excellent overview of the problems and the various voices weighing in on the discussion (ranging from Heidegger to Levinas to Derrida), see Ward, *Barth, Derrida, and Theology*, 53–78, 126–46. Ward's conclusion is perhaps an adequate summation for the current purposes. Ward points out that an address, to be an address, has to be understood by the addressee as a linguistic event to which one can respond. It therefore must be understood as having signs that refer to or signify something: "The significance of the exchange [between I and Thou] cannot be separated from the referential content of the exchange" (Ward, *Barth, Derrida, and Theology*, 76). Consequently, "Immediacy cannot logically be immediate and yet to admit mediacy is to admit defeat, because it admits a subject-object split" (Ward, *Barth, Derrida, and Theology*, 76). In brief, the problems are the apparent inconsistencies between Buber's Hasidic pansacramentalism and Buber's dialogical philosophy, not inconsistencies between Buber's Hasidic theology and Dillard's pansacramentalism.

CHAPTER 3

The Emptying God

Kabbalah, Creation, and Kenosis

"To create, God did not extend himself but withdrew himself;
he humbled and obliterated himself, and left outside himself
the domain of necessity, in which he does not intervene."

—Annie Dillard, *For the Time Being*

Introduction

The previous chapter discussed how from Dillard's first work of literary non-fiction to her last she draws upon the literature and doctrines of Jewish mysticism to affirm the role of the senses in mystical experience and to present a pansacramental view of the world. Her apprehension of the divine through rather than apart from her senses raises epistemological as well as theological questions. What exactly is the relationship between God and the world? How is God mediated in it? The previous chapter demonstrated that the corpus of Dillard's work consistently portrays an immanent but hidden God, and the language of mystical descent features prominently in each of her major works.

Dillard's artistic and theological witness to God's pansacramental presence leads immediately, however, to theodicean questions arising from classical Western notions of divine attributes such as God's omniscience and omnipotence. If a spark of God's holiness is present but exiled within creation, does God remain omnipotent? What kind of God, as Dillard asks in *Holy the Firm*, allows a child's face to be burnt off in a plane crash while her father escapes unscathed? Such questions about pain and suffering are of central concern in Dillard's work for the whole of her career. In the afterword to *Pilgrim at Tinker Creek*, written twenty-five years after it was first published, Dillard recounts how the book began. She remembers thinking, "Why not write some sort of nature book—say, a theodicy? In November, back in Virginia, I fooled around with the idea and started filling out five-by-seven index cards with notes from years of reading."[1] The intellectual structure for *Holy the Firm*, published three years later, arose from the idea of writing about whatever happened to Dillard within a three-day span. On day two, a neighbor's small aircraft crashed in the pines near Dillard's cabin on an island in Puget Sound, badly burning his young daughter. Dillard explains, "On the second day an airplane crashed nearby, and I was back where I had been in *Pilgrim*—grappling with the problem of pain and dying. I had no intention of dealing with that issue at first, but it became unavoidable."[2] In her collection of essays, *Teaching a Stone to Talk*, themes of sorrow, suffering and death are explicit in essays such as "The Deer at Providencia," "Total Eclipse," "Sojourners," "A Field of Silence" and implicit in others such as "Aces and Eights." Dillard's final book of literary non-fiction, *For the Time Being*, is perhaps her most grim and exacting in its tenacious examination of human and natural evil, suffering, and death. Both of her novels, *The Living* and *The Maytrees*, examine without nostalgia the clarifying power of time and death.

Questions about God's sovereignty arising from evil and unjust suffering expose perhaps more quickly than any other existential problems the difficulties accompanying the orthodox Christian claims within the Western church that God possesses "omni" attributes such as omniscience, omnipotence, and omnipresence. The "problem" of evil is only a problem if one presupposes that God is entirely good, omniscient, and omnipotent. If he is all-knowing and all-powerful as well as loving and good, why does he let a little girl's face get destroyed by fire? Christian kenotic theology is one notable attempt to re-examine God's relationship to the world by exploring what it might mean for God's presence in Christ to be self-limiting in it. More recently, panentheistic theologies have emerged, which Vanhoozer labels "new kenotic-perichoretic relational ontotheologies,"[3] that develop a relational, metaphysical paradigm expanding the notion of kenosis beyond

---

1. PTC, 279.

2. Yancey, "Face Aflame," 16.

3. Vanhoozer, *Remythologizing Theology*, 139. Vanhoozer provides an incisive critique of this school of thought from the perspective of "classical" theism. Vanhoozer defines "the new kenotic-perichoretic relational orthodoxy" as one that "maintains that God, out of love for the world, freely limits himself for the sake of a genuine relationship with free human creatures" (Vanhoozer, *Remythologizing Theology*, 163).

Christology to an entire ontotheology. They are undergirded by the premise that God's relationship to creation is predicated upon love—a mutual indwelling, reciprocal relationship in which God elects to grant freedom or "space" to his creation and thereby allows it to choose and develop as it is drawn toward the fulfillment of its potentialities by his providential luring. This inevitably allows humans freedom to choose evil and for nature to go awry.[4] Process theologians such as A. N. Whitehead, Charles Hartshorne, and, more recently, John Cobb and David Ray Griffin, fall into this broader category of panentheism, which includes thinkers from Jewish, Western, and Eastern Orthodox Christian traditions such as Martin Buber, Arthur Peacocke, Philip Clayton, Jürgen Moltmann,[5] and Kallistos Ware.

Dillard's work does in fact express a kenotic panentheistic view, and she insists throughout her works of non-fiction on the unreasonableness of the belief that God is in every circumstance omnipotent. Moreover, in Dillard's understanding of the relation of God to creation, as in her accounts of mystical encounters with God, she employs with surprising frequency and consistency motifs from Jewish mysticism, particularly *tsimtsum*, and *shevirat ha-kelim*, that speak of God's self-limiting acts and being in creation. This chapter will therefore explore Dillard's explicit and implicit challenges to the classical Western notions of God's omniscience and omnipotence

---

4. Michael Brierley calls this "panentheistic turn" in contemporary theology a "doctrinal revolution" that "subverts the priorities of classical theism" and "challenges classical theism's imperium" (Brierley, "Naming a Quiet Revolution," 4). The list of ancient and modern thinkers and theologians, indeed entire movements, which are now classified as or identify themselves as panentheistic, is vast. For an excellent overview of the "dramatis personae" and common themes that emerge despite differences in eras or religious traditions, see Brierley, "Naming a Quiet Revolution."

5. There is some question as to whether Moltmann's theology can be properly labeled panentheistic given ambiguity in his work about whether God is in creation eucharistically or creation is contained within God. In *God in Creation*, he uses absolute terms to describe the God-forsakenness of creation at the moment in which God conceded space in order for the world to come into being: "The space which comes into being and is set free by God's self-limitation is literally God-forsaken space" (Moltmann, *God in Creation*, 87). How there can be a God-forsaken place within God is not made entirely clear. Shortly thereafter Moltmann declares that "God is the eternal dwelling place of his creation. . . . God and the world are related to one another through their mutual indwelling and participation: God's indwelling in the world is divine in kind; the world's indwelling in God is worldly in kind" (Moltmann, *God in Creation*, 150). What can perhaps be said is that Moltmann's assertion that creation existed within God at the creation event and continues to do so in its historical unfolding suggests some sort of perichoretic relationship between God and creation, even if it is not entirely clear to what extent creation is "in" God and God is "in creation." It is worth noting that theologians both sympathetic to and critical of Moltmann classify him as a panentheist. See Cooper, *Panentheism*. He devotes an entire section to Moltmann. See also Vanhoozer, *Remythologizing Theology*; Brierley, "Naming a Quiet Revolution," 1–15.

through her literary synthesis of the Kabbalistic notions of *tsimtsum* and *shevirat ha-kelim* with Christian kenotic theology to create within her literary cosmos a God who elects to be self-limiting.

Although the question of God's kenotic relationship to creation will be examined throughout this chapter and the next, a few preliminary comments should be made about why elements of Jewish mystical thought, particularly the Lurianic idea of *tsimtsum*, are amenable to Dillard's theological and artistic purposes. Briefly, it seems they allow Dillard to wrestle with theodicean questions within a pre-messianic theological and existential space conceded by a God who has chosen to be self-limiting, or, in Judaic terms, a God who journeys in exile with his creation, without diminishing that tension by appealing to Christ's victory over death and evil in his resurrection. This not-yet-realized messianic vision compels Dillard to wrestle with the world *as it is* (not as it *will be* in the *parousia*) and thereby to hold in tension two equally binding yet often conflicting fiduciary claims on her life—her conviction that "God is all good"[6] and her knowledge of unjust and unmitigated suffering—without closing the gap between them. This gap is, in effect, a theodicean space within which questions about evil and suffering are raised but not answered. In Dillard's work as in Judaism there is no messianic denouement, only fervent watchfulness and waiting.

Given that the themes of kenosis, *tsimtsum*, and theodicean spaces are closely interconnected, this chapter and the next will have multiple points of intersection and should be viewed as two parts of an extended analysis. The aim of the current chapter is to establish the foundation for those discussions by examining the kenotic God Dillard constructs within her literary universe and how a generalized notion of kenosis can illuminate Dillard's aesthetic principle of gaps and absences. Chapter 4 will focus more specifically on the theological and aesthetic rationale for theodicean spaces and their manifestation in Dillard's asyndetic style. Chapter 5 will begin the argument's arc toward themes of redemption by examining the ways gaps, absences, and asyndeton function in Dillard's work as epistemic blank spaces that, paradoxically, engender mystery and meaning.

The Emptying God: Kenosis Defined

Before embarking on an analysis of Jewish and Christian kenotic elements in Dillard's texts, a brief overview of the categories of theological meanings present in recent discussions of kenosis is needed. The topic is vast and its

---

6. HTF, 47.

complexities far beyond the scope of this discussion.[7] However, relevant to it are three general categories within which theological discussions about kenosis can be framed. These categories are the Christological, Trinitarian, and more generalized meanings of the word and phenomenon of kenosis that allow theologians like Polkinghorne and Moltmann to speak of "creation as kenosis."[8] Christological discussions about kenosis center on Paul's Christic hymn in Philippians 2:5—11, in which Paul speaks of Christ emptying himself (*ekenōsen*) in Philippians 2:7.[9] Both exegetical and theological controversies remain. Does "emptying," for example, refer to the moment of incarnation, or to Christ's journey toward, or death on the Cross?[10] Even more fundamentally, arguments persist about whether the notion of kenosis is even orthodox.[11] Within Trinitarian theologies of kenosis, the term used in Philippians becomes a metaphysical construct for speaking of the perichoretic relationships within the Godhead, a Trinity of self-giving, reciprocal, self-surrendering Persons.[12] Thus, the meaning of kenosis broadens to refer not merely to a Christological event but to the nature of God himself. This is the point from which recent creation-as-kenosis theologies (what Coakley calls "generalized approaches" to kenosis) emerge.[13]

Exegetical debates aside,[14] the features common to creation-as-kenosis theologies relevant to the current discussion can best be summarized by Vanhoozer's category name of which they are a subset—"kenotic, perichoretic,

---

7. For a superb historical overview of the development of kenotic theology, as well as a compelling argument for its necessity in modern theological thought, see Brown, *Divine Humanity*. It provides a thorough and fascinating historical overview that is exceptionally readable and that meets the need in current scholarship for a comprehensive, coherent analysis of the historical development of kenotic theology.

8. Coakley, "Kenosis," 193.

9. David W. Brown's analysis offers an historical overview of the range of meanings possible for the Greek term in light of Paul's context and the various concerns of the early church councils from which orthodox creeds proceeded. See Brown, *Divine Humanity*, 3–35.

10. Coakley, "Kenosis," 194.

11. See Evans, *Exploring Kenotic Christology*. The chapters by Thomas R. Thompson, Stephen T. Davis, and C. Stephen Evans are particularly helpful. See Thomson, "Nineteenth-Century Kenotic Christology," 74–111; Davis, "Is Kenosis Orthodox?," 112–38; Evans, "Kenotic Christology and the Nature of God," 190–217; Brown, *Divine Humanity*.

12. Coakley, "Kenosis," 198–200.

13. Coakley, "Kenosis," 200.

14. For an excellent analysis of the diversity of theological approaches to creation as kenosis, just within one volume of essays, see Sarah Coakley's analysis of the various perspectives represented by Polkinghorne, *Work of Love*, in Coakley, "Kenosis," 200–204.

relational" theologies.[15] They are kenotic in the sense that they maintain that God, from love, elects to limit the exercise of his omni-attributes (omniscience, omnipotence, omnipresence, etc.) in order "that a cosmos of free finite agents should exist,"[16] and this affords creation the freedom and autonomy to evolve and make real choices that affect the destiny of creation, humanity, and even God himself. Moltmann, for example, argues that God's self-determining choice prior to the event of creation *to* create and allow something other than himself to exist is inherently kenotic: "It is therefore correct to see God's self-determination to be the Creator of a non-divine world as already a self-limitation on God's part."[17] Similarly, John Polkinghorne can conclude that the evolutionary process is "clearly kenotic in its character" because it allows creation "to make itself."[18] Consequently, God, humans, and the processes of creation participate in a "kenotic sharing of power" that "has implications for theodicy. No longer can God be held to be totally and directly responsible for all that happens. An evolutionary world is inevitably one in which there are raggednesses and blind alleys. Death is the necessary cost of new life."[19] However, which divine attributes are limited, as well as how (and when) they are limited, has been debated since kenotic Christian theologies first emerged in nineteenth-century Germany.[20] These theologies are perichoretic (and thereby panentheistic) in that, to one extent or another, the world is conceived as being in God or contained by God, and therefore, what happens within the world has in some sense a real effect upon the being of God. Thus, God is seen as passible, and his relationship with the world is reciprocal. It is this final, "generalized" category of creation as kenosis that will be central to this chapter's discussion since one finds each of these three broad features in Dillard's work.

A few points need clarifying at the outset. Though Dillard uses the term "kenosis" and is obviously familiar with its various theological meanings, she is an artist not a theologian and draws upon the term's meanings as evocative and open-ended motifs rather than as theological dogma. This chapter's argument therefore is not concerned with identifying precisely where Dillard registers among kenotic theologies, creating a taxonomy of Dillard's thought, or considering the orthodoxy of Dillard's panentheistic

---

15. For a helpful summary of the features common to panentheistic theologies, see Brierley, "Naming a Quiet Revolution," 1–15; Clayton, "Panentheism Today," 249–64.
16. Ward, "Cosmos and Kenosis," 160.
17. Moltmann, "God's Kenosis," 145.
18. Polkinghorne, "Kenotic Creation," 95.
19. Polkinghorne, "Kenotic Creation," 95.
20. Thompson, "Nineteenth-Century Kenotic Christology," 74–111.

views in general. It is concerned, rather, with the unexplored intersections between Jewish and Christian kenotic theologies in her work, particularly in their common assertions that the creation of the world and God's ongoing relationship to it can be seen as events of divine self-definition, self-limitation, and self-humiliation.

It should also be acknowledged that in recent discussions of kenosis, the term is no longer used merely to refer exclusively to the nature of Christ or even to the Christian Trinity. As the volume of essays, *The Emptying God: A Buddhist-Jewish-Christian Conversation*, indicates, "kenosis" is now a term used within Jewish and Buddhist theological discussions to refer to elements within those traditions that speak to God's choice to be self-limiting.[21] Scholars as distinguished as Jürgen Moltmann speak of "Jewish kenotic theology."[22] Obviously, because Christ is not understood to be God in Judaism, and the New Testament is not its scripture, the phrase "Jewish kenoticism" is nonsensical if one insists on the term's strictly technical meaning in Philippians 2:7 and its Christological context. However, for ease of reference and to remain in keeping with recent discussions that make use of more generalized sense of the term, kenosis will be used throughout this discussion to mean the self-limiting being and acts of the God of Israel as well as of the Christian Trinity.

Furthermore, while a detailed history of kenotic thought is not necessary for this discussion, one aspect of its development is. Kenotic theology emerged in nineteenth-century Germany in part because of problematic aspects of classical interpretations of God's nature arising from assumptions about "the attributes of deity related to the world (omnipotence, omnipresence, omniscience, immortality, impassibility, and immutability)."[23] Those who challenge these tenets of classical theism, such as Jürgen Moltmann, argue they derive from Greek philosophy, namely "Aristotle's general metaphysics," and are inconsistent with the God of the Bible and inadequate for the realities to which the scientific world now points.[24] In other words, the difficulties of reconciling faith in an omniscient and omnipotent God with God's failure to exercise these attributes in response to human suffering, as well as with what is known of evolutionary processes, make them untenable. Likewise, it is Dillard's theodicean concerns that precipitate similar conclusions. In *For the Time Being*, Dillard informs readers that to equate God's omnipotence with his all-causingness is fatal—and infantile—reasoning,

---

21. See Cobb and Ives, *Emptying God*.
22. Moltmann, "God's Kenosis," 137.
23. Moltmann, "God's Kenosis," 139.
24. Moltmann, "God's Kenosis," 139–40.

and suggests that those who reject God on the basis of such a mental error have probably not re-examined their views of divinity since childhood. "It is not the toothfairy," she grumbles.[25] She begins the chapter's following section, entitled "Evil," by commenting that each time she hears a minister say to God during a service, "All your actions show your wisdom and love," she longs to "rise and shout, 'That's a lie!'—just to put things on a solid footing."[26] Because of Dillard's fidelity to apparently contradictory fiduciary claims—that God is all good and that unspeakable suffering and evil go unchecked—it is perhaps no surprise that she finds kenotic panentheistic theologies, including those of Jewish mysticism, particularly attractive and amenable to her purposes. As suggested at the outset, Isaac Luria's inherently kenotic concept of *tsimtsum* and the Hasidic understanding of God's wandering Shekinah allow Dillard to suggest that evil and suffering exist within a space God has conceded to his creation.

A Jewish-Christian Synthesis

One finds in Lurianic Kabbalism and Hasidism the notions of God's self-definition at creation in the Lurianic idea of *tsimtsum*, and God's self-limitation and self-humiliation in the cosmic tragedy of *shevirat ha-kelim* that resulted in the exile of God's Shekinah. Though these concepts were explained in chapter 1, we will briefly review them here given this chapter's focus on ways their kenotic dimensions inform Dillard's work.

Briefly, in Lurianic Kabbalism, God's first creative act in primordial history was not an outflow or emanation of his divine power but a withdrawal, or *tsimtsum*,[27] in which God exiled himself from part of himself to make space for creation to exist. The brilliant logic of Luria's symbolism explains how an eternal and infinite God can create *ex nihilo* a temporal and finite world that is both independent from him but still present to him.[28] To return to Scholem, *tsimtsum* means that the "God who revealed himself in firm contours was superseded by one who descended deeper into the recesses of His own Being, who concentrated Himself into Himself, and had done so from the very beginning of creation."[29] After this first motion in Luria's dialectical concept of creation, God's light emanated from him bringing order to the void's chaos and filling its nothingness with all that

25. FTB, 85.
26. FTB, 85.
27. Scholem, *Major Trends*, 260.
28. Dan, *Teachings of Hasidism*, 11; Scholem, *Major Trends*, 260–61.
29. Scholem, *Major Trends*, 261–62.

exists.[30] Every following act of creation followed this dynamic motion of concentration (or withdrawal) and emanation.[31]

However, as God's light went forth from him, its power shattered the finite forms meant to contain it, and *shevirat ha-kelim*, or the "breaking of the vessels, occurred."[32] As the vessels shattered, "fragments of divine light (termed *nizonot*, or 'sparks') clinging to them, fell downward, while the remaining lights ascended back toward the En Sof.[33] These holy sparks animate all that exists and remain imprisoned within their material form until liberated by prayer and devout acts. Importantly, therefore, God is understood not only to have suffered exile from himself in primordial history during these two events, but he continues to suffer exile, since fragments of his own eternal light even now wander the earth, suffering the world's vicissitudes with it. While Luria's theosophy hinted at gnostic dualism,[34] focusing on the imprisoning dark shells, the Hasidic masters, beginning with the Baal Shem Tov and his disciples, emphasized the holy sparks instead, concluding that because God's Shekinah inhabits all that is, even the most humble and mundane of events and objects could be considered sacred.[35] This is what Martin Buber labels the "pan-sacralism" of the Hasidic worldview.

Taking the Lurianic and Hasidic views of *tsimtsum* and *shevirat ha-kelim* together, one finds inherent in them the broad features outlined in current kenotic theologies. *Tsimtsum* is kenotic in that it requires the self-limitation of God. It is perichoretic in that the world is viewed as emanating from within God and is intimately related to God through the exiled presence of his Shekinah within it. Finally, it is relational, since God wanders with his creation in exile and suffers the world's exigencies with it.

While the discussion of kenosis here is necessarily limited in scope, it is important to identify the salient features of kenotic theology shared by Judaism and Christianity relevant to an analysis of Dillard's work.[36] Because Jürgen Moltmann's Christian kenotic theology borrows from Kabbalistic and Hasidic thought, it proves a fitting voice for articulating the ways Jewish and Christian kenotic images intersect and illuminate each other in

---

30. Scholem, *Major Trends*, 263.
31. Scholem, *Major Trends*, 263.
32. Dan, *Teachings of Hasidism*, 11.
33. Dan, *Teachings of Hasidism*, 12.
34. Scholem, *Major Trends*, 260, 267–68.
35. Potok, Foreword, xi.

36. This is not meant to suggest that Dillard is systematically developing a kenotic Christology, only that she includes kenotic motifs, both Jewish and Christian, that seem well suited to her artistic and theological purposes.

Dillard's work. Broadly speaking, both kenotic traditions conceive of God as self-defining, self-limiting, and self-humiliating.

Tsimtsum asserts that before a finite world can come into being, God must will his own self-definition by exiling himself from himself within his own being.[37] In *God in Creation*, Moltmann borrows from the Lurianic doctrine of *tsimtsum* to emphasize this inward action of God upon his own being: "Before God issues creatively out of himself, he acts inwardly on himself, resolving *for himself,* committing *himself,* determining *himself.*"[38] This primal act of self-definition that allows free, autonomous beings to exist is a primordial act of self-humiliation and God's "first act of grace."[39] Out of all the "infinite possibilities God realizes this particular one" and "renounces all others"; furthermore, he has elected to grant it "space and time and its own movement, so that it is not crushed by the divine reality or totally absorbed by it."[40] Second, *tsimtsum* posits an ontologically kenotic view of God: "prior to any *thing* is an original emptiness in the fullness of *Ein-Sof.*"[41] Exegetical debates about Philippians 2:6–11 aside, the passage suggests that in the incarnation, the uncreated God elected to become "other" to himself by becoming a creature in the midst of his creation, subject to its limitations and predations—hunger, fatigue, perplexity, and ultimately alienation from God on the cross as one who has become radically other—sin—for the sake of the world. As noted earlier, creation-as-kenosis theologies maintain that God did not "become" kenotic at the incarnation but that the incarnation evidences an ontologically kenotic Trinity. Moltmann asserts, "there was already a cross in the heart of God

---

37. Scholem, *Major Trends*, 261.
38. Moltmann, *God in Creation*, 86.
39. Moltmann, *God in Creation*, 88; "God's Kenosis" 145. One of the challenges to the spacial metaphor employed in Kabbalistic thought and adopted by Moltmann is that it is based on an incompatibilist presupposition—the false premise that God and creation compete for "space" within which to exist. For both to exist, one or the other must somehow limit or diminish itself. Vanhoozer asks "must the God who enters into dialogical relationship with human beings be always less than fully himself?" (Vanhoozer, *Remythologizing Theology*, 167). Coakley notes the gender connotations of such a view. Libertarian ideas of freedom, which presuppose creaturely freedom necessitates limitations on God's part, are premised upon the ideas of total autonomy and freedom from "conditioning, or the admission of dependence." In psychoanalytical terms, it symbolizes a "normative, 'masculine' self" who becomes independent by severing ties to life-giving and sustaining entities (Coakley, "Kenosis," 205).
40. Moltmann, "God's Kenosis," 145.
41. Bauerschmidt, "Wounds of Christ," 85.

before the world was created" for according to Revelation 18:8, Christ was "the Lamb slain from the foundation of the world."[42]

Inhering in such self-definition is self-limitation. In Luria's notion of *tsimtsum*, God limited himself by contracting his presence within himself. Similarly, most modern kenotic Christian theologies presuppose that the enfleshed Christ "emptied himself"—to one degree or another—of the "omni" attributes of the eternal Logos. Such limitation makes God vulnerable to suffering and humiliation. In Jewish terms, the wandering Shekinah suffers in exile along with Israel. Moltmann summarizes succinctly this kenotic attribute in both Jewish and Christian thought: "[God] opens himself in his Shekinah for the sufferings of his people, and in the incarnation of the Son for the sufferings of the love which is to redeem the world."[43]

Moreover, both Jewish and Christian kenotic symbols suggest God's relationship to his creation is perichoretic. The Jewish Kabbalistic notion of the indwelling Shekinah provides a potent and theologically rich symbol for understanding what it might mean for the world to be "in" God. Moltmann notes that "if we follow the doctrine of the Shekinah and the Christian doctrine of the incarnation, we have to speak of the marvel that the infinite God himself should dwell in his finite creation, making it his own environment. . . . God is the eternal dwelling place of his creation. . . . God and the world are related to one another through their mutual indwelling and participation: God's indwelling in the world is divine in kind; the world's indwelling in God is worldly in kind."[44] Appealing to *tsimtsum*, he goes on to clarify that the world does not exist in the absolute space of God but "*in the emptiness of God ceded for it through his creative resolve. So the space of creation precedes both creation and the spaces fashioned within creation, yet without being identical with the uncreated, eternal omnipresence of God.*"[45] Thus, in the Lurianic and Hasidic idea of *tsimtsum* one finds not only the Jewish counterpart to the Christian doctrine of creation *ex nihilo* but also orthodox Christianity's insistence, since Nicea,[46] on the ontological

---

42. Moltmann, "God's Kenosis," 146–47.

43. Moltmann, "God's Kenosis," 148.

44. Moltmann, *God in Creation*, 150.

45. Moltmann, *God in Creation*, 156. Moltmann's theology has been challenged on many fronts, not the least of which is the charge that these Kabbalistic ideas are not biblical. For an incisive critique of Moltmann, in the context of a larger critique of kenotic-perichorietic relational ontotheology, see Vanhoozer, *Remythologizing Theology*.

46. See Andrew Louth's analysis of the break between early Christian Platonism and orthodox Christianity at the Council of Nicea over the issue of creation *ex nihilo* in Louth, *Origins*, 73–79.

gap between God and His creation that makes possible the kenotic idea of God's self-definition in the act of creation.

Moltmann also notes that the Hasidic tradition preserves the sacral nature of creation. Seeing "all [God's] creatures as fundamentally eucharistic," Moltmann cites biblical examples to demonstrate that not just humans but all of God's creation offers the Creator praise. Hasidism, he argues, is one tradition that has preserved in its notion of God's Shekinah being hidden within the splintered vessels of creation, the "splendid" idea that all of creation is "a sacrament of God's hidden presence," which humans can therefore understand as "a communication of God's fellowship."[47]

Finally, both Jewish and contemporary Christian kenotic theologies affirm that a self-limiting God who makes himself vulnerable to his creatures cannot be impassible. The wandering, exiled Shekinah, participates in Israel's misery. As Isaiah 63:9 states, "In all their distress he too was distressed." Likewise, if Christ is the eternal Logos intersecting time and space, a Trinitarian kenotic approach would maintain that his human life and death happened within the Godhead as well as on earth. This is what David W. Brown's *Divine Humanity: Kenosis Explored and Defended* defines as a "modern kenotic view" in which the divine nature is seen "to be committed in the incarnation not merely to a symbolic drawing alongside humanity but also to an actual ontological entering into the human condition, with some real change in divinity itself."[48]

Shevirat ha-Kelim and Christ's Kenosis

Kenotic motifs appear in Annie Dillard's earliest published works. In the poem "Christmas," appearing in her 1974 publication *Tickets for a Prayer Wheel*, the speaker announces Christ's birth and incarnation: "This is the hour / God loosens and empties. Rushing, consciousness comes / unbidden, gasping, and memory, wisdom, grace."[49] Within the same volume, one finds images highly evocative of the Hebrew Bible's indwelling Shekinah paired with a christologically kenotic image in "Feast Days." In the poem's final section, the narrator tells readers that if they ever wonder why "soil and fresh-water lakes / also rejoice" or the reason for nature's bizarre diversity, the answer "is that the universal / loves the particular / that freedom loves to live / and live fleshed full."[50] The subsequent stanza begins "God empties

---

47. Moltmann, *God in Creation*, 70–71.
48. Brown, *Divine Humanity*, 1.
49. TPW, 103.
50. TPW, 33.

himself / into the earth like a cloud. / God takes the substance, contours / of a man, and keeps them, / dying, rising, walking, / and still walking / wherever there is motion."[51] The image of the cloud hearkens to the Hebrew scripture's narrative of the indwelling presence of God in the cloud that led the Israelites through the desert by day. Significantly, this is conjoined in the following line with images alluding not only to the single event of the incarnation of Christ, but also to the perpetual indwelling of God who elects to continue to die, rise, walk, within all that has life. One finds a similar image in the title poem "Tickets For A Prayer Wheel." The narrator asks, "Did God dilute / even his merest thought / . . . shrink and cross / to an olive continent / and eat our food at little tables for a time?"[52] The verbs "dilute" and "shrink," connoting a contraction of God's being *prior* to the incarnation's crossing over to temporal life, are highly suggestive of *tsimtsum*, portraying God as self-limiting and humbly condescending to the terms of mortal existence, even eating "our food at little tables."[53]

In *Holy the Firm*, one finds a powerful synthesis of Jewish and Christian kenotic theology depicting an ontologically kenotic Christ. The book's second section begins to frame a theodicy in terms of Christ's kenosis and its Jewish equivalent, *shevirat ha-kelim*. On November 19, a neighbor's young daughter is badly burned by exploding jet fuel when her plane crashes near Dillard's cottage. The event leads Dillard to ask theodicean questions about time, space, reality, and God's connection to them. She cannot accept, in the end, the gnostic premise that all life's loves and pains are an illusion and the spirit alone is real. In that case, she asks "where are we?"[54] With, she protests, a universe "obedient only to its own gross terms, meaningless, out of mind, and alone," and a God who "knows himself blissfully as flame unconsuming, as all brilliance and beauty and power and the rest of us can go hang."[55]

Her dissatisfaction with the universe on these terms seems an implicit rejection of the Platonic view of God as static perfection who draws humans toward his beauty yet who is impassible and indifferent. It seems also to be a rejection of classical theism's view of God as one who "presides serene over the assured unfolding of a predetermined purpose, Whose triumph is assured before His activity begins, and Who, in the appearance of giving, is

---

51. TPW, 33–34.
52. TPW, 125.
53. TPW, 125.
54. HTF, 46.
55. HTF, 48, 46.

ever maintaining, intact and unimpaired, His own supremacy."[56] Instead, she suggests that faith, if she had any, would have to be kenotic. She writes:

> Faith would be that God is self-limited utterly by his creation—a contraction of the scope of his will; that he bound himself to time and its hazards and haps as a man would lash himself to a tree for love. . . . That God is helpless, our baby to bear, self-abandoned on the doorstep of time, wondered at by cattle and oxen. . . . Faith would be, in short, that God has any willful connection with time whatsoever, and with us.[57]

Dillard seems to have both Jewish and Christian kenotic traditions in mind here. The idea of *tsimtsum*—suggested by the phrase "the contraction of the scope of his will"—is paired with allusions to both the crucifixion and incarnation of Christ, each described in kenotic terms. As the reflexive pronouns make clear ("*self*-limited, "bound *himself* to time and its hazards," "*self*-abandoned") this is a voluntary not necessary kenotic act of love. The passage is also unequivocal in its assertion that God has given himself up entirely to the "hazards and haps" of his creation. Dillard claims God is "self-limited *utterly* by his creation," and "*helpless*, our baby to bear."[58] God in Christ, like the exiled Shekhinah, becomes a creature bound within time and space. His omnipotence and omniscience are therefore limited by temporal terms, terms which expose him to suffering, rejection, alienation, and death.

This leads Dillard to the central theodicean question in *Holy the Firm*: "Did Christ descend once and for all to no purpose, in a kind of divine and kenotic suicide, or ascend once and for all . . . Is there no link at the base of things?"[59] The answer comes in the book's third and final section. Reflecting on the burned child, Dillard returns to the theme of kenosis and tells the reader that, like it or not, Julie's tragedy serves a painful but spiritually efficacious purpose. It reminds us "not of what God can do, but of what he cannot do, or will not, which is to catch time in its free fall and stick a nickel's worth of sense into our days."[60] In terms of Polkinghorne's kenotic theology, God "will not" intervene in time's free fall because he is bound by love to be one cause among many causes that exert power in human lives.[61] Exploding jet fuel happens also to be one of them.

56. Vanstone, *Love's Endeavor*, 73.
57. HTF, 46–47.
58. HTF, 46.
59. HTF, 47–48.
60. HTF, 61.
61. Polkinghorne, "Kenotic Creation," 104.

Shortly hereafter is Dillard's account of a mystical event that commences when she returns home from an errand to buy communion wine. The passage was discussed in chapter 1 as illustrative of a Hasidic pansacramental view of creation and Jewish unitive mystical experiences. Yet, it is important to note here that the passage also illustrates powerfully Dillard's blending of Jewish and Christian theology to describe God in kenotic terms: "Here is a bottle of wine with a label, Christ with a cork. I bear holiness splintered into a vessel, very God of very God, the sempiternal silence personal and brooding, bright on the back of my ribs."[62] The Kabbalistic image of *shevirat ha-kelim* with which *Holy the Firm* began—days "splintered down, splintered down and wrapped in time like a husk"[63]—resurfaces and is linked to the Eucharistic blood of Christ. Both "Christ with a cork," and "holiness splintered into a vessel" are kenotic images, the latter alluding specifically to the Lurianic idea of *shevirat ha-kelim*, the "splintering of the vessels," that occurred in the second phase of the cosmic process of creation. The images reinforce not only the idea that God is self-limited (the eternal Logos is "corked" within a bodily vessel) but also hint at an ontologically kenotic Christ by linking Christic images with the primordial events of Luria's creation cosmogony. Indeed, the words from the Nicene Creed ("very God of very God") affirm that Christ is the eternal, pre-existent Logos. Nicene orthodoxy, forged in response to Arianism, affirms emphatically the full divinity *and* humanity of Christ, and by implication, affirms the potential for God to be contained within a creature. Christ was the fullness of God splintered into a clay vessel. Though there are of course significant and irreconcilable differences between Jewish mysticism and Nicene orthodoxy, their metaphors and symbols provide Dillard with rich and varied strata to mine from the same theological terrain. The splintered Shekinah of God, the Eucharistic presence of Christ, and the Nicene Creed all speak to the self-emptying of God that makes holiness both present and perceptible in creation. Dillard grafts theological root to branch, and a robust Judeo-Christian pansacramentalism emerges.

The Exiled Shekinah, The Suspended Christ

Dillard's darkest and most fragmented long work of non-fiction is *For the Time Being*, published in 1999. The book's seven chapters each have ten identically titled and ordered sections and its themes, as Dillard states outright in the "Author's Note," center on theodicean questions: "Does God

62. HTF, 64–65.
63. HTF, 11.

cause natural calamity?"; what is the relationship between God and creation (especially the particular individual)?; and "given things as they are, how shall one individual live?"[64] It seems hardly coincidental that Dillard's book most focused on questions of evil and suffering also relies more than any previous work on Jewish mystical theology, primarily the ideas of Isaac Luria and the Baal Shem Tov. As suggested at the outset, Isaac Luria's inherently kenotic concept of *tsimtsum* and the Hasidic understanding of God's wandering Shekinah allow Dillard to suggest that evil and suffering exist within a space God has conceded to his creation.

In the second chapter of *For the Time Being*, Dillard introduces the Lurianic concept of *tsimtsum*.[65] Dillard concludes, "Luria's Kabbalist creation story, however baroque, accounts boldly for both moral evil and natural calamity.... This is our bleak world. We see only the demonic shells of things. It is literally sensible to deny that God exists. In fact, God is hidden, exiled, in the sparks of divine light the shells entrap."[66] Dillard returns to Luria's idea of *tsimtsum* several chapters later in the parallel sections "Evil" of chapters 5 and 6. In these, she synthesizes Lurianic Kabbalism with Christian kenoticism in a highly evocative and theologically potent image of an eternally crucified Christ.

In the section "Evil" of chapter 6, Dillard has been considering to what extent God intervenes in natural processes and how prayer affects them. She concludes the section with this paragraph and its startling, final image: "Nature works out its complexities. God suffers the world's necessities along with us, and suffers our turning away, and joins us in exile. Christians might add that Christ hangs, as it were, on the cross forever, always incarnate, always nailed."[67]

The parallel clauses, "God joins us in exile" and "Christ hangs on the cross" clearly link Jewish and Christian kenotic traditions. The images of the wandering Shekinah and the eternally nailed Son express dramatically God's self-limitation as a creature and challenge classical theology's notions of God's impassibility, immutability, and omnipotence. If "God suffers the world's necessities with us," Dillard seems to be suggesting he is not impassible.[68] If He also "suffers our turning away," neither is he immutable.[69] Likewise, Abraham Heschel insists on the pathos of God and contends in

64. FTB, x.
65. FTB, 50–51.
66. FTB, 50–51.
67. FTB, 169.
68. FTB, 169.
69. FTB, 169.

The Prophets that the choices of humans have a real effect upon God: "The predicament of man is a predicament of God Who has a stake in the human situation.... Man's alienation from God is not the ultimate fact by which to measure man's situation. The divine pathos, the fact of God's participation in the predicament of man, is the elemental fact."[70] By joining his creation in exile, God becomes a participant in human suffering and alienation within this world and makes himself vulnerable to it.

Perhaps most significantly, Dillard's choice to leave Christ "*always* incarnate, and *always* nailed" argues radically for an ontologically kenotic God.[71] If Christ is *always* nailed, within the eternal Trinity hangs a man whose body is pierced and broken forever by creatures he loves. This is no triumphant, resurrected Christ[72] but an eternally bound and slain God, whose choice to limit the scope of his omnipotence made "room" for evil and suffering within his own body and thus within the eternal Trinity itself.

The image also seems to signal Dillard's doubts as to whether God will exercise his omnipotence to spare his creatures from violence and pain. For if Christ still hangs, his hands are rather tied (as she puns earlier in the book).[73] God-in-Christ's self-emptying on the cross and God's self-abandonment in the cry of dereliction seems to her good (or good enough) evidence that God is unlikely to violate the terms of the universe or his own nature by intervening with miracles.[74] This is in fact what she has deduced in the preceding paragraphs. Reflecting on the power of prayer, she asks, "Does God stick a finger in, if only now and then? Does God budge, nudge,

---

70. Heschel, *Prophets*, 226.

71. FTB, 169 (emphasis mine).

72. Given Dillard's theodicean concerns, the omission of any mention of the resurrection not only in this passage but in the entire canon of her work is a conspicuous absence. Chapter 5 will return to this image of the eternally suspended Christ to argue that by eclipsing the resurrection ending to the gospels, Dillard suspends the end of the story, as it were. Doing so allows her to argue that the time of redemption is the present rather than the *parousia*.

73. See her comment in response to the thinking of Simone Weil (FTB, 168). Previously, in chapter 5, she concludes, "After all, the semipotent God has one hand tied behind his back" (FTB, 140).

74. Dillard states that Teilhard de Chardin, whom she frequently quotes in *For the Time Being*, believed in the Gospels in spite of rather than because of the miracles (FTB, 71). She also notes that according to his biographer, de Chardin was not really concerned with "who moved the stone" from Christ's grave (FTB, 71, 163). Because de Chardin often speaks for Dillard, one could surmise that like him she eschews basing her faith on the miraculous and finds it confirmed instead in the physical world. She quotes de Chardin's confession that "If I should lose all faith in God . . . I think that I should continue to believe invincibly in the world" (de Chardin in FTB, 44).

hear, twitch, help?"⁷⁵ Her answer is a hugely qualified "maybe." With the help of Paul Tillich, she walks a theological tightrope and proposes that the prayer of "willing surrender" to God perhaps "changes the situation a jot or two by adding power which God can use . . . I don't know."⁷⁶

In this respect, Dillard's theological position shares striking similarities to the kenotic theologies of Jürgen Moltmann and John Polkinghorne. Moltmann insists "We look in vain for God in the history of nature or in human history if what we are looking for are special divine interventions. Is it not much more that God waits?"⁷⁷ Polkinhorne suggests that one might understand God's choice to limit his omnipotence in the world's activities as a "kenosis of causal status," the most dramatic instance of which is the incarnation whereby "in first-century Palestine, God submitted . . . to becoming a cause among causes."⁷⁸ Likewise, Dillard believes that God has a hand in the world,⁷⁹ but so do mutant genes, exploding airplanes, and tsunamis. Thus, she observes:

> It need not craze us, I think, to know we are evolving, like other living forms according to physical processes. Statistical probability describes the mechanism of evolution. . . . In order to live at all, we pay a "mysterious tribute of tears, blood, and sin." It is hard to find a more inarguable explanation for the physical catastrophe and the suffering we endure at chance from the material world.⁸⁰

Though elliptical rather than discursive in her presentation of ideas, Dillard's clear thesis by the end of *For the Time Being* is that it does craze us—and rightly so—especially when that statistical probability turns up in one's own home, when a pregnant mother discovers *she* is carrying a severely deformed child, or when a husband discovers *his* wife drowned in a tsunami. Herein is the theological problem: "Do we believe the individual is precious, or do we not?" Dillard asks. "My children and your children

---

75. FTB, 168–69.
76. FTB, 169.
77. Moltmann, "God's Kenosis," 149–51.
78. Polkinghorne, "Kenotic Creation," 104.
79. See Dillard's aside in FTB, 140–41. After claiming that God has one hand tied behind his back, she admits parenthetically that "I cannot prove that with the other hand he wipes and stirs our souls from time to time, or that he spins like a fireball through our skills, and knocks open our eyes so we see flaming skies and fall to the ground and say, 'Abba! Father!'"
80. FTB, 87.

and their children? Of course."[81] Yet because she also believes in an ontologically kenotic God, in Christ forever nailed, she knows that "nature works out its complexities" and many events derive not from God's wisdom and love "but only from blind chance."[82] In Moltmann's view, "In his relation to the world, God is not almighty in the sense that as *causa prima* he effects everything in everything through the *causae secundae*—good and evil, becoming and passing away, genesis and dissolution."[83] Dillard has little patience with those who confuse kenosis with causality. Taking up Teilhard de Chardin's view, Dillard concludes, "It is 'fatal'" to believe "that we suffer at the hands of an omnipotent God. The omnipotence of God makes no sense if it requires the all-causingness of God."[84] Near the end of *For the Time Being*, she declares emphatically: "God is no more blinding people with glaucoma, or testing them with diabetes, or purifying them with spinal pain . . . than he is jimmying floodwaters or pitching tornadoes at towns. . . . The very least likely things for which God might be responsible are what insurers call 'acts of God.'"[85]

One is left with the question, what *does* God do? Dillard asks, "If God does not cause everything that happens, does God cause anything that happens? Is God completely out of the loop?"[86] The answer a few paragraphs later combines the idea of *tsimtsum* with a kenotic image that will be introduced here and examined at length in the next chapter. Dillard concludes:

> Mostly, God is out of the physical loop. Or the loop is a spinning hole in his side. Simone Weil takes a notion from Rabbi Isaac Luria to acknowledge that God's hands are tied. To create, God did not extend himself but withdrew himself; he humbled and obliterated himself, and left outside himself the domain of necessity, in which he does not intervene.[87]

The allusion to Christ's hole-pierced side on the cross makes clear Dillard's kenotic, perichoretic panentheism. The universe with all its beauty and pain is spinning *within* the body of God and is therefore embraced within his own kenotic suffering. The strong, active verbs in the following sentence underscore the depth of God's own agony and suggest the power of weakness; he "withdrew," "humbled," and "obliterated" himself. Moreover, the explicit

81. FTB, 59.
82. FTB, 87.
83. Moltmann, "God's Kenosis," 148.
84. FTB, 84–85.
85. FTB, 167.
86. FTB, 167.
87. FTB, 166.

link made between the crucified Christ, the Lurianic notion of *tsimtsum*, and God as the creator affirms the ontologically kenotic nature of the Godhead. God at creation endured the self-inflicted wound of exile, humiliation, and alienation in the process of the world's coming into being. In doing so, God conceded it space, a theodicean space, that allows it freedom not only to inflict injustice and suffering upon itself but also upon its creator.

Dillard's fusion of Kabbalistic thought, specifically the ideas of *tsimtsum* and *shevirat ha-kelim*, with Christian kenotic images and symbols allows her to construct a powerful literary and theological instrument for exploring the difficult terrain of moral and physical evil. With her art instrument, she has carved out a theodicean space within which questions can be asked about God's omni-attributes and yet tensions preserved between often conflicting existential and spiritual realities. The next chapter will examine how the multiplicity of gaps, absences, and spaces function theologically in Dillard's work and how Dillard's asyndetic style not only reflects those gaps but locates readers within their unsettling silences.

CHAPTER 4

Tsimtsum, Theodicean Spaces, and Annie Dillard's Asyndetic Style

"For the world is as glorious as ever, and exalting, but for credibility's sake let's start with the bad news."

—ANNIE DILLARD, *FOR THE TIME BEING*

Introduction

DILLARD'S INQUIRIES INTO THE relationship of eternity to time and thereby of God's relationship to creation become problematic when she attempts to reckon with the fallen-ness of creation and the metaphysical reality of evil. Of enduring interest to Dillard are the apparent and intractable absurdities that arise from God's creating humans to be moral creatures in an amoral natural world and the acute suffering that ensues. The previous chapter's analysis focused on Dillard's challenges to the classical Western notions of an omnipotent God and on her literary arguments, made in part through appeals to both Jewish and Christian kenotic theologies, for a God who has elected to be self-limiting. As Dillard explains in a 1999 interview with Maureen Abood, "I say God has one hand tied behind his back. If you deal with the problem of evil in an honest way, it seems to me that eventually you will have to tinker with the doctrine of God's omnipotence."[1]

Dillard's attempt to deal honestly with the world results in the suspension or holding in tension of apparently contradictory but equally binding epistemic and theological truths. Stan Goldman notes that "the notion

---

1. Abood, "Natural Wonders," 31.

of unresolvable dualities" is "central to Dillard's theological and literary vision."[2] These manifest themselves in various oppositional motifs and structural elements in her work: God as both present and absent, the horrors and beauties of nature, being and non-being, self-awareness and self-forgetfulness, just to name a few.[3] Dillard also expresses these apparently unresolvable dualities as twinned elements. In *Pilgrim at Tinker Creek*, for example, they appear as the world's "twin fiords" of corruption and beauty and the twinned Shadow Creek and Tinker Creek.[4] In *For the Time Being*, they emerge in the contrasting personalities of the "gloomy [Isaac] Luria" and "the exuberant Baal Shem Tov."[5] Critics such as Jim Cheney,[6] Joseph DeRoller,[7] David Lavery,[8] Margaret Loewen Reimer,[9] and Robert Paul Dunn[10] have explored these elements in her work at length. However, to date, an overlooked dimension of this feature in Dillard's work is its theological function and the frequency with which Dillard draws upon Jewish mystical theology to explore the tensions between contradictory realities, particularly God's goodness and the presence of evil and unjust suffering within His creation.

The preceding chapter explained that Dillard's holding in tension of these contradictory realities creates what is being called in this argument "theodicean spaces"—existential and theological gaps within which evil and suffering can exist. While chapter 3 demonstrated that the God Dillard depicts within her literary world is a kenotic one whose choice to limit the scope of his intervention creates theodicean spaces, the current chapter will focus on the theological and aesthetic rationale for such gaps or absences, as well as the various ways they are manifested rhetorically in Dillard's asyndetic style. Furthermore, it will continue the discussion begun in chapter 3 of ways in which Jewish mystical theology suits well these artistic and theological purposes. The imagery and theology of *tsimtsum* and *shevirat ha-kelim* allow Dillard not only to create theologically resonant images of a kenotic God, but they also allow her to grapple with questions about evil and suffering within the tension of a pre-messianic

2. Goldman, "Sacrifices to the Hidden God," 196.
3. Goldman, "Sacrifices to the Hidden God," 196.
4. PTC, 245.
5. FTB, 22.
6. See Cheney, "Waters of Separation."
7. See DeRoller, "Recommended."
8. See Lavery, "Noticer."
9. See Reimer, "Dialectical Vision."
10. See Dunn, "Artist as Nun."

interval in which eschatological hope is suspended in theological and, quite literally, textual space.

This chapter will first explore the theological and aesthetic origins of Dillard's habit of "minding the gap" and how her doing so creates quite deliberately what Martin Buber calls a "holy insecurity" that is both reflected in and evoked by Dillard's asyndetic style. It will then explore how Dillard draws from Kabbalistic imagery to create multi-layered motifs of shadows and gaps that give shape to Dillard's metaphysical questions, inform readers of humanity's existential exile "here in the flickering shade of the nothingness between me and the light,"[11] and articulate her assumptions about the origins of evil in creation. The chapter will then consider Dillard's own question found in the author's note of *For the Time Being*, of what, if the world is like this, is the relationship between the Absolute and the concrete particulars of life, especially all the particular griefs and horrors one human life might have to endure? It will suggest that although Dillard's texts never present an answer, they do present a recurring image—that of a clay man, the crucified Christ, within whom the universes spin, an image introduced in chapter 3 and returned to here for a final and full analysis in light of both chapters' discussion of theodicean spaces. Finally, and perhaps most importantly, it will be suggested that Dillard not only inhabits tensions created by theological ellipses or the negative spaces evoked by her asyndetic style but also insists that it is especially in them that God is to be found.

Throughout the chapter's sections, it will be argued that Dillard's asyndetic style plays a significant theological role not only in reflecting the gaps she perceives but also in locating readers within theodicean spaces that are deliberately unsettling, suspending readers over textual silences, stammerings, and ellipses that resist closure. In short, features of Dillard's asyndetic style will be read as both a mimesis and the genesis of theodicean spaces.

Minding the Gap

By refusing to reconcile logical (and concomitantly, theological) contradictions, Dillard is, one might conclude, committed not only to minding the gap but also to maintaining the tension between these contradictions. This determination to "mind the gap" arises from her commitment to both spiritual and artistic integrity. In a 1978 interview with Michael Burnett, she explains, "Even to talk about God in the first place for me takes a whole lot of sincerity and it's hard even to begin, and once I do I am of course

---

11. PTC, 63.

committed to being absolutely honest, which is very, very difficult."[12] When Philip Yancey asked Dillard about her work's oscillations between "hope and despair, anger and love," Dillard accounted for them this way:

> I must stay faithful to art. I get in my little canoe and paddle out to the edge of mystery; it is unfortunately true that words fail, reason fails, and all I can do is to create a world which by its internal coherence makes a degree of sense. I can either do that or hush. And then I learn to make statements about that world, to furrow deeper into mystery.
>
> Every single thing I follow takes me there, to the edge of a cliff.[13] As soon as I start writing, I'm hanging over the cliff again. You can make a perfectly coherent world at the snap of a finger—but only if you don't bother being honest about it.[14]

This commitment to create tightly structured works of art that preserve (and actually create) epistemic and theological gaps results in literature calculated to be unsettling and sometimes profoundly disturbing. Peter Fritzell asserts that *Pilgrim at Tinker Creek*, more than any other book associated with nature writing in America, proves that the human attempt to domesticate life and the landscape "is finally an epistemological and metaphysical struggle, an ongoing psychobiotic and philosophic scramble in which virtually every moment of innerving belief and hope is met with a coordinate moment of unnerving doubt, each instance of stabilizing facticity ... followed by a meditation on the indeterminacy of fact."[15] In his review of *Holy the Firm*, Frederick Buechner remarks, "'the violence is sometimes unbearable.'"[16] Ray Kelleher warns his audience that "Some readers will find *For the Time Being* brutalizing " and "will be driven away."[17] Dillard risks doing so quite deliberately. Speaking to Maureen Abood, Dillard asserts that if readers know that *she* knows "how grim it can get," her Christian "belief is a lot more convincing."[18] In fact, she warns readers at the beginning of

---

12. Burnett, "Interview," 90.

13. This sort of epistemic insecurity is described vividly in *Writing Life*. Dillard recounts, "As I walk about this enclosed bay on Cape Cod, or as I scroll down a computer file to a blank screen, then from time to time the skies part ahead of my path, or the luminous photons on the screen revert to infinite randomness, and I balk again on the brink. The irrational haunts the metaphysical" (TWL, 89).

14. Yancey, "Face Aflame," 17.

15. Fritzell, *Nature Writing*, 219.

16. Buechner, "Island Journal," 12.

17. Kelleher, "In the Face of Brutality," 58.

18. Abood, "Natural Wonders," 30.

For the Time Being, "the world is as glorious as ever, and exalting, but for credibility's sake let's start with the bad news."[19]

The resolve to maintain the absurdities of logical and theological contradictions rather than attempt to reconcile them is what Martin Buber identifies as the heart of Hasidic piety. In *The Origin and Meaning of Hasidism*, Buber explains that Hasidism differs from Kabbalistic thought in a foundational assumption that life lived in authentic relationship with God means assenting to life lived in suspension over the abyss of its manifold contradictions, in a posture of what Buber calls "holy insecurity."[20] Because God is entirely Other, this relationship is predicated not upon finding intellectual solutions to life's contradictions but upon encountering a living mystery in a dialogical relationship. It is a relationship that is neither safe nor fully comprehensible, but fraught with risk, vulnerability, and instability. Buber explains:

> It is precisely in stopping short, in letting itself be disconcerted, in deep knowledge of the impotence of all "information," of the incongruence of all possessed truth, in the "holy insecurity," that Hasidic piety has its true life.... One may "clamber about in the upper worlds"—suddenly it touches him and all is blown away, and in infinite pathless darkness one stands before the eternal presence. Only the defenseless outstretched hand of the insecure is not withered by the lightning. We are sent into the world of contradiction; if we soar up away from it into spheres where this world seems translucent to us, we forsake our mission.... The absurd is given to me that I may endure and sustain it with my life; this, the enduring and sustaining of the absurd, is the meaning which I can experience.[21]

Importantly, Dillard quotes this very passage in *For the Time Being*.[22] Her doing so reveals that near the end of her writing career, Hasidic thought continues to voice her commitment to sustain the contradictory and to endure rather than explain the absurd.

For both Dillard and the Hasids, "holy insecurity" arises in part from a deep sense of the ontological gulf between God and humans. Buber insists that for this reason, the Baal Shem Tov and his followers endured the gap rather than attempted to "get behind the problematic" as the Kabbalists did

---

19. FTB, 8.
20. Buber, *Origin and Meaning*, 179.
21. Buber, *Origin and Meaning*, 179.
22. FTB, 141.

through gnosis or number and letter magic.[23] More broadly, Buber asserts in *Eclipse of God*, that the fear of God is the proper starting place for religion:

> All religious reality begins with what Biblical religion calls "the fear of God." It comes when our existence between birth and death becomes incomprehensible and uncanny, when all security is shattered through the mystery. . . . Through this dark gate . . . the believing man steps forth into the everyday which is henceforth hallowed as the place in which he has to live with the mystery.[24]

Buber insists that "he who begins with the love of God without having previously experienced the fear of God,[25] loves an idol which he himself has made, a god whom it is easy enough to love. He does not love the real God who is, to begin with, dreadful and incomprehensible."[26]

This "fear of the Lord," or "holy insecurity," is depicted frequently in the Hasidic tales, and these legendary anecdotes appear often in Dillard's work. One of the tales first appears in Dillard's essay "An Expedition to the Pole,"[27] and she uses it again in *The Writing Life*.[28] In "An Expedition to the Pole," Dillard writes:

> On the whole, I do not find Christians, outside of the catacombs, sufficiently sensible of conditions. Does anyone have the foggiest idea what sort of power we so blithely invoke? Or, as I suspect, does no one believe a word of it? . . . The eighteenth-century Hasidic Jews had more sense, and more belief. One Hasidic slaughterer, whose work required invoking the Lord, bade a tearful farewell to his wife and children every morning before he set out for the slaughterhouse. He felt, every morning, that he

23. Buber, *Origin and Meaning*, 178–81.

24. Buber, *Eclipse of God*, 36.

25. Interestingly, in Moses' public exhortation regarding obedience to the Ten Commandments, fearing God precedes loving Him. He asks, "And now, Israel, what does the Lord your God ask of you but to fear the Lord your God, to walk in obedience to him, to love him, to serve the Lord your God with all your heart and with all your soul, and to observe the Lord's commands and decrees that I am giving you today for your own good?" (Deut 10:12–13).

26. Buber, *Eclipse of God*, 37.

27. TST, 52–53.

28. Dillard writes this version of the same tale: "I admire those eighteenth-century Hasids who understood the risk of prayer. . . . A ritual slaughterer . . . every morning bade goodbye to his wife and children and wept as if he would never see them again. His friend asked him why. Because, he answered, when I begin I call out to the Lord. Then I pray, 'Have mercy on us.' Who knows what the Lord's power will do to me in that moment after I have invoked it and before I beg for mercy?" (TWL, 9).

would never see any of them again. For everyday... the words of his prayer carried him into danger. After he called on God, God might notice and destroy him before he had time to utter the rest, "Have mercy."[29]

In the chapter "The Present" in *Pilgrim at Tinker Creek*, Dillard confesses, "This is *the* fear. It often feels best to lay low, inconspicuous, instead of waving your spirit around from high places like a lightning rod... For if God is in one sense the igniter... God is also in another sense the destroyer... impartial as the atmosphere."[30] In the book's final pages, Dillard warns the reader that if one wants to have dealings with God, one had best "read the fine print. 'Not as the world giveth, give I unto you.'"[31] He will "catch you up, aloft, up to any gap at all, and you'll come back... dribbling and crazed," and at death you will finally understand that "you're dealing with a maniac."[32]

B. Jill Carroll, in a perceptive and convincing analysis of Dillard's God in *The Savage Side*, argues that if one is serious about taking "'the cosmos as the context for doing theology'" one has to reckon with "discomforting" images of God as well as the "healing and nurturing" ones: "To do otherwise is to do violence to otherness, to reduce the wildness and cruelty of the natural world—and the deity modeled upon it—to what in Levinasian[33] terms might

---

29. TST, 52–53.
30. PTC, 90.
31. PTC, 275.
32. PTC, 275.

33. The philosophical connections between Buber and Levinas are highly complex and even a cursory analysis would go well beyond the scope of the current discussion. However, a few words about their similarities and differences are warranted. Atterton, Calarco, and Friedman point out in the introduction to the excellent volume, *Levinas and Buber: Dialogue and Difference*, that although Levinas's phenomenology, by his own admission, was enormously indebted to Buber's thinking, determining how it is so is quite difficult. At the same time Levinas was reading Buber, he was also reading the dialogical philosophies of Franz Rosenzweig and Gabriel Marcel. Further, Levinas's own assessment of Buber's *I-Thou* construction changed markedly over time, most noticeably following Derrida's critique of Levinas's reading of Buber in the 1964 essay, "Violence and Metaphysics" (Atterton et al., *Levinas and Buber*, 6–8). That being said, certain parallels between Buber and Levinas can fairly confidently be drawn: "Both... place the relationship with otherness—or the readiness for such an encounter—at the beginning of experience. Both consider the encounter as oriented toward the other prior to theoretical understanding and knowledge," and "both posit the relationship with the Thou as in some sense incorporating or deriving from the relation with the absolutely Other called God" (Atterton et al., *Levinas and Buber*, 6). Furthermore, as Stephan Strasser points out in his very helpful overview in the same volume, both philosophers espouse a humanism deeply rooted in Judaism, both endeavor to revitalize religious and cultural life in an era each understands as hostile to genuine encounters with the other, and both place speech at the center of the dialogical movement toward

be called a representation of the same"; this results in a God who becomes merely an instrument to be used for one's own utilitarian purposes.[34] Dillard's insistence on the ontological gulf between God and human reason serves as a hedge against domesticating Him[35] and thereby against collapsing an I-Thou relationship suffused with holy insecurity into an I-It objectification of a false god. In so doing, her practice of "minding the gap" could perhaps be understood as a literary enactment of the Deuteronomic command "to fear the Lord your God" (Deut 10:12). Since the staggering incomprehensibility of the world and the God who made it brings Dillard quickly to the end of her own reason, it is, *de facto*, the "beginning of wisdom" (Prov 9:10). "My God, what a world," Dillard exclaims in *Pilgrim at Tinker Creek*. "There is no accounting for one second of it."[36] When, as Buber observes, "all security is shattered through the mystery,"[37] Dillard refuses to construct from the remaining fragments of human reason a theological or philosophical structure

---

the Other (Strasser, "Buber and Levinas," 37).

Where the current argument's point is concerned—the radical otherness and incomprehensibility of God—the two philosophers' views essentially correspond, and where they differ, the difference is a matter of degree not of kind. In the Postscript to the 1958 edition of *I and Thou*, Buber is careful to note that any speech about God is inherently paradoxical and limited. Yet, he insists that "whatever else he may be," God is a "Person," not "a principle," or "an idea"; therefore, "God enters into a direct relation with us men in creative, revealing and redeeming acts, and thus makes it possible for us to enter into a direct relation with him" (Buber, *I and Thou*, 135). Buber is careful to preserve the radical otherness of God—God is the only *Thou* that can never become an It—while at the same time allowing for there to be a genuine meeting between the I and *Thou* that sanctifies and redeems all of life. Strasser points out that while Levinas would agree that in the "face" of the other one "meets" God, God is "no existing being," nor a hidden "noumenon." Consequently, "there are no real existing bridges that can be built to Him" (Strasser, "Buber and Levinas," 44). In short, Buber's God, though Other, is not sufficiently Other for Levinas. Buber, in his estimation, fails to preserve the radical otherness of God (Strasser, "Buber and Levinas," 44). Similarly, Levinas's primary criticism of Buber's articulation of the I-*Thou* relationship is that it suggests a reciprocal and therefore symmetrical relation. Levinas argues that because the other is fundamentally unlike me, the relation is by nature asymmetrical. This confers upon the other the orientation of height, a height that makes me always responsible to and for the other. Buber's I-*Thou* relation, Levinas asserts, does violence against height by suggesting that through dialogue, the relation of I to *Thou* is symmetrical and reciprocal. See Kelley, "Reciprocity and the Height of God," 226–32.

34. Carroll, *Savage Side*, 77.

35. In *For the Time Being*, these sentiments are expressed succinctly in the words of the contemporary hermit, Theresa Mancuso: "'The thing we desperately need is to face the way it is'" (FTB, 19).

36. PTC, 267.

37. Buber, *Eclipse of God*, 36.

to traverse the gaps. Instead, she passes through the "dark gate,"[38] and brings readers along with her through an asyndetic style.

A Stammer Bore it Onward: Holy Insecurity and Asyndeton

Dillard's efforts to "mind the gap" also manifest themselves in her asyndetic style[39] and, more generally, in her own aesthetic convictions about the intellectual structure of literary works of art. While excellent scholarly work has been done on the ways in which her texts' surface ruptures and their highly stylized, painterly prose[40] functions epiphanically, little attention has been devoted to how it functions theologically. These asyndetic disjunctions echo the epistemological and theological concerns of her body of work. On a syntactic level, these asyndetic gaps take the form of omitted transitions between sentences and narrative segments, sudden shifts in tone and grammatical mood (from indicative to imperative, for example), and prose shaved down to the barest syllable. On a structural level, they take the form of the juxtaposition of disparate literary genres (e.g., Eskimo mythology abuts data from a scientific manual), and fragmented narrative sequences.[41] Dillard explains her aesthetic strategy in an interview with Michael Burnett, revealing that even at a structural level, she conceives of the text as an art object with a void or space at the center which defines the contours of the whole. Commenting on *Holy the Firm*, she explains that her work is "reflexive" in that "the whole meaning is structural.... It refers back to itself, so the various elements in the structure of this kind of thing pertain to themselves. It is like the Rutherford model of the atom: held together by the strongest forces in the universe . . .

---

38. Buber, *Eclipse of God*, 36.

39. Asyndeton is defined here as the omission of conjunctions and/or connecting elements that express the logical relationships between words, clauses, and structural elements. Defined as such, technically, it includes the figure of speech "brachylogia," the absence of conjunctions between single words.

40. See Scheick, "Annie Dillard"; Humble Johnson, *Space Between*, esp. 127–97.

41. The fragmentation exists within meticulously wrought structures. Dillard's mentor, writing instructor and the chair of the English Department at Hollins College, Louis Rubin, was a New Critic. His influence on Dillard seems manifest in her painstaking crafting of structure and syntax. *Pilgrim at Tinker Creek*, has a bilateral symmetry, the first half structured upon the *via positiva* and the second half on the *via negativa* (Dillard, "Drawing," 32). *Holy the Firm* has a tripartite structure that corresponds to creation, the fall, and redemption (Burnett, "Interview," 88). *For the Time Being* has seven chapters, each with ten identically titled and ordered sections: Birth, Sand, China, Clouds, Numbers, Israel, Encounters, Thinker, Evil, and Now.

all the elements . . . are spinning like crazy around the center, but the center exists only for them and they exist for the center."[42]

Similarly, in *Living by Fiction*, she describes a present but absent structure in interpretive fiction that could apply equally to her own prose works. She asserts that in order for writers "to make a world in which their ideas might be discovered, [they] must embody those ideas in materials solid and opaque, and thus conceal them. In the process of fleshing out a thought, they brick it in."[43] She goes on to explain that the better artists they are, "the more completely their structures will vanish into the work" and, thus, writers are left in the paradoxical position of laboring to craft a structure only then carefully to "obliterate" all traces of it.[44] Thus, it seems that an abiding aesthetic feature in Dillard's work is the silent center or invisible structure around which and for which the entire work exists—in other words, an affective absence. Though wordless itself, the structure determines every word on the page, and is, therefore, an absence necessary for the created work to exist.

In like fashion, Dillard describes the short sentences of "plain prose" as having "a good deal of blank space around them" that "erupt against a backdrop of silence."[45] This style of writing, Dillard insists, has "one supreme function, which is not to call attention to itself, but to refer to the world. This prose is not an end in itself, but a means. It is, then, a *useful* prose."[46] In other words, Dillard understands and means this prose style to engender certain effects, and in so doing it has a didactic element. Dillard's own prose style can be categorized as such and increasingly so as it evolves to the clean, spare prose of *For the Time Being*, her most narratively fragmented but in many ways most structurally precise book. Given that this book deals most frankly with the problem of evil, it seems hardly coincidental that its sentences have "a good deal of blank space" around them; in fact, its short paragraphs and fragmented structure quite literally create a great deal of white space on the pages themselves. As she describes its style in the Author's

---

42. Burnett, "Interview," 88.

43. LBF, 156.

44. LBF, 156. Perhaps for this reason, Dillard frequently gives her readers cues as to how to approach her texts. In the first chapter of *Holy the Firm*, she states, "Nothing is going to happen in this book. There is only a little violence here and there in the language, at the corner where eternity clips time" (HTF, 24). The "Author's Note" beginning *For the Time Being* warns readers it will be fragmented and difficult. It outlines its major themes and structural elements, promising the reader that after several chapters, these "disparate" elements "will be growing familiar" (FTB, x).

45. LBF, 116–17.

46. LBF, 117.

Note, "it is not intimate, and its narratives keep breaking. . . . Its pleasures are almost purely mental."[47]

There is a strong parallel between Dillard's aesthetic aims and her epistemological and theological concerns. Prose that seamlessly guides readers from one thought to the next by providing clear transitions, conjunctions, subordination, and coordination of syntactical elements can foster the illusion of control and mastery of the ideational content the grammar embodies. Thus, the apparent effortlessness lent to the apprehension of meaning by the logic of syntactical elements that connect and express the relationships between components can be transferred to the concepts themselves, and one can come away believing one has understood what is ultimately incomprehensible and mysterious. Because Dillard so often grapples with unanswerable questions, the disruption of logic, ruptures in narrative sequence, and erasure of structural connectors guard against easy, unimpeded reading and thereby against the illusion that human reason (expressed in grammatically coherent syntax) can secure meaning in the face of realities that far exceed the capacity of language to express.[48] Dillard's asyndetic elements simultaneously reflect and elicit a "holy insecurity" and thereby parallel uncannily Buber's description of Biblical and Hasidic piety. Her texts "stop short"; they let the reader be "disconcerted, in deep knowledge of the impotence of all 'information;'" and textual ruptures both reflect and enact "the incongruence of all possessed truth."[49] Moreover, the gaps created by the logical and syntactic ellipses force the reader to "endur[e] and [sustain] the absurd"[50] rather than have it collapsed or bridged by grammatical elements. Dillard carries readers to the cliff edge with her, precipitating a "holy insecurity" about the act of reading itself that translates to an existential insecurity about one's ready-made answers to life's contradictions. Anyone who has read Dillard knows how frequently one asks with her "What in the Sam Hill is going on here?"[51]

Interestingly, Martin Buber often refers to the stopping short of language in response to encounters with mystery as "stammering."[52] Buber claims that Hasidism sprang to life out of a "stammer" and "a stammer

---

47. FTB, ix.

48. This section is indebted to the thinking of Catherine Pickstock in *After Writing: On the Liturgical Consummation of Philosophy* for the general ideas expressed here about the ways asyndeton can function in discourse about God. See her argument in Pickstock, *After Writing*, 220–28, esp. section three, "Christic Asyndeton."

49. Buber, *Origin and Meaning*, 179.

50. Buber, *Origin and Meaning*, 179.

51. HTF, 60.

52. Buber, *On the Bible*, 11.

bore it onward—from generation to generation."⁵³ Further, in his analysis of the Genesis creation account, Buber asserts, "what is unutterable *can* only be uttered, as it is here expressed, in the language of men. . . . Man cannot but stammer when he lines up what he knows of the universe into a chronological series of commands and 'works' from the divine workshop."⁵⁴ It should be noted that the stammer of "holy insecurity" is a stammer not because of the words and syllables but because of the silences, the fractures between them, which register the snapping of reason, the acute sense that speaking itself is a contradiction. One is trying to utter the unutterable. Dillard's asyndetic style could be understood, therefore, to be a voice shaped as much by its gaps, ruptures, and silences, as by its words and thus is, as it were, an expressive stammering. As such, it mirrors her keen awareness of the theological abyss of silence out of which arise both praise and lament. How *can* she speak, her texts seem to ask, of a cedar tree whose cells are "charged like wings beating praise"⁵⁵ or, conversely, of a little girl whose face has been burned off in a plane crash, except in stumbling syllables that fade into silence?

The *Shema* of the Shadows

Gaps and absences are also at the heart of Dillard's metaphysical questions about the nature of reality and the existence of evil and suffering within it. While it is a given, as Dillard observes midway through *Pilgrim at Tinker Creek*, "here we—so incontrovertibly—are," what is not a given is the meaning of being here. "This is our life, these are our lighted seasons, and then we die," she states.⁵⁶ Within life's brief span one can endeavor to discover if not why, at least "*where* we so incontrovertibly are."⁵⁷ By *Pilgrim*'s chapter 13, Dillard's observations of the suffering and apparently senseless waste of life in nature leads her to conclude, "The only way I can reasonably talk about all this is to address you directly and frankly as a fellow survivor. Here we so incontrovertibly are. . . . Here may not be the cleanest, newest place, but that clean timeless place that vaults on either side of this one is no place at all."⁵⁸ In other words, the attempt to make sense of one's life must begin from the fact that a flawed, corporeal existence embedded in time and space is the only

53. Buber, *Legend of the Baal Shem Tov*, 10.
54. Buber, *On the Bible*, 11.
55. PTC, 245
56. PTC, 129.
57. PTC, 129.
58. PTC, 243.

context one has for making meaning; that "clean and timeless" place either side of birth and the grave is "no place at all."⁵⁹ The attempt to engage difficult metaphysical questions therefore necessitates an honest reckoning *during* life's brief span with all that one endures and observes.

This engagement, as noted earlier, begins for Dillard with the "bad news," namely that humans live in a world in which death and suffering are not anomalies but are, in her view, the conditions of its very existence. Dillard conceives of death, suffering, and loss as existing within a void or space located at the center of life, ranging from the cosmic to the microscopic levels. On a cosmic scale, all of creation exists within the space God concedes to it as he kenotically elects to limit his omni-attributes. In short, it exists within a theodicean space. Yet Dillard also locates such voids or absences at the microscopic level. In an illustrative passage, she notes, "And we the people are so vulnerable. Our bodies are shot with mortality. Our legs are fear and our arms are time. These chill humors seep through our capillaries, weighting each cell with an icy dab of non-being."⁶⁰ Physical courage is therefore essential: "it fills, as it were, the holes."⁶¹ Various metaphors recur over the course of *Pilgrim at Tinker Creek*—and indeed over the course of her writing career—that signify such holes or spaces at the center of everything from cells to the cosmos. They are referred to variously as shadows, Shadow Creek, gaps, splits, holes, chasms, blue streaks or dabs of nothingness, or a shaded emptiness, just to name a few.⁶² Moreover, Dillard frequently appeals to the imagery and theology of absence found within Lurianic Kabbalism's notions of *tsimtsum* and *shevirat ha-kelim* rather than to Christian doctrines of creation and the fall to create a literary *shema* of the shadows.⁶³ For at the heart of Isaac Luria's creation and redemption

---

59. PTC, 243.
60. PTC, 91.
61. PTC, 91.

62. A particularly apt example occurs in her essay, "Expedition to the Pole," found in *Teaching a Stone to Talk*. At one point, Dillard speaks metaphorically of a holy spiritual and existential insecurity induced by the blank spaces on cartographers' maps, called "'sleeping beauties.'" She quotes polar explorer Lieutenant Maxwell, who observes, "'You never feel safe when you have to navigate in waters which are completely blank'" (TST, 59).

63. Dillard tells readers in *The Writing Life* that at the time she was writing *Pilgrim at Tinker Creek* she "was reading, among other things, Hasidism." Only slightly tongue in cheek when joking about her nocturnal writing habits, she adds, "If you stay awake one hundred nights, you get the vision of Elijah—the same revelation, earthquake and all. I was not eager for it, although it seemed to be just around the corner. I preferred this: 'Rebbe Shmelke of Nickolsburg, it was told, never really heard his teacher, the Maggid of Mezritch, finish a thought because as soon as the latter would say 'and the Lord spoke,' Shmelke would begin shouting in wonderment, 'The Lord spoke, the Lord

process is a profound sense of exile that for the first time in Kabbalistic thought became both cosmic and micro-cosmic in scope. In Luria's myths, exile was not just a national and political reality for Israel; it existed within the forms of all created things and even within God himself.[64] Likewise, Dillard identifies at the heart of all that exists a theodicean space, conceded by God, within which evil and suffering are manifest.

One of the most significant motifs of voids or absences early in Dillard's work is that of shadows in *Pilgrim at Tinker Creek*. In its well-known meditation on seeing in chapter 2, Dillard concludes that "I live now in a world of shadows that shape and distance color."[65] As this book's discussion in chapter 3 explained, shadows here represent lost cognitive innocence, an irrevocable separation between pure sensory input and the brain's ordering processes. This inability to see what is *really* there, before the brain's filtering and sense-making processes remake it, becomes a metaphor for one's inability to have direct epistemic access to physical and spiritual realities. Yet this sense-making is necessary, since it is the condition for seeing anything at all. Two chapters later, Dillard includes a grim reprise of this earlier meditation on shadows and sight:

> So shadows define the real. If I no longer see "dark marks," as do the newly sighted, then I see them as making some sort of sense of the light. They give the light distance; they put it in its place. They inform my eyes of my location, here, here O Israel, in the world's flawed sculpture, here in the flickering shade of the nothingness between me and the light.[66]

If "shadows" do indeed "define the real," they possess a dark efficacy, a paradoxical ability to map metaphysical and material boundaries. In doing so, they articulate the borders not only between darkness and light, but also between reality and non-reality. Thus, absence possesses a metaphysical power to expose or make manifest the real. To underscore the point, Dillard notes that shadows do not "have" color; they merely look blue because their spaces, devoid of light, reflect the sky's blue.[67] Yet shadows are a *potent* "nothingness," possessing the power to shape and distance light, even "put it in its place"—in

---

spoke,' and continue shouting until he had to be carried from the room'" (TWL, 35). She was also reading Lurianic Kabbalism at the time, as she tells readers at the beginning of *For the Time Being* (FTB, 22).

64. Scholem, *Messianic Idea in Judaism*, 43–45.
65. PTC, 32.
66. PTC, 63.
67. PTC, 63.

other words, reveal it for the illusion-maker that it is.[68] The proliferation of active verbs in this passage is telling: shadows "define" "[make] sense," "give," "put," "shape," and "distance."[69] Shadows are one symbolical form of what might be identified in Dillard's work as "affective absences," voids or spaces crucial to physical and spiritual perception, and, as shall be explored later in the chapter, to the existential center of life itself.

Moreover, shadows also disclose the nature of life's realities. Shadows "inform" one of his or her existential and spiritual location as "here . . . in the world's flawed sculpture" where flickering spiritual and intellectual insight illuminates only intermittently the vast "nothingness" between the God Dillard knows well enough to praise and the silence that separates her from him.[70] Dillard puns on the word "here" in "here, here O Israel," to create her own version of the *Shema* found in Deuteronomy 6:4: "'Hear, O Israel: The Lord our God, the Lord is one.'" Spoken by Moses to the Israelites just prior to their crossing the Jordan to possess Canaan, the *Shema* is a declaration of Israel's distinctive monotheism and a recapitulation of the first commandment to love God alone. In return for Israel's obedience and faithfulness, God promises abundant material and spiritual blessings to the nation and its descendents. Dillard's shift from "hear" to "here" in her *shema* of the shadows seems a wry twist intended to expose the irony that humans find themselves not in a promised land but exiled within "the world's flawed sculpture." The paradoxical facts of beauty and cruelty are twinned opposites in an amoral creation and remind humans that both they and God are exiled within its shadowed brokenness.

So Dillard offers up in stammering voice a *shema* of the shadows; "here" is repeated four times within the paragraph's final sentence in which parallel clauses crescendo to a lament on nothingness: "[Shadows] inform my eyes of my location, here, here O Israel, here in the world's flawed sculpture, here in the flickering shade of the nothingness between me and the light."[71] Perhaps this could be understood as the stammer of a holy insecurity born, as Buber asserts it must, of enduring and sustaining the irony that not light but "shadows define the real."[72] It is darkness and absences that shape the metaphysical landscape humans inhabit, and only by living in holy insecurity within the gaps created by paradox in this often treacherous, exilic terrain is meaning to be discovered.

68. PTC, 63.
69. PTC, 63.
70. PTC, 63.
71. PTC, 63.
72. Buber, *Origin and Meaning*, 179.

Dillard reinforces the link between exile and shadows in the paragraph immediately following. Dillard alludes to de Chirico's painting "Nostalgia of the Infinite" in which "cast shadows stream across the sunlit courtyard, gouging canyons. There is a sense in which shadows are actually cast, hurled with a power, cast as Ishmael was cast, *out*, with a flinging force."[73] The work of De Chirico, originator of the "Metaphysical School" of painting early in the twentieth century, is known for its melancholy, and it frequently depicts classical gods, mute and turned away from human figures who are exiled within deeply shadowed and unspeakably lonely landscapes.[74] Linking "Nostalgia of the Infinite" to the biblical story of Ishmael, who with his mother was exiled from the family by his own father, Abraham, creates a text freighted with multiple layers of anguish as well as longing to be welcomed into eternal mysteries, a longing that is frustrated by existential and spiritual banishment within the "flickering shade" of a theodicean space.

Suffering and exile is, Dillard goes on to note, the "blue strip running through creation."[75] Dillard frequently links the motifs of blue ribbands,[76] streaks, or threads with shadows and gaps. In the sentences immediately following her allusions to de Chirico and Ishmael, Dillard identifies Shadow Creek as life's icy stream of terrors and losses:

73. PTC, 64.

74. Conway Morris, "De Chirico"; Toohey and Toohey, "Giorgio de Chirico," 286–89. See, for example, de Chirico's paintings "Enigma of the Oracle" and "Melancholy of a Beautiful Day" (as well as Kathleen Toohey's analysis of them) in Toohey, *Melancholy, Love, and Time*.

75. PTC, 64.

76. In many passages throughout the canon of Dillard's work, Dillard identifies the color blue with the abyss of life's mysteries—both incomprehensible evil, suffering, or death, and less frequently, with beauty, often describing mystery's presence in creation as "ribbands," or "streaks," or "speckles" of blue. Earlier in *Pilgrim at Tinker Creek*, in yet another exilic lament, she likens mystery to the blue threads woven into the Jewish prayer shawl, the *talith*: "Terror and beauty insoluble are a ribband of blue woven into the fringes of garments of things both great and small. No culture explains, no bivouac offers real haven or rest" (PTC, 27). Likewise, in *Holy the Firm*, at the climax of her outcry at the end of section two against Julie Norwich's unjust suffering, Dillard notices on the horizon a heretofore unseen "land blue beyond islands . . . a blue chunk fitted just so beyond islands" to which she gives several names, including "Time's Bad News; I name it Terror" (HTF, 51). The tragic incident has necessitated a remapping of Dillard's inner landscape in light of this new horizon of suffering and terror: "as if we needed a new thing," she remarks (HTF, 50). The old map's naïvely drawn boundaries of what God will allow must be redrawn. Dillard asks, "How long can this go on? But let us by all means extend the scope of our charts" (HTF, 50). In "Total Eclipse," Dillard recounts the terrifying experience of a total solar eclipse, during which the valleys "were dissolving into the blue light" (TST, 16). The apex of the experience is her sense of impending extinction as the shadow cone sweeps over her with astonishing speed: "We saw the wall of shadow coming, and screamed before it hit" (TST, 16).

> Shadow Creek is the blue subterranean stream that chills Carvin's Creek and Tinker Creek; it cuts like ice under the ribs of the mountains, Tinker and Dead Man. Shadow Creek storms through limestone vaults under forests, or surfaces anywhere. . . . I wring it from rocks; it seeps into my cup. Chasms open at the glance of an eye; the ground parts like a wind-rent cloud over stars. Shadow Creek: on my least walk to the mailbox I may find myself knee-deep in its sucking, frigid pools.[77]

One finds a nearly identical passage in the final chapter of *Pilgrim at Tinker Creek*, "The Waters of Separation," where Dillard again links Shadow Creek with gaps and voids:

> Somewhere, everywhere, there is a gap, like the shuddering of Shadow Creek which gapes at my feet, like a sudden split in the window or hull of a high-altitude jet, into which things slip, or are blown, out of sight, vanished in a rush, blasted, gone, and can no more be found. For the living there is a rending loss at each opening of the eye, each *augenblick*.[78]

In both passages, Dillard connects blue with blue shadows, shadows with gaps or absences, and these with suffering and loss. Additionally, both passages allude to earlier chapters' motifs of seeing in nearly identical clauses: "Chasms open at the glance of an eye"[79] and "there is a rending loss at each opening of the eye."[80] In doing so they also echo her previous meditations on the inevitable and paradoxical loss entailed by life in time and space. If one wants to perceive light, at least in this world, one must perceive shadows and dwell in their flickering shade. Dillard's use of Kierkegaard's term *Augenblick*, meaning literally the "eye blink," or "moment," is telling.[81] As Koral Ward notes, it describes "the instant of time from which [one] can never escape" as one is "inexorably within the temporal world."[82] Yet it also connotes something momentous, often described as the intersection of eternity with time in which one "partakes in the transcendence of Being itself."[83] In the terms of the current discussion, each *Augenblick* is a darkly efficacious absence running through the heart of creation that, paradoxically, evidences a metaphysical presence.

77. PTC, 64.
78. PTC, 270.
79. PTC, 64.
80. PTC, 270.
81. Ward, *Augenblick*, 7.
82. Ward, *Augenblick*, xi.
83. Ward, *Augenblick*, xi.

Additionally, the biblical allusion in the second passage, points to a shadowy absence, an elided text behind Dillard's text. The phrase "can no more be found" comes from Job 20:9 in which Job's friend Zophar speaks of the ephemerality of the wicked:

> Though [the wicked] be magnified up to the heaven, so that his head reacheth into the clouds: yet he perish at the last like dung: In so much that they which have seen him, say: Where is he? He vanisheth as a dream, so that he can no more be found, and passeth away as a vision in the night. So that the eye which saw him before, getteth now no sight of him, and his place knoweth him no more. (Job 20:6–9, Matthew's Bible 1537)

Though Dillard quotes only the phrase "can no more be found," given the recurring motif of sight and *Augenblick*, she surely had in mind the omitted following sentences from Job which speak of the eye not seeing that which it beheld just moments before. Thus, the passage speaks of gaps or ellipses in both its structure and content. The observations of Zophar about the ephemerality of human and creaturely life that "vanisheth" like a dimly lit "vision in the night" give literary and spiritual gravity to Dillard's meditations on the shadowy gap of death into which living things every second are cast from created time and space. Simultaneously, the ghostly echoes of the rest of Zophar's speech, removed structurally but present in memory, become a textual space in which the missing sentences "can no more be found" but nevertheless linger allusively around the edges of the passages' motifs of sight.

These nearly identical passages that span the length of *Pilgrim at Tinker Creek* seem to provide clear literary evidence for the link between shadows, gaps, hollows, spaces, chasms, with the metaphysical reality of suffering and death as well as with humanity's exile within "the world's flawed sculpture."[84] What remains to be explored is the theological significance of these literary motifs. More specifically, it remains to be asked what is the connection between shadows, gaps, and absences and the Lurianic creation myths?

The answer emerges in a passage found in chapter 10, "Fecundity," that uses familiar motifs of shadows and gaps to give voice to Dillard's metaphysical conclusions about the reality of evil and suffering within creation. The passage takes a surprising turn away from orthodox Christian and Hebrew thought and toward Lurianic Kabbalism. Rather than attributing evil's origin to Adam's fall, Dillard suggests that evil and brokenness come into being at creation and are necessary to its very existence:

---

84. PTC, 63.

> That something is everywhere and always amiss is part of the very stuff of creation. It is as though each clay form had baked into, fired into it, a blue streak of nonbeing, a shaded emptiness like a bubble that not only shapes its very structure but that also causes it to list and ultimately explode.... The world has signed a pact with the devil; it had to. It is a covenant to which every thing, even every hydrogen atom, is bound. The terms are clear: if you want to live, you have to die; you cannot have mountains and creeks without space.... The world came into being with the signing of the contract.[85]

The motifs of shadows and voids ("a blue streak of nonbeing," "a shaded emptiness like a bubble") once again signify theodicean spaces where the world's brokenness and the predations of evil exist within a space conceded to creation by God. What is novel, however, is the text's claim that evil is part of the "very stuff of creation."[86] This observation is underscored emphatically in an equally significant and surprising declaration two chapters later in which Dillard exults, "Creation itself was the fall, a burst into the thorny beauty of the real."[87] Both passages imply a very different explanation of "the fall" from that articulated in Genesis 3. Its creation story ascribes the world's fallen-ness to the sin of Adam, not to God's act of creation itself. The movement within her literary cosmos away from the orthodox Hebrew and Christian story of creation is intriguing.

A brief word about the various interpretations of Genesis' creation myth is perhaps necessary to underscore how arresting Dillard's observations in these passages seem to be. Long-standing debates within Christianity exist regarding how to interpret the opening lines of Genesis, in part because the Hebrew lacks clarity about "where" God was in relation to creation when it began. Was he "outside" time and space and did he create out of nothing, or did he impose order upon chaotic, pre-existent primordial matter? Furthermore, whether matter was pre-existent or created *ex nihilo*, was it inherently good, seeded with the latent potential for evil, or fallen by nature, given its corporeality? The various answers to these questions far exceed the scope of this discussion, but it is sufficient to note that by the end of the second century CE, the doctrine of *creatio ex nihilo* had been fully and clearly articulated by Theophilus and Irenaeus, largely in response to the growing influence of gnosticism and philosophical and

---

85. PTC, 183.
86. PTC, 183.
87. PTC, 218–19.

intellectual developments within Christianity itself.[88] It became "with astonishing speed the self-evident premise of Christian talk of the creation."[89] As fully articulated by Ireneaus, the doctrine of *creatio ex nihilo* maintains that God in his goodness created with a free and unconstrained will out of nothing. He did not create by shaping pre-existent materials like a human craftsman or by subduing the primordial forces of chaos in battle.[90] It will therefore be assumed for the purposes of this argument that an historically orthodox Christian reading of the opening lines of Genesis and the subsequent narrative of the fall in Genesis 3 can be understand to mean that God created humans and the physical world *ex nihilo*, and they were "very good" (Gen 1:31), containing neither moral nor physical evil. Only *after* humans sinned, did disease, hardship, killing, and death become endemic to human and creaturely life.[91]

This orthodox Christian view is clearly not, however, the position Dillard adopts in these passages.[92] As Dillard attempts to come to terms with

88. May, *Creatio Ex Nihilo*, 148–78.

89. May, *Creatio Ex Nihilo*, 177–78.

90. May, *Creatio Ex Nihilo*, 148–78; Copan and Craig, *Creation Out of Nothing*, 33–34. See also Moltmann, *God in Creation*, 72–93.

91. This is not to suggest no other sound or compelling interpretations of Genesis 1 exist, merely that the position articulated by Irenaeus has predominated historically. As Brian D. Robinette correctly observes, "The doctrine of *creatio ex nihilo* has come under sharp criticism in recent years by those who see in it an alien imposition of metaphysics upon biblical theologies of creation. Noting as a matter of historical record that the doctrine's formal development comes subsequent to the biblical tradition, such critics argue that while ostensibly designed to affirm the sovereignty of God and the goodness of matter in the mid-second-century disputes with Middle Platonism and gnosticism, 'creation from nothing' in fact represents a capitulation to a metaphysical view of God in which power (omnipotence) serves as its governing predicate" (Robinette, "Difference Nothing Makes," 525).

See also Jon D. Levenson's fascinating and compelling arguments in *Creation and the Persistence of Evil*. He asserts that the Hebrew Bible emphatically affirms that God is indeed almighty and will triumph over evil. Yet, because at creation the primordial forces of chaos were merely given boundaries, not finally and irrevocably overcome by God, they still threaten existence and challenge biblical faith in a triumphant and good God. His exegesis, particularly of Psalms 74, 89, and Isaiah 54, argues for a dialectical "religious vision" wherein "the present is bereft of the signs of divine triumph" but hopelessness does not prevail. For through cultic ritual, Israel can summon—and reproach—its God, petitioning Him to arise again and overcome evil. Thus, one sees in the Hebrew scriptures the resolute holding in tension of "simplistic faith" and "stoic resignation" (Levenson, *Creation*, 25). He concludes, "The cognitive pressure on faith and realism to fly apart from each other is, in every generation, so intense that the conjunction of the two in these texts continues to astound" (Levenson, *Creation*, 25).

92. This is not to suggest Dillard overlooks or rejects entirely the Genesis story. She mentions elsewhere in *Pilgrim at Tinker Creek* pre-lapsarian Eden (PTC, 30) and

the existential facts of life, she relies not upon Genesis for an explanation of moral and physical evil but upon the Lurianic creation concepts of *tsimtsum* and *shevirat ha-kelim*. In Lurianic thought, evil came into reality not with the fall, though in Kabbalistic thought, the sin of Adam had catastrophic consequences for the process of redemption,[93] but in the first movement of creation in which God withdrew himself into himself in order to make a space in which to create *ex nihilo*. Scholem explains:

> The first act [of creation], the act of *Tsimtsum*, in which God determines, and therefore limits, Himself, is an act of *Din* [judgment] which reveals the roots of this quality in all that exists; these "roots of divine judgment" subsist in chaotic mixture with the residue of divine light which remained after the original retreat or withdrawal within the primary space of God's creation. Then a second ray of light out of the essence of *En-Sof* brings order into chaos and sets the cosmic process in motion, by separating the hidden elements and moulding them into a new form. . . . In the final resort, therefore, the root of all evil is already latent in the act of *Tsimtsum*.[94]

Second, though evil has its origins in the process of *tsimtsum*, it became an intrinsic part of the physical world during the second movement of creation when God's emanating light shattered the discrete vessels meant to hold, and thereby give order and place to, every created thing in the cosmos. This "shattering of the vessels," or *shevirat ha-kelim*, resulted in *qelipot*, or demonic shells of non-being, uniting with shattered sparks of God's Shekinah.[95] Evil influences "crept into all stages of the cosmological process," and this is how "the good elements of the divine order came to be mixed with the vicious ones."[96] The shattering of the vessels "is the cause of that inner deficiency which is inherent in everything that exists."[97]

The similarities between the Lurianic notion that with *creation*, not with human sin, evil came into being and Dillard's parallel claims that "creation itself was the fall," that "something is everywhere and always amiss is

---

Adam's fall (PTC, 223). However, when speaking of the presence of evil within creation, she borrows heavily from Hasidic and Lurianic ideas and imagery in order to express poetically the metaphysical reality of evil, its all-pervasiveness, and God's kenotic self-limitation.

93. Scholem, *Messianic Idea in Judaism*, 46.
94. Scholem, *Major Trends*, 263.
95. Scholem, *Major Trends*, 266–67; Dan, *Teachings of Hasidism*, 12.
96. Scholem, *Major Trends*, 268.
97. Scholem, *Major Trends*, 268.

part of the very stuff of creation," are striking. The claims' links to Lurianic thought are all the more convincing precisely because they are a departure from orthodox Christian doctrine concerning the original goodness and perfection of creation prior to human sin. Likewise, Dillard's image of the "clay form" that has fired into it a "blue streak of nonbeing" seems to be a poetic reimagining of the Lurianic idea of the *qelipot*.[98] Moreover, in Dillard's assertion that the world's coming into being is contingent upon its making a "pact with the devil" one hears echoes of the Lurianic notion that from its inception, the material world has "fired into it" a tragic flaw, namely the contractual terms of its life—suffering, decay, and death.[99] Scholem's analysis, once again, makes this connection explicit:

> Kabbalists [following Luria] connected the "Breaking of the Vessels" with the law of organic life in the theosophical universe. Just as the seed must burst in order to sprout and blossom, so too the first bowls had to be shattered in order that the divine light, the cosmic seed so to speak, might fulfill its function.[100]

---

98. Scholem's full explanation makes the similarities even more clear: "For Luria, the deepest roots of the *Kelipot*, or 'shells,' i.e., the forces of evil, existed already before the breaking of the vessels and were mixed up, so to speak, with the lights of the Sefiroth and the . . . *Reshimu*, or residue of *En-Sof* in the primordial space. What really brought about the fracture of the vessels was the necessity of cleansing the elements of the Sefiroth by eliminating the *Kelipot*, in order to give a real existence and separate identity to the power of evil" (Scholem, *Major Trends*, 267). Furthermore, "According to Luria, these waste products were originally mixed with the pure substance of *Din* (sternness), and it was only after the breaking of the vessels and the subsequent process of selection that the evil and demonic forces assumed real and separate existence in a realm of their own" (Scholem, *Major Trends*, 267). Some of Luria's disciples had difficulty accepting this since it suggested a dualistic concept of God. He contains both evil and good. Therefore, they modified the concept and "held to the view that the powers of evil developed out of the scattered fragments of the vessels which have sunk into the lower depths of the primordial space . . . in which the spirit of evil dwells" (Scholem, *Major Trends*, 267).

99. PTC, 183. In Dillard's view, as in Luria's, creation's brokenness does not prevent it from revealing God's goodness and glory. Dillard's ecstatic moments (beholding the cedar tree buzzing with eternal light, for example) make this self-evident. Luria also held that, despite the fact that through the "breaking of the vessels" evil came into being and the *qelipot* were formed, there was still a vestigial remnant of divine glory in every created thing. Scholem explains that "Not only is there a residue of divine manifestation in every being, but under the aspect of *Tsimtsum* it also acquires a reality of its own which guards it against the danger of dissolution into the non-individual being of the divine 'all in all' [pantheism]. Luria himself was the living example of an outspoken theistic mystic" (Scholem, *Major Trends*, 262).

100. Scholem, *Major Trends*, 268.

For Dillard, as for Luria, moral and physical evil are intrinsic to and a necessary part of the creation process itself. As Dillard states bluntly: "[Death] is a covenant to which every thing, even every hydrogen atom, is bound. The terms are clear: if you want to live, you have to die."[101]

Additionally, when Dillard declares that "you cannot have mountains and creeks without space," she is asserting that in order for creation to exist God had to have conceded it space. As the previous chapter's discussion of kenosis explains, in a kenotic act of self-limitation, God elects to withdraw or limit the scope of his omni-attributes and allows an autonomous, free, finite creation bounded by time and space to exist. This idea of God contracting himself to concede space within which a finite creation can exist originates not in the Genesis creation accounts but in Luria's notion of *tsimtsum*, the withdrawal of God within God that created space in which God could create *ex nihilo*. Scholem notes that "but for this perpetual tension, this ever repeated effort with which God holds Himself back, nothing in the world would exist."[102] For Dillard as for Luria, it is in the dialectical process of conceding the world space (*tsimtsum*) and giving it creaturely definition (*shevirat ha-kelim*) that physical matter and a "blue streak of nonbeing" are linked, thereby building into each atom of the universe a void that shapes its very structure but also causes it "to list and ultimately explode."[103] In short, within the space God has conceded to his creation, cells go rogue and planes fall out of the sky.

To summarize, at the heart of all creation is, paradoxically, a theodicean space. According to Dillard, there are no coherent theological or intellectual arguments available to fill in the enormous blank spaces created by life's manifold contradictions, most notably for Dillard, the gap between the equally binding but often conflicting fiduciary claims of knowledge and faith. In response to the suffering of a burned child, Dillard declares in *Holy the Firm*, "Of faith I have nothing, only of truth that this one God is a brute and traitor, abandoning us to time, to necessity and the engines of matter unhinged. This is no leap; this is evidence of things seen: one Julie, one sorrow, one sensation bewildering the heart and enraging the mind."[104] Yet faith proclaims only one paragraph later, "For I know it as given that God is all good."[105] Reckoning honestly with the validity of these twinned yet seemingly irreconcilable assertions requires living in a state of holy insecurity

---

101. PTC, 183.
102. Scholem, *Major Trends*, 261.
103. PTC, 183.
104. HTF, 46.
105. HTF, 47.

precipitated by "a deep knowledge of the impotence of all 'information,' of the incongruence of all possessed truth."[106]

In *I and Thou* Buber expresses this holding in tension of contradictory realities as living with and through "antinomy": "Man's religious situation, his *being there* in the Presence, is characterized by its essential and indissoluble antinomy. The nature of its being determines that this antinomy is indissoluble."[107] Buber goes on to argue that intellectual strategies to reconcile seemingly contradictory realities will not do, for such efforts destroy the gravity and integrity of the situation. For Buber, no matter the intellectual method—reconciliation of opposites, Hegelian synthesis, relativism—each "abolishes the significance of the situation."[108] In one's relationship with God and its concomitant realities for life on earth, Buber asserts that "I cannot try to escape the paradox that has to be lived by assigning the irreconcilable propositions to two separate realms of validity; nor can I be helped to an ideal reconciliation by any theological device: but I am compelled to take both to myself, to be lived together."[109] In maintaining the integrity of these two separate realms, Dillard and her readers move into a sphere of religious reality that, as noted earlier, Buber identifies as "the fear of God," which comes "when our existence between birth and death becomes incomprehensible and uncanny, when all security is shattered through the mystery."[110]

This is also a metaphysical space within which evil and suffering manifest their reality and their power. By drawing from Lurianic rather than primarily Christian thought, Dillard creates a radical sense of existential and spiritual exile at the heart of all that exists[111] and thereby confers upon evil and suffering a metaphysical reality that preserves their potency and, in consequence, preserves the dignity of those who suffer. If evil and suffering are real and God has kenotically elected to concede space to his creation thus exiling it and himself from his omnipotent intervention, one must take seriously one's own as well as others' suffering and death. For if one maintains, as Dillard does, that evil and suffering are endemic to one's creaturely

---

106. Buber, *Origin and Meaning*, 179.
107. Buber, *I and Thou*, 95.
108. Buber, *I and Thou*, 95.
109. Buber, *I and Thou*, 96.
110. Buber, *Eclipse of God*, 36.
111. PTC, 63. In *For the Time Being*, Dillard quotes Rabbi Yehuda Aryeh Leib Alter of Ger, a nineteenth-century Hasidic rabbi, who daringly asks "How can evil exist in a world created by God, the Beneficent One? It can exist, because entrapped deep inside the force of evil there is a spark of goodness. This spark is the source of life of the evil tendency." Dillard adds, "It was the Baal Shem Tov who taught this vital idea" (FTB, 139).

existence "here, here O Israel, here in the world's flawed sculpture,"[112] human and creaturely suffering are not the interplay of random causes and effects nor the wrath and judgment of God but a principle intrinsic to life itself. If inherent in creation is its own fallen-ness, she can indeed conclude, "It is death that is spinning the globe."[113]

The Clay Man in Whom the Universes Spin

Given that this is the way the world is, Dillard asks in *For the Time Being*, "What might be the relationship of the Absolute to a lost school girl in a plaid skirt?"[114] In other words, if God has kenotically conceded space so that the world exists, is he present in, or to, the concrete particularities of the world, especially the particular griefs each human suffers? A daughter lost in the woods, a beloved rabbi skinned alive by a Roman torturer, a child born terribly deformed, to cite but a few examples from *For the Time Being*.

An evocative image used four times in publications spanning twenty-five years and the length of Dillard's writing career suggests an answer to the question. It is the image of a clay man with a hole in his side within which the universe spins, introduced briefly at the end of chapter 3. The centrality of this image to Dillard's theodicean concerns can hardly be overemphasized. It appears in both of Dillard's 1974 publications, *Tickets for a Prayer Wheel* and *Pilgrim at Tinker Creek*, and twice again in *For the Time Being* published a quarter of a century later. This chapter will conclude with a careful analysis of this image, for through it, Dillard once again reveals the centrality of Lurianic thought throughout the course of her career to her theological concerns with the problem of evil and also demonstrates yet again her habit of "minding the gap."

---

112. PTC, 63. It should be noted that though the terms used here, including "stammering," may suggest similarities between negative theology and theodicean spaces, they differ. This discussion is concerned solely with elucidating Dillard's understanding of the nature and relationship of evil to creation, not of unspeakable or unknowable attributes of God. She crafts poetic images of spaces, gaps, and absences to depict existential and epistemic gaps in human experience and understanding, created by God's apparent choice to limit his omnipotence. It is within the "space" he concedes to his creation that moral and physical evil can exist. Moreover, these poetic renderings consistently depict these voids as having their own agency or potency. Thus, evil and "empty" gaps or spaces are portrayed as things engendering effects. Shadows *shape* and *distance* color, blue threads *run* through creation, a blue-streak of non-being causes the clay vessel to *list and explode*.

113. PTC, 182.

114. FTB, x.

The 1974 poem, "Tickets for a Prayer Wheel," recounts a family's petition for God to "Teach us to pray."[115] Its prayer is gradually answered, but as God begins to fill the house, their souls become etiolated and spare, their home is wrecked, and their bodies vanish. The poem's dominant images of God are of Christ incarnate, and in a question that alludes most explicitly to the Word made flesh, Dillard echoes the idea of *tsimtsum*. The speaker asks, "Did God dilute his merest thought / and . . . shrink and cross / to an olive continent."[116] "Dilute" and "shrink" hint at the kenotic self-limitation and contraction of God in Luria's theosophy as well as in the incarnation of Christ. The subsequent stanzas broaden God's kenosis to cosmic dimensions. Recounting a dream her sister had of the shape of God, the speaker states, "He has no edges, / and the holes in him spin. . . . and all things lie in him"; God "moves around" the "solar systems hollowed in his side."[117] The image seems clearly to connect creation with kenosis and these with the crucified Christ; the solar systems abide within a space conceded by God and that space is the sword-pierced side of the Son on the cross.

An identical image is used in the chapter "Intricacy" in *Pilgrim at Tinker Creek*. Dillard describes a man of "unformed clay" who "completely surrounds the holes in him, which are galaxies and solar systems. The holes in him part . . . circle, spin. . . . Here is a ragged hole, our earth, a hole that makes torn and frayed edges in his side, mountains and pines."[118] This Christ-image suggests that God is intimately present *to* fallen creation (in fact, it exists within his own body), and yet he is kenotically self-limited *within* creation, for it has the freedom to tear ragged holes in his own flesh.

Dillard returns to this kenotic image of the fallen world-as-wound twenty-five years later in *For the Time Being*. The image first appears in

115. TPW, 113.
116. TPW, 125.
117. TPW, 125–27.
118. PTC, 132. The discussion in chapter 3 explains that this image no doubt expresses among other things Dillard's interest in and affinity for panentheism. The image of the created world existing within an unformed clay man who is malleable thus affected directly by the vicissitudes of the creation he contains, seems derived directly from the general tenets of panentheism, its various modes not withstanding (e.g., soteriological panentheism, dipolar panentheism, etc.). As such, it embodies the generic principles of panentheism as defined by Niels Henrik Gregersen: "1. God contains the world, yet is also more that the world. Accordingly, the world is (in some sense) 'in God'" and "2. As contained 'in God,' the world not only derives its existence from God but also returns to God, while preserving the characteristics of being a creature. Accordingly, the relations between God and world are (in some sense) bilateral" (Gregersen, "Three Varieties of Panentheism," 22). Chapter 1 also explains Dillard's interest in the pansacramental panentheism of Hasidic thought. She makes explicit her avowal of panentheism in *For the Time Being*.

chapter 5, "Evil." Dillard, again reflecting on the relationship between God and creation, suggests that it is merely tangential: "God is—for the most part—out of the physical loop of the fallen world he created, let us say. Or God is the loop, or pervades the loop, or the loop runs in God like a hole in his side he never fingers."[119] Asyndetic features of Dillard's style are readily apparent here. The interrupting qualifiers, "for the most part" and "let us say," bespeak hesitancy about ultimate claims and indicate she is groping, testing out ideas. The repeated "or" phrases are quite literally a stammer; the same word and beginning syntax is repeated three times. The inversion of subject and object in the final clause ("loop" becomes subject, "God" becomes object) suggests Dillard is shifting the logical pieces trying to find a syntax that can interrupt the stammer. The pace of the sentences is slow, their logic is retrenched with each subsequent clause, and the tone is conjectural. Who knows whether God is the loop, pervades the loop, or loop runs through him? Reason is insufficient to span the gap between evil and God's omnipotence.

Dillard repeats the passage nearly verbatim in the identical section, "Evil," of the following chapter. There she asks, "If God does not cause everything that happens, does God cause anything that happens? Is God completely out of the loop?"[120] She answers, "Mostly, God is out of the physical loop. Or the loop is a spinning hole in his side."[121] As noted in chapter 3, Dillard subsequently connects the image to the Lurianic doctrine of *tsimtsum*. She writes, "Simone Weil takes a notion [*tsimtsum*] from Rabbi Isaac Luria to acknowledge that God's hands are tied. To create, God did not extend himself but withdrew himself; he humbled and obliterated himself, and left outside himself the domain of necessity, in which he does not intervene."[122] A few paragraphs later, she concludes with yet another image linking Jewish kenotic theology with Christian kenotic images: "God suffers the world's necessities along with us, and suffers our turning away, and joins us in exile. Christians might add that Christ hangs, as it were, on the cross forever, always incarnate, and always nailed."[123] Dillard's use of the clay man image four times in three major works spanning the length of her career seems clear evidence of its centrality to her understanding of the relationship of the Absolute to the particular, a relationship that is both intimate and seemingly distant.

119. FTB, 140.
120. FTB, 167.
121. FTB, 168.
122. FTB, 168.
123. FTB, 169.

So the "answer" to the metaphysical question Dillard poses at the book's outset, "What might be the relationship of the Absolute" to his creatures and creation?,[124] is yet another paradox. God is both present and absent to a world which spins within a wound his kenotic love allowed it to inflict. Catholic theologian Frederick Bauerschmidt's essay, "The Wounds of Christ," also links the hole in Christ's side to Luria's notion of *tsimtsum*, expressing well the paradox inherent in Dillard's theodicean spaces:

> The wound [of Christ] is the emptiness that is God's own self which God withdraws in order to make room for creation.... All that is stands on gracious emptiness.... It is the space provided by God's eternal renunciation of being, before all time and throughout all time. And out of this space, this gracious emptiness, which stands like a tear, a gaping hole in creation, flows all existence, all presence.[125]

Dillard would perhaps add that within this space, conceded by an all-good God, loops a suffering creation whose brokenness God carries within his own body.

In the Coils of Absence, We Meet Him

At the end of *Pilgrim at Tinker Creek*, Dillard asserts, "What I have been after all along is not an explanation but a picture."[126] This is true of the entire body of her work, including *For the Time Being*. Dillard attempts not to create a theodicy but to construct in stammering prose an image that bodies forth something of an unspeakable mystery—the mystery of an ontologically kenotic God who has conceded space within himself for a fallen universe, thereby allowing evil and suffering to enter, literally to pierce, his own being. In short, within God Himself exists a theodicean space—a place where the wound of God's infinite love and the wound of His creation's unchecked violence have made a hole that "fights against closure."[127] As Bauerschmidt envisions it, "There is the wound of love, which is a self opening [sic] or self emptying [sic].... This is the wound of the *kenosis* of the Logos in creation," and there is the "wound of violence" that fills the wound with a

---

124. FTB, x.
125. Bauerschmidt, "Wounds of Christ," 85.
126. PTC, 181.
127. Bauerschmidt, "Wounds of Christ," 84.

nail of "presence."[128] "To the eye is displayed only the wound of violence," he adds, "but to the believing soul is displayed the wound of love."[129]

Dillard's keen eye perceives the world's wounds of violence, but her soul's eye sees an equally inarguable reality—Christ's wound of love. For this reason the void or absence her work preserves is not a *nihil*.[130] Rather, the gap the two forms of perception create is *requisite* for authentic lament and praise. One cannot lament the violence one refuses to see, nor can one offer authentic praise to a household idol. To return to Buber, one must love the "real God who is, to begin with, dreadful and incomprehensible," and one would surely despair "of God and the world if God does not take pity on him ... and bring him to love Him Himself."[131]

Dillard's texts suggest he *does* bring individuals to love himself, not by providing answers to theodicean questions but by encountering individuals in the gaps. God's kenotic absence is therefore a beneficent absence, for in it "he finds us"; in the "coils of absence we meet him."[132] In John 16:7, Jesus assures his disciples, "It is for your good that I am going away." By withdrawing, the eternal Logos concedes a space for faith, but it is a potent space. "The wound is fecundity," Bauerschmidt maintains, for it graciously makes room for human freedom and creaturely potential.[133] One could also say it is an affective absence. When words and reason fail before inexplicable evil or unspeakable beauty, the silence that ensues actually defines the contours of faith and provides belief with its context. Thus, the shape given to the questions one asks about life and God must take its form, at least in part, from "the

---

128. Bauerschmidt, "Wounds of Christ," 87.

129. Bauerschmidt, "Wounds of Christ," 88.

130. This is precisely Scholem's conclusion in his analysis of Kabbalistic thought about the creation event as put forth in *The Book of Creation*. Referring to the "tree of God" constructed from the ten *sefiroth* that emanate from Him at creation, Scholem explains, "[in] the meaning of the *sefiroth* and the tree of the *sefiroth*, there is no room in this world for the *nihil* of the theological conception. Emerging from His hiddenness, God appears in His potencies, in the trunk and branches of the theogonic and cosmogonic 'tree,' extending his energy to wider and wider spheres. . . . If there were a breach, a nothing, in the earliest beginning, it could only be in the very essence of God" (Scholem, *On the Kabbalah*, 102). He goes on to explain that as later Kabbalists further developed the idea of *creatio ex nihilo*, they concluded that "this nothing had always been present in God, it was not outside Him, and not called forth by Him. It is this abyss within God, coexisting with His infinite fullness, that was overcome in the Creation, and the Kabbalistic doctrine of the God who dwells 'in the depths of nothingness,'" that exemplifies the Kabbalists' mythical transformation of the idea of God at least since the thirteenth century (Scholem, *On the Kabbalah*, 102).

131. Buber, *Eclipse of God*, 37.

132. FTB, 139.

133. Bauerschmidt, "Wounds of Christ," 85.

evidence of things not seen" (Heb 11:1, KJV), for what is *not* seen, paradoxically, constitutes the very *substance* of faith. At the heart of authentic belief, therefore, is a hole, a beneficent and efficacious theodicean space.

Consequently, it is possible to conceive of this absence as a well-spring of hope. For, as Bauerschmidt explains, "It is the free place of possibility because in it all possibility is not filled with the actuality of a presence. It is unending space in which can live, not a particular hope, neither a general state of hopefulness, but an unending hope."[134] The world's possibilities and tragedies loop together but are compassed by the bruised and broken body of God himself.

In the final pages of *Pilgrim at Tinker Creek*, Dillard tells the reader "Ezekiel excoriates the false prophets as those who have 'not gone up into the gaps.' The gaps are the thing. The gaps are the spirit's one home. . . . Go up into the gaps."[135] Going up into them, one risks being wounded as Christ was wounded, but one also might hear there a voice speaking the most profound contradiction of all: "I wound to heal."[136]

---

134. Bauerschmidt, "Wounds of Christ," 83–84.

135. PTC, 274. This is one of very few instances in which Dillard describes the movement of the spirit and intellect toward God as an ascent. One might gather, therefore, that it suggests the movement into the epistemic darkness of gaps and absences is indeed a shift to an elevated mode of consciousness or being. However, in the same passage, she describes grace as *descending* into the gaps: "It is so self-conscious, so apparently moral, simply to step aside from the gaps where the creeks and winds pour *down*, saying, I never merited this grace" (PTC, 274 [emphasis mine]).

136. Dillard uses this phrase in "Tickets for a Prayer Wheel" when describing the family's discovery that under their hearth is a sea and that "Under the water grew eglantine, / standing either for Poetry / or the saying 'I wound to heal'" (PTC, 117).

CHAPTER 5

"It Could Be That We Are Not Seeing Something"

Affective Absences and Asyndeton

> "No culture explains, no bivouac offers real haven or rest. But it could be that we are not seeing something."
>
> —ANNIE DILLARD, *PILGRIM AT TINKER CREEK*

Introduction

THE PREVIOUS CHAPTER'S ANALYSIS examined a persistent feature of Annie Dillard's literary non-fiction—the suspension or holding in tension of apparently contradictory and yet equally binding epistemic and theological truths to create theodicean spaces which are resolutely held open. It was argued that Dillard employs throughout the duration of her career the symbols and theology of Jewish mysticism to construct a pre-messianic theological space within which to explore questions about evil and suffering without collapsing it through an appeal to the redemptive eschatological end promised through the resurrection of Christ or to an ecstatic flight away from life's gritty realities to the Neoplatonic One. This refusal to reconcile apparently incongruous logical and theological claims arises from Dillard's commitment to artistic and spiritual integrity. Dillard's tenacious refusal results in texts that are frequently unsettling and deliberately calculated to engender what Martin Buber calls a "holy insecurity" through textual ruptures, ellipses, and gaps that create an asyndetic style.

One finds that in addition to gaps and spaces functioning as theological ruptures created from existential and spiritual contradictions, they also function in Dillard's work as epistemic gaps or ellipses. These epistemic spaces are perhaps most obvious when Dillard openly identifies the endpoint of reason and knowledge. Not infrequently, Dillard will conclude a long meditation on the nature of God or life with abrupt and seemingly disingenuous statements, expressing her ignorance on the subject. For example, in *For the Time Being*, after reflecting on the efficacy of prayer, she gives up, concluding, "I don't know. I don't know beans about God."[1] Similarly, in the final paragraph of *Living by Fiction*, Dillard asks a series of existential and metaphysical questions only to end the book with the two clauses, "I am sorry; I do not know."[2] At the end of "A Field of Silence," Dillard tells the reader she "would go to the lions" for her conviction that there were angels in a field, but "what all this means about perception, or language, or angels, or my own sanity, I have no idea."[3] Although critics have accused Dillard of being at best coy and at worst insincere in such statements, they may be seen as the epistemic counterpart to the theological gaps Dillard creates and sustains throughout the canon of her work. It shall be argued in the present chapter that these epistemic ruptures are therefore entirely consistent with her practice of "minding the gaps."

While the previous chapter examined how Dillard's insistence on "minding the gap" defines and amplifies her theodicean concerns, this chapter's analysis will focus on ways Dillard's texts suggest the potential spiritual and epistemic plenitude of those spaces—what shall be referred to as "affective absences." Like the theodicean spaces Dillard constructs, these epistemic gaps function both at the level of content and style. To summarize the last chapter's introduction to Dillard's asyndetic style, it features gaps and ellipses at the syntactic level in the form of broken narratives, abrupt shifts in tone and style, jarring juxtapositions of subject matter, and shifts in grammatical mood and person (from first to second person, from declarative to interrogative, for example). At a deeper level, one finds an abiding aesthetic principle of gaps and absences, that of the transparent intellectual structure of a work that gives shape to its entirety but whose traces have been completely obliterated so that its skeleton "vanish[es] into the work."[4] In *Living By Fiction*, Dillard explores questions arising from the intersection of epistemology and art in the final section titled, with characteristic daring,

1. FTB, 169.
2. LBF, 185.
3. TST, 136.
4. LBF, 156.

"Does the World Have Meaning?" Literary objects, Dillard argues, are instruments, just like microscopes and space craft, constructed for the purpose of probing and interpreting the world in the effort to discover if there is any meaning "out there" to be had.[5] Paradoxically, literary texts, good ones at least, create meaning by concealing it, she contends. Their power is in their allusivity. "The writer 'conceals,' as it were, his interpretation inside literary materials which feign lifelikeness on one hand or elaborately wrought surfaces on the other," Dillard explains.[6] Authors "discover that in order to write fiction that anybody might want to read, they must painstakingly conceal what is to them its very point. . . . In the process of fleshing out a thought, they brick it in."[7] In the fiction of pure aestheticism, she remarks, "the writer . . . finds himself by losing himself."[8] Dillard notes in the section "Find the Hidden Meaning" that "Sadly, the interpretative aspects of fiction absolutely require further interpretation by a reader in order to exist. They are simply not present to the senses," like raw experience, "but rather concealed behind materials."[9] Hence, for Dillard the "meaningfulness" of a text requires an inherently reciprocal or dialogical relationship with its readers who must probe its structures to unearth the "hidden meaning." Because Dillard presupposes both that meaning is to be had and that someone will inevitably read her work, her aesthetic principles and practices have a didactic element. Given this, one can assume the asyndetic disjunctions that characterize her work are meticulously crafted not only to create theodicean spaces which provoke stammers and silence, but also affective absences out of which might erupt epistemic plenitude and plurivocal meanings.[10] These

---

5. To make a similar point in "Teaching a Stone to Talk," Dillard quips, "What is the difference between a cathedral and a physics lab? Are not they both saying: Hello?" (TST 89).

6. LBF, 152.

7. LBF, 156.

8. LBF, 156. Dillard alludes here to Matthew 16:25, where Christ cautions those wanting to be his disciples that doing so requires taking up their cross and following him: "For those who want to save their life will lose it, and those who lose their life for my sake will find it." These self-emptying terms and allusions hint at Dillard's kenotic understanding of the artist's vocation as sacrificial and costly, most vividly illustrated in Part II of *Holy the Firm*. There she likens the artist's tasks to the kenotic self-emptying of Christ on the cross that enables time and eternity to intersect.

9. LBF, 155.

10. Dillard's fastidiousness about visual space in manuscripts is illustrated vividly (and humorously) in a long-running argument she has with her editors at Alfred Knopf about the typeface chosen for *For the Time Being*. The book's proofs, now in Yale University's Beinecke Library, contain Dillard's zealous and lengthy notes in the margins, explaining her dislike of the font because it leaves too little blank space at the ends of sentences. Dillard writes: "The only problem with this typeface . . . is the recurring

epistemic gaps that define the contours of both art and life, and through which one gains at least partial epistemic access to knowledge, constitute "affective absences" and will be the focus of this chapter.

Further, the chapter will explore the striking parallels between Dillard's aesthetic principle of the epistemic and theological plenitude of absence and Kabbalistic and Hasidic thought on the white spaces within the written Torah. It will return to an examination of how Dillard's asyndetic style—its white spaces, fragmented narrative sequences, silent-but-effectual intellectual structures, grammatical ellipses, and stammering—locates readers within epistemic and theological "white spaces" in order to position them for encounter.

The Shape of the Air: Reversing Positive and Negative Spaces

It should be noted that, for Dillard, "minding the gap" is not ancillary to other forms of perception but an epistemological strategy essential for apprehending one's true condition in life and positioning oneself to receive revelation. For this reason, Dillard's texts frequently position readers—or urge them to position themselves—within epistemic and theological gaps. Dillard tells readers emphatically at the end of *Pilgrim at Tinker Creek*, "the gaps are the thing" and commands them to "Go up into the gaps."[11] For they are "the spirit's one home" where a soul can "discover itself for the first time like a once-blind man unbound."[12] One of the primary ways Dillard enables readers to "mind the gap" so that they might regain epistemological sight is by steering her audience directly into them.

Dillard's most frequent intellectual and poetic modes for making readers cognizant of a present and affective absence is the imaginative reversal of

---

sensation it gives me that there is a one en—no—a one em space missing between sentences. Could that possibly be fixed with some keystrokes? Each sentence as a unit gets lost because the sentences stumble over one another. The period carries no weight or pause because the next sentence begins on the same breath—all because a one en [sic] space is missing at the end of every sentence—no matter on what punctuation mark the sentence ends. The sentences seem actually to interrupt; they step on one another's heels. I try to craft these babies, and without that extra space it seems all in vain." On the following page, the argument continues: "lordy [sic] it goes against the grain to have such tiny spaces at sentences' ends. A sentence's end should have a little hollow space following, in which it might—in its fullness, rhythm, and import—sink in. Especially in this difficult book. We must defend against the 'jumbled' charge with every means we have. Spacing is a big one" (Dillard, *Annie Dillard Papers*).

11. PTC, 274.
12. PTC, 274.

positive and negative space. Her early poem, "The Shape of the Air," included in *Tickets for a Prayer Wheel*, explores this perceptual mode. The poem begins with the narrator, speaking in the imperative mood, telling the reader how to make visible the shape of the air. "Cut a hole through the roof of your house," she instructs, "pour plaster down" and once it dries, "Remove with hooks. / Split. Remove the clothes; / discard. / This is the shape of part of the air."[13] The poem depicts various inverted visions of the shape of the air over mountains, within trees, over creatures and grasses. Importantly, the air is a potent and active though invisible entity that defines the contours of the visible world. The poem's muscular verbs reveal the creative power of nothing: it "sticks in a craw of a wave," "press[es] just so on the reeds, hovers," and "closes the space where [the muskrat] stood." It "loops like an acrobat," "cups," "spread[s]," "sways and fills," and "swells in a cone."[14]

This imagery and epistemic process is repeated nearly verbatim in *Pilgrim at Tinker Creek*'s chapter 8, "Intricacy." Early in its first section, Dillard explains the Kabbalistic doctrine of *shevirat ha-kelim*, "'the Mystery of the Splintering of the Vessels.'"[15] Dillard defines the Lurianic concept of the breaking of the vessels as "the shrinking or imprisonment of essences within the various husk-covered forms of emanation or time. The Vessels splintered and solar systems spun; . . . Not only did the Vessels splinter: they splintered exceedingly fine. Intricacy, then, is the subject, the intricacy of the created world."[16] Earlier chapters explained that the cosmic event of *shevirat ha-kelim*, according to Luria, is actually the second part of a divine movement that began with *tsimtsum*, a contraction within God that conceded space to allow creation to exist; in the process of God's emanation, the vessels meant to contain the *sefirot* or creative, emanating power, shattered, sending husks of matter cascading into physical reality with a divine spark or fragment of God exiled inside. Thus, the animating core of all that exists is the invisible but present Shekinah of God, exiled within his own creation. Not only does this doctrine depict Dillard's interest in the staggering detail of creation, it also provides further evidence for her epistemological habit of "minding the gaps." The gaps, in Lurianic cosmogony, afford in the first movement of creation, a space for God to create *ex nihilo*, but also provide in its second movement a space *within* a fallen world, at its very core no less, for the potent and enlivening divine spark—the unseen and affective absence.

13. TPW, 55.
14. TPW, 55–61.
15. PTC, 130.
16. PTC, 130–31.

Interestingly, this discussion of the "Splintering of the Vessels" is followed immediately by a section in which Dillard speaks of the reversal of positive and negative space in a series of five disconnected paragraphs exemplifying her asyndetic style. Their ideational content is linked only by parallel beginning declarative sentences. Each paragraph begins with a direct address of the reader in the second person who is then abruptly transmogrified into radically incongruous beings. Dillard tells the reader in the first paragraph "You are God" while in the last "You are a chloroplast."[17] Within this section of *Pilgrim*, Dillard reprises images and ideas from the earlier poem, "The Shape of the Air." The fourth paragraph begins, "You are a sculptor," and provides instructions on how to build an inverted sculpture of air in the shape of a longleaf pine tree. Methodically, she tells the reader how to prepare the tree, build the cofferdam, pour the plaster. The narrative then shifts into the imperative mood and states, "Now open the walls of the dam, split the plaster, saw down the tree, remove it, discard, and your intricate sculpture is ready: this is the shape of part of the air."[18] The thought cycle comes full circle with the last sentence of the fifth paragraph stating, "You are God—are you tired? finished?"[19]

The explanatory paragraph immediately following these five "you" paragraphs makes Dillard's epistemological aims in them clear. She is training the mind to see the presence of intricacy more fully by focusing the mind's eye on absence. "Intricacy means," Dillard asserts, "that there is a fluted fringe to the something that exists over against the nothing. . . . She then commands the reader to "mentally reverse positive and negative space":

> Imagine emptiness as a sort of person, a boundless person consisting of an elastic, unformed clay. (For the moment forget that the air in our atmosphere is "something," and count it as "nothing," the scuptor's negative space. The clay man completely surrounds the holes in him, which are galaxies and solar systems. The holes in him part, expand, shrink, veer, circle, spin."[20]

This figure within whom exists a space for creation, an exceedingly intricate creation, alludes not only to the incarnate Christ but also to the God of Lurianic creation cosmogony and its doctrines of *tsimtsum* as well as *shevirat ha-kelim*.[21] Moreover, by instructing the reader to reverse

17. PTC, 131–32.
18. PTC, 132.
19. PTC, 131–32.
20. PTC, 132.
21. As noted in chapter 4, the image of a clay man with a hole in his side, within which the universes spin, appears in four of Dillard's major works, spanning twenty-five

positives and negatives, presence and absence, something and nothing, Dillard invites the reader to participate imaginatively in an epistemic exercise in paradox. A sculpture of "nothing" in the shape of a pine tree, can allow one to apprehend more fully the "something" pine tree one thinks one sees. Nothingness, therefore, is the operative element in gaining both visual and spiritual acuity.[22] As Lurianic creation cosmology suggests, absence or withdrawal of presence makes it possible for the created world to exist. Dillard moves the doctrine to epistemological ground and suggests that these imaginative maneuvers are necessary for the mind to concede or make room for new perceptual modes that allow one to perceive absence and thereby presence more accurately. The sculptor who builds a tree in the shape of the air creates *ex nihilo*. Forging sculptures of air and mentally reversing positive and negative space are the games one has to play to unravel the mind's incessant normalizing of the miraculous and its generalizing of the particular, both of which prevent one from seeing the world as it *really is*. Making absence visible is therefore the means of bringing into being—of moving into one's perceptual field as it were—a more accurate vision of the world's expansive beauty as well as an unfathomable wonder that there is something rather than nothing.

It could be argued that present and affective absences are the operative elements rhetorically as well. The passage typifies Dillard's asyndetic style. The declarative "You" paragraphs not only lack transitions between them to provide logical links, but the first three paragraphs of the section are also separated from each other by additional spacing and from the final two paragraphs by a section break indicator (three asterisks). Each lacks paragraph indents. Further, the entire five-paragraph section is separated from the following explanatory paragraph by additional spacing. The blank spaces on the page amplify as well as repeat the thematic attention to the "shape" of absence and make more emphatic (in fact, more visually conspicuous) the abrupt declarative sentences at the beginning of each paragraph. The lack of interrupting space in the final two paragraphs, as well as the rapid piling on of "you are" sentences within the last paragraph, accelerate toward the

---

years, and alludes to the incarnate and crucified Christ. For a discussion of the kenotic aspects of this image, see chapter 3. For a discussion of how this image becomes crucial to an understanding of the absence of a resurrected Christ in Dillard's body of work, see chapter 6.

22. British sculptor Rachel Whiteread's work is in many ways the physical embodiment of this sort of imaginative reversal. Perhaps her most famous work, *House*, was created by pouring liquid concrete into the interior of a demolished terrace house in east London. The result was a visible sculpture of the previously invisible space that had filled the home's interior. See Nicholas Wroe's tribute to her life and art in Wroe, "Rachel Whiteread."

breathless "are you tired? finished?" and leave the reader hanging, grammatically and visually, over blank space on the page.[23] Because these spaces make conspicuous certain features of the text and interrupt reading, absence becomes a rhetorical device that shapes and defines presence by isolating the paragraphs on the page as well as by augmenting the import of their content. Thus, the power of the paragraph's opening declarative sentences is generated in large part by the blank spaces surrounding them. Further, the asyndeton precipitates epistemic disorientation, causing the reader to stumble from the transitionless shift from being God one moment and a starling or chloroplast the next. The vast range of physical scale alone causes imaginative and cognitive dissonance through rapid alterations in perceptual perspective. The world looks markedly different to a chloroplast than it does to God. Dillard forces the reader to make these sudden shifts with nothing to guide them except grammatical parallelism in the hope, it seems, that the gaps might engender newness of sight in the reader.

Dillard concludes this first section of the chapter by stating outright that the terrible and beautiful intricacies of the world do not "all [fit] together like clockwork."[24] In other words, an honest and full appraisal of the world's infinite particulars causes the discrepancies between two contradictory but equally binding epistemic claims to become more pronounced; the world is both staggeringly beautiful and savagely indifferent to cruelty and suffering. Look closely, she says, and the epistemic gap only widens, and it becomes less reasonable than ever to say it "all fits together like clockwork." Dillard repeats this conclusion in chapter 13, "The Horns of the Altar": "I am not washed and beautiful, in control of a shining world in which everything fits, but instead am wandering awed about on a splintered wreck I've come to care for."[25] The image of the world as "splintered" and therefore wrecked is strongly suggestive of the Lurianic doctrine of the splintering of the vessels that Dillard draws upon in the previous chapter. The shattering of the vessels created a world exceedingly intricate and terribly broken. To return to Scholem, the breaking of the vessels "is the cause of that inner deficiency which is inherent in everything that exists."[26] The "lack of control" cannot signify a lack of power, for certainly Dillard knows she does not control what goes on at Tinker Creek much less the world. It must signify therefore a lack of epistemological control, the inability to reconcile and make sense of the world by making all the disparate pieces fit neatly together.

23. PTC, 132.
24. PTC, 139.
25. PTC, 245.
26. Scholem, *Major Trends*, 268.

Although several scholars such as Sandra Humble Johnson suggest that the "space between" contradictory realities gets traversed or filled in the moment of epiphany,[27] countless images as well as Dillard's narrative interpretation of them seem to insist they do not. As noted at this and the previous chapter's outset, a hallmark of her texts is the holding in tension of irreconcilable realities. In *Pilgrim*'s chapter 13 Dillard surveys the chasm between conflicting epistemic claims. She recalls for the reader her ecstatic experience of seeing the cedar tree suddenly aflame with eternal lights and concludes that the epiphanic moment does *not* result in epistemic certainty:

> I know what happened to the cedar tree, I saw the cells in the cedar tree pulse charged like wings beating praise. Now it would be too facile to pull everything out of the hat and say that mystery vanquishes knowledge. Although my vision of the world of the spirit would not be altered a jot if the cedar had been purulent with galls, those galls *actually do matter* to my understanding of this world. Can I say then that corruption is one of beauty's deep-blue speckles, that the frayed and nibbled fringe of the world is a tallith, a prayer shawl, the intricate garment of beauty? It is very tempting, but I honestly cannot.... I can, I think, call the vision of the cedar and the knowledge of these wormy quarryings twin fiords cutting into the granite cliffs of mystery.[28]

Her language here could hardly be stronger in its insistence that epiphanic moments are *not* unifying, nor do they narrow one centimeter the abyss between beauty and pain or reconcile competing fiduciary claims by locating them in some quasi-transcendent reality. They remain as doggedly separate as ever for Dillard. By stating that her knowledge of the world's corruption matters enormously, she declares her commitment to epistemological integrity. She is unwilling to pretend that pain and beauty are not both real and irreconcilable, nor will she attempt to reconcile them by suggesting that the corruption of death and suffering is somehow beautiful, purposeful, or dignifying.

---

27. See Humble Johnson, *Space Between*, 24, 48–49. She suggests that the epiphanic moment for Dillard offers her "the comfort, the solace, of that entity which cannot be defined" (Humble Johnson, *Space Between*, 24). Similarly, she argues that Dillard's epiphanic moments "are supreme moments of unification.... Chaos, or at least chaotic antilogic, is dominant until unity ... [is] clearly and suddenly apprehended in an illumination, a brightening of the mind" (Humble Johnson, *Space Between*, 48). However, it is difficult to find a single example in Dillard's work when a heightened spiritual encounter brings unity. In fact, Dillard seems to go to great lengths to insist that these moments do *not* blunt, temper, or displace the tension of conflicting realities. If anything, such moments heighten her sense of their discrepancy.

28. PTC, 245 (emphasis mine).

Pain and beauty are *twin* fiords. Mystical experiences reinforce her belief in the spirit, but those experiences do not budge the granite cliffs. Beauty is still ineffable, and the world's suffering is still inexplicable. The most she is willing to concede is "that corruption is not beauty's very heart."[29]

Admittedly, the twinning of beauty and pain could be said to suggest a wholly absent yet metonymically posited resolution of the tension between them at some level beyond sight and intellect. Even if this were the case, a connection presupposed by faith does not invalidate the reality that as humans *experience* beauty and pain, no explanation derived from reason can bridge the epistemic gap between them, as *Holy the Firm*, for example, illustrates. There is the exquisite beauty of Puget Sound, and there is a burnt child. Dillard juxtaposes them but does not resolve the tension created by these two facts. In like fashion, by minding the epistemic gap through the reversal of positive and negative space, Dillard resists contorted metaphysical and intellectual explanations as a matter of intellectual and spiritual integrity.

Shadows Define the Real

In addition to the motif of the reversal of positive and negative space, Dillard also quite frequently invokes the images and science of shadows to explore the notion of affective absence. In the chapter, "Seeing," in *Pilgrim at Tinker Creek* Dillard meditates on the irony that one's ability to distinguish shapes from one another and thus see clearly relies on the brain's ability to separate light from shadow. In chapter 4, "The Fixed," Dillard returns to the discussion about sight begun in chapter 2, "Seeing," in which she explains that shadows "shape and distance color," and as the brain's reasoning capacities develop, they allow the mind to distinguish one thing from another and make sense of the world.[30] Paradoxically therefore, the processes of the rational mind—a process that separates light from shadow—means living in an epistemologically precarious position. The only thing one knows with absolute certainty is that what one sees is not what is there. Dillard laments that "a nightmare network of ganglia . . . cuts and splices what I do see,

---

29. PTC, 245.

30. PTC, 32. See chapters 2 and 3 for a full discussion of this passage and its links to Jewish mystical thought. Dillard draws upon both Kabbalistic and Hasidic thought, as well as upon one of the Hasidic tales and Martin Buber's *I and Thou*. In the chapter "Seeing," the darker of *Pilgrim's* two meditations on sight, she employs symbols and narratives from Kabbalism and Hebrew scripture to raise theodicean questions.

editing it for my brain,"[31] and thus, "there is rending loss at each opening of the eye."[32] Dillard informs the reader that "When you see fog move against a backdrop of deep pines, you don't see the fog itself, but streaks of clearness floating across the air in shreds. So I see only tatters of clearness through a pervading obscurity."[33] The "tatters of clearness" express metaphorically the ephemeral and partial nature of epistemic clarity. Repeatedly in the chapter Dillard insists on the precariousness of what one seems to see and comprehend. The stammering clauses, "I can't distinguish," "I can't be sure," "I reel in confusion; I don't understand what I see," "I can't see," and "I'm blind as a bat" all illustrate her uncertainty.[34]

When Dillard takes up the subject again in chapter 4, she links shadows to gaps, observing "The shadow's the thing."[35] She explains that "shadows define the real. If I no longer see shadows as 'dark marks,' as do the newly sighted, then I see them as making some sort of sense of the light. They give the light distance; they put it in its place."[36] The first line, "The shadow's the thing," parallels grammatically her assertion in the final pages of the book, "The gaps are the thing."[37] Her linking the two assertions through identical syntax argues for reading them as concomitant ideas. Both shadows and gaps are affective absences. Shadows, like the shape of the air, afford perceptual acuity by allowing the eye to distinguish objects one from another. Shadows here as elsewhere are also indicative of the fallen state of creation, an idea which was discussed at length in the previous chapter. For now, it is significant to note that in Dillard's thinking, without the absence of light, light itself becomes imperceptible. Shadows are paradoxically affective absences.

The discussions of light and seeing in chapters 2 and 4 of *Pilgrim at Tinker Creek* reveal the *potential* of absence. The prelude to Dillard's conclusion that "the shadow's the thing" is a story told by Pliny of a young woman in ancient Corinth whose lover was often away for long periods. When he was home, she sketched the shadow his face made on the plaster wall. When he was away, she chipped away at the plaster under the tracing of his shadow

31. PTC, 21.
32. PTC, 270.
33. PTC, 21.
34. PTC, 21–27.
35. PTC, 63.
36. PTC, 63.

37. PTC, 274. Both sentences allude to Hamlet's line in Act 2, Scene 2 of *Hamlet*: "The play's the thing / Wherein I'll catch the conscience of the king." The allusion reinforces the sense in this passage that gaps and spaces can become places where hidden things are revealed.

until she had created an inverted, three-dimensional likeness. Her father one day pressed clay into it and invented, so the legend goes, clay modeling.[38] Paradoxically, the beloved becomes present to the woman only as she hollows out space behind the etched shadow. A double absence, the removal of both lover and plaster wall, is therefore the necessary prerequisite for the work of art to exist. Dillard concludes the paragraph declaring, "If I went back and found the shadow of that face there on the wall by the fireplace, I'd rip down the house with my hands for that hunk."[39] Both Dillard's humor and her passionate avowal of the positive potential of absence are evidenced in this final sentence. The man's shadow, created by his body eclipsing light, has potency because it makes manifest or "seeable" his likeness when he is absent. The work of absence is so valuable Dillard would sacrifice the whole house for the fragment of plaster which contains a nothing that is yet a something—the "hunk" on the wall. Dillard's humorous pun on "hunk" (both a handsome man and a chunk of the clay cast) is directed toward herself. She readily admits that like a rock star groupie, she would tear down the house for an image of a shadow. Yet it serves to underscore the zealousness of her conviction that "the shadow's the thing," which can be understood also to mean the shadow *is* the thing. If so, she has got to have it, for if she has the shadow-sculpture, she has the man.

Perhaps Dillard's most succinct affirmation of the epistemic potential of absence occurs in chapter 2, "Seeing." In the midst of expressing her spiritual and perceptual disorientation from both darkness and light, "terror and beauty," she adds, "But it could be that we are not seeing something. . . . This is *fertile* ground."[40] Dillard reminds the reader that many things once thought to be illusions are now known to exist: "Galileo thought comets were an optical illusion."[41] So, "What if there are *really* gleaming castellated cities hung upside-down over the desert sand? What limpid lakes and cool date palms have our caravans always passed untried? Until, one by one, by the blindest of leaps, we light on the road to these places, we must stumble in darkness and hunger."[42] Her tentative claim that perhaps "we are not seeing something" cannily suggests that, counter to normal reasoning which concludes that if nothing is seen, nothing is there, the perceptual blanks or shadowed distortions might just be a something. Her hopeful conjectures about the potential reality of what one is tempted to dismiss as unreal makes

38. PTC, 63.
39. PTC, 63.
40. PTC, 27 (emphasis mine).
41. PTC, 27.
42. PTC, 27.

this clear, and her "what if" question argues for holding open a space for mystery and for valuing the potentially unseen something.

In a subtle way, even the sentence "But it could be that we are not seeing something" plays with ambiguity and plurivocality. Given the context of the sentence in a chapter on shadows and sight and the example of Galileo, "we are not seeing something" could mean that one is overlooking something, or it could mean that the something that is there cannot be perceived by available modes of seeing. Or, conversely, it could mean that what one is seeing is not a "something" but an ineffable *Thou*. Thus, the sentence itself suggests the potential fertility, the semantic plenitude, of the affective absence.

The Tale of Hidden Teachings: Black Letters and White Spaces

There is an intriguing convergence between Dillard's epistemology of absence and a significant body of thought in Kabbalistic and Hasidic literature on the meaning of the white spaces between the black letters in the written Torah. Although many Jewish rabbis meditated on the meaning of the white spaces and black letters, the Hasidic master Rabbi Levi Isaac of Berditchev, according to Moshe Idel, seems to have devoted "more attention to this topic than any other Jewish thinker.[43] Martin Buber includes in the *Tales of the Hasidim* Rabbi Isaac's story of the "Hidden Teachings," and Annie Dillard has certainly read this tale given how frequently and consistently throughout her career she has expressed admiration for Buber's book.[44] Additionally, Idel discusses Rabbi Levi Isaac of Berditchev at length in *Hasidism: Between Ecstasy and Magic*, a book Dillard read when researching *For the Time Being*.[45] Although Dillard is quite familiar with Lurianic Kabbalism, it is less clear whether she is familiar with Kabbalistic interpretations of the meaning of the white and black letters. Since fascinating parallels exist between Dillard's epistemological and theological concerns regarding presence and absence and Kabbalistic and Hasidic thought on the blank spaces, both traditions will be considered. However, given that the literary

---

43. Idel, *Absorbing Perfections*, 60.

44. For example, the list of "good books" Dillard supplies for Karen Fitzgerald's column, "Good Books: Writer's Choices," includes Martin Buber's *Tales of the Hasidim* and Heschel's work on Hasidism. Incidentally, the other two are Simone Weil, a Jewish woman, who, though not formally a convert, felt great affinity with Roman Catholicism, and Ralph Waldo Emerson. Tellingly, three of the four authors Dillard names are Jewish.

45. Dillard, *Annie Dillard Papers*.

and extra-literary evidence suggests a closer connection between Dillard and Hasidism on the subject, the analysis will focus primarily on the views of Hasidic master Rabbi Levi Isaac of Berditchev.

As Moshe Idel explains, historically the idea of the significance of the white spaces and black letters arose from questions about the origins and authority of the written Torah, a book that emerged out of an oral culture. While the rabbinic literature preserved the primacy of the "vocal form of the creative process," it also came to suggest that God created not by writing but by "contemplating the Torah as the paradigm of the world."[46] The written Torah, therefore, came to be understood as essential to God's primordial act of bringing order from chaos. Consequently, "the intermediary status of the written Torah now shares with the divine the status of preexistence, and it cooperates in the process of creation."[47] In the pre-Kabbalistic text *Sefer Yetzirah*, or *Book of Creation*, the idea of the creative and preexistent text burgeoned into elaborate speculations on the process of creation occurring through the "*sefiroth*, or ten original numbers, and of the twenty-two consonants of the Hebrew alphabet."[48] But these ideas led to further questions. If the written Torah was preexistent, on what was it written? It came to be suggested that the Torah was "black fire" written on the "white fire" of the arm of God himself.[49] The white spaces become synonymous with the Holy One.[50] So the mystic who contemplates the Torah contemplates not merely the meaning of the words on the page but also the white spaces between them, for those gaps signify divine presence. Idel is careful to point out here as well as in his discussion about Rabbi Levi Issac's interpretation of the black letters and white spaces that such thinking does not constitute a negative theology. The white spaces do signify the absence of black letters, but because they are equated with the white fire of God, a theology of plenitude not of absence develops.

Furthermore, several Kabbalistic fragments from the thirteenth and fourteenth centuries indicate an adoption of an ancient anthropomorphic view of the white fire as the divine skin, thus sacralizing the blanks in the text.[51] This has both hermeneutical and practical consequences for the mystic.[52] The hermeneutical significance is two-fold. First, by equating the divine

---

46. Idel, *Absorbing Perfections*, 46.
47. Idel, *Absorbing Perfections*, 46.
48. Scholem, *On the Kabbalah*, 167; Idel, *Absorbing Perfections*, 47.
49. Idel, *Absorbing Perfections*, 47–48.
50. Idel, *Absorbing Perfections*, 49–50.
51. Idel, *Absorbing Perfections*, 55.
52. Idel, *Absorbing Perfections*, 55–56.

realm with blank spaces which have no linguistic signification, the Kabbalists suggest that the more potent or theologically plentiful divine space is the ambiguous one, whereas the black fire, the written letters, are less pregnant with mystical meaning because they are limited by their very signification. "The written, namely the limited, aspects of the text," Idel explains, "are the lower ones, whereas the higher ones [the white spaces], which reflect the divine essence, are less definite."[53] Second, such a view allowed Kabbalists to maintain a conservative and orthodox position about the authority of the Bible while simultaneously allowing endless interpretations of the written words in it, for its "authority" was held within the white spaces, in the "mystical authority" of those blanks, since they were understood symbolically to be the white fire or the body of the Most High God.[54]

The Kabbalists' understanding of the potential plenitude or potency of absence as well as its mystical significance seems consonant with Dillard's convictions about affective absences. Her injunction in *Pilgrim at Tinker Creek* to mind the gaps for they are "the spirit's one home" and her urging the reader to "stalk the gaps,"[55] for in them one might encounter God, seem entirely in harmony with the Kabbalists' assertion that the blank spaces of the Torah are where one potentially encounters the white fire of God. Both Dillard and the Kabbalists seem to privilege the gaps as the more spiritually fertile realm to inhabit than fixity and certitude. Of course, the ambiguity and elusiveness of certitude in the gaps make one's epistemic and spiritual position within them precarious. But as was discussed in the previous chapter, Dillard seems to know full well that being honest about God requires living in "holy insecurity."

Hasidic thought about the white spaces finds its origins in Rabbi Levi Isaac of Berditchev. Within Martin Buber's first volume of *Tales of the Hasidim* one finds the story "Hidden Teachings" attributed to Rabbi Levi Isaac of Berditchev concerning a question about Isaiah 51:4. The verse is variously translated in the tale as "For instruction shall go forth from me," "A Torah shall go forth from me," or "A new Torah will go forth from me."[56] Rabbi Levi Isaac's commentary proceeds as follows:

> How shall we interpret this? For we believe with perfect faith that the Torah, which Moses received on Mount Sinai, cannot be changed, and that none other will be given. It is unalterable

---

53. Idel, *Absorbing Perfections*, 55–56.

54. Idel, *Absorbing Perfections*, 56.

55. PTC, 274.

56. Buber, *Tales of the Hasidim*, 232; Idel *Absorbing Perfections*, 60; Scholem, *On the Kabbalah*, 82.

and we are forbidden to question even one of its letters. But, in reality, not only the black letters but the white gaps in between, are symbols of teaching, only that we are not able to read those gaps. In time to come God will reveal the white hiddenness of the Torah.[57]

Scholem interprets Rabbi Levi Isaac's explanation as potentially antinomian and unorthodox in that it seems to suggest that in a future messianic age a missing, or "'vanished,'" book of the Torah will be revealed.[58] He concludes that since such a view "left room for all manner of heretical variants and developments" it was "daring" and slightly heretical.[59] Idel takes a different view. He interprets the tale in light of earlier Kabbalistic thought as well as the general outlook of both Hasidic mysticism and the biographical facts of the Rabbi of Berditchev's life, reputation, and contemporaries to gain a contextual, and thereby, in Idel's opinion, a more accurate understanding of the tale. Idel links the tale to thirteenth and fourteenth-century Kabbalistic thinkers who reason symbolically that just as the black letter on the page is joined to a white letter (the parchment) that sustains it, spiritually the white and black letters are linked "so that from the lower [black letter] one can perceive the higher [white letter]."[60] Rabbi Levi Isaac can be understood to mean, therefore, that God will issue forth not a new document but will reveal the hidden meanings (white spaces) of the Torah already in hand.[61] If this is the correct reading, the rabbi was far from heretical.

From Idel's analysis of Rabbi Levi Isaac's interpretation, three aspects of Hasidic thought about the white spaces emerge that seem to throw considerable light on Dillard's understanding of affective absences.[62] First, the tale of "The Hidden Teachings" as well as other documents written by the rabbi suggests not that there will be a future change in the Torah but an epistemic

---

57. Buber, *Tales of the Hasidim*, 232.
58. Scholem, *On the Kabbalah*, 81; Idel, "White Letters," 171.
59. Scholem, *On the Kabbalah*, 82; Idel, *Absorbing Perfections*, 61.
60. Idel, *Absorbing Perfections*, 55.
61. Idel, *Absorbing Perfections*, 61.
62. Idel's interpretation of Rabbi Levi Isaac's tale has been chosen for this analysis rather than Scholem's for several reasons. Idel's extraordinarily thorough analysis, supported by compelling historical evidence and primary sources, probes more deeply into the particular subject at hand than Scholem's. Further, Idel's analysis reveals aspects of Rabbi Levi Isaac's thought that appear highly consistent with the values and patterns within eighteenth-century Hasidism in general. Finally, the aspects of early Hasidic mysticism Idel highlights are very much in harmony with Dillard's thinking about the link between what is present and what is hidden. Martin Buber's translation of the tale rather than Scholem's or Idel's has been selected simply because Buber's translation is the one Dillard read.

change in the mystic contemplating it. For the Hasid, Idel explains, there is no "ontic change of the founding document"—no new book will emerge to supplement, reinterpret, or replace the existing Torah.[63] Instead, the revelation of the meaning of the white spaces will entail "an epistemological change that opens the eyes, or hearts, of the people."[64] If this is the case, the tale also suggests that such an epistemological change is perhaps possible now, not in some future or messianic era.[65] This sort of epistemological transformation seems to be the central aim of Dillard's entire artistic and spiritual enterprise. Her vigorous thrusting of the reader into the disparate roles of God and chloroplast, her command to "mentally reverse positive and negative space," her insistence that shadows of nothingness "define the real," and her asyndetic style that leaves readers contemplating white space and logical blanks in her own books, all testify to how seriously she takes the business of epistemological change. Moreover, as each of these examples illustrates the change happens when one *enters* the gaps, sustains the absurd, and holds open the possibility that "we might not be seeing something."

Second, Hasidic thinking in general focuses on the interpenetration or influx of the divine with the material world, and this vision of the divine presence flowing into the physical realm is reflected in Rabbi Levi Isaac's understanding of the relationship between the black letters and white spaces. Idel notes that "Rabbi Levi Isaac claims that 'the letters point to the influx of '*Elohim* within the world of nature'" and that "'the shape of the letters'" reveal the clues as to how the emanations of divine light from Holy One "operate within the corporeality [sic] and nature.'"[66] Thus, in contrast to Kabbalistic thought which often sees the divine light as inaccessible to humans and completely beyond this world, the Hasids envision the two as intimately linked, and the black letters become "pipes or channels" for incursions of the divine into the corporeal world.[67]

As explained in chapter 2, this is indeed the mystical paradigm Dillard seems to have adopted throughout the body of her non-fiction. The movement of the holy is downward, and it manifests itself invariably through the senses and the world, never obliterating the world or transporting Dillard

---

63. Idel, *Absorbing Perfections*, 63.

64. Idel, *Absorbing Perfections*, 63.

65. Idel, *Absorbing Perfections*, 64. The idea that the present hour is the moment of choice bears resemblances to what Martin Buber identifies as the prophetic stance in Judaism. See Buber, *Pointing the Way*, 192–207. For a full discussion of the prophetic stance and its relation to Dillard's understanding of redemption, see chapter 6.

66. Idel, "White Letters," 178.

67. Idel, "White Letters," 180, 178.

from it but transforming her vision momentarily within it.⁶⁸ A brief return to an example in *Holy the Firm* illustrates the point. When Dillard carries communion wine, "Christ with a cork," up a hill on her back, she begins to experience an unfolding vision of the world transformed, with "its infinite particulars" charged with energy and light.⁶⁹ The life within "blackberry brambles, white snowberries, red rose hips," becomes visible like "banked fires"; mountains are "raw nerves, sensible and exultant; the trees, the grass, and the asphalt below [her] are living petals of the mind, each sharp and invisible, held in a greeting or glance full perfectly formed."⁷⁰ When God's glory has filled everything, "There is no speech nor language; there is nothing, no one thing, nor motion, nor time. There is only this everything."⁷¹ The effacing of language reflects the ineffability of the moment, but Dillard is also careful to link absence with plenitude. "There is nothing" *and* "There is only this everything."⁷² Indeed, one is not seeing a "something" but a plenitude that fills and vivifies the particularity of every single thing. As the Hasidic master suggests, the ineffable moment reveals what was hidden all along; it does not entail an "ontic change" in the existing book of creation. Rather, the visible aspects of creation—rocks, beach, wine—become "pipes or channels" like the black letters of the Torah for the influx of *Elohim*.

Third, in Rabbi Levi Isaac's thinking, the white space, or the "Nought," is not a *nihil* or void signifying meaninglessness or the absence of God.⁷³ For the Jew as well as the Christian, such a state is theologically and existentially impossible since the withdrawal of God's presence from any atom of creation would mean it would cease to exist. Instead, the white spaces represent the unseen but immanent presence of God and imply an

---

68. In *Kedushat Levi*, a well-known treatise by Rabbi Levi Isaac, the Hasidic master tells readers that the one who gazes upon the "Nought," the divine nothingness, "is like a dumb man, because his intellect is effaced" (Idel, "White Letters" 179). Thus, it hints at the epistemic limitations of intellectual knowledge in the face of the divine blanks. Again, this seems very like Dillard's assertion near the end of *Pilgrim at Tinker Creek*, "my God, what a world. There is no accounting for one second of it" (PTC, 276) as well as her own tendency to throw up her hands and claim she knows nothing of God.

69. HTF, 64, 65.

70. HTF, 64. It is worth noting how the language of "greeting" and "glance" here seems to reflect Buber's conviction that it is possible to experience moments of mystical relation with nature, in which one beholds the "Face" of the *Thou* in it. For example, "He who forgets all that is caused and makes decision out of the depths . . . and naked approaches the Face, is a free man" (Buber, *I and Thou*, 53).

71. HTF, 68.

72. HTF, 68.

73. Idel, "White Letters," 179, 181.

"inherent fullness" or "semantic pregnancy" held within a blank space.[74] Even so, it is a deeply paradoxical plenitude. The white spaces of the Torah do not "contain" linguistic signifiers and therefore cannot "mean" any one thing but can potentially mean everything. For the blanks cannot be "decoded" through conceptual reasoning[75] but must be engaged spiritually and imaginatively for the fullness of their meaning to be disclosed through an encounter with divine presence.[76] Thus, in the terms Dillard sets forth, when the mystic contemplates the white absences of the world, "it could be that [she] is not seeing something."[77]

It is perhaps necessary at this point to underscore an important distinction between Dillard's understanding of the affective absence, Jewish mystical thought on the white spaces, and the language of presence and absence that emerges in the discourse of postmodern literary theorists who have also been influenced directly or indirectly by the teachings of Rabbi Levi Isaac. The influence of Kabbalistic and Hasidic thought on Jacques Derrida has been noted by scholars such as Elliot R. Wolfson,[78] John Caputo,[79] Kevin Hart,[80] Harold Bloom,[81] Moshe Idel,[82] and Gideon Ofrat,[83] among others. In addition, Umberto Eco and George Steiner both quote Rabbi Levi Isaac's views on the white letters.[84] The language of these theorists, particularly Derrida, when speaking of the "trace" that is neither a presence nor an absence and of the endlessly generated meanings of the plurivocal text, sounds very close to Kabbalistic interpretations of the white letters and Rabbi Levi

---

74. Idel, "White Letters," 179–81.

75. See Scholem, *On the Kabbalah*, 96–99; Buber, "Symbolic and Sacramental Existence" 173–81.

76. Idel, "White Letters, 182. This is true to some degree even in Kabbalistic literature and thought. See Scholem's discussion about the Kabbalah and myth in *On the Kabbalah*. He points out that "conceptions such as the *Shekinah*, the *tsimtsum*, the breaking of the vessels, to mention only a few examples . . . can be truly understood only as symbols. The discursive thinking of the Kabbalists is a kind of asymptotic process: the conceptual formulations are an attempt to provide an approximate philosophical interpretation of inexhaustible symbolic images, to interpret these images as abbreviations for conceptual series" (Scholem, *On the Kabbalah*, 96).

77. PTC, 27.

78. See Wolfson, "Assaulting the Border."

79. See Caputo, *Prayers and Tears*.

80. See Hart, *Trespass of the Sign*.

81. See Bloom, *Kabbalah and Criticism*, 24–25.

82. See Idel, *Absorbing Perfections*; "White Letters."

83. See Ofrat, *Jewish Derrida*.

84. Idel, "White Letters," 182–87.

Isaac's tale of the "Hidden Teachings."[85] In *The Jewish Derrida*, Ofrat contends that "Deconstruction and negative theology are thus allied" and both are connected to Kabbalism:

> Bottomless chasms separate the seeker after-truth [sic] from the primary truth. Any additional abyss leaves the seeker after-truth with an additional ruin of truth. This approach entails a theological position, no less than a hermeneutic one, as it condemns the concept of God (as source, *logos*) to everlasting division, everlasting separation, or—to resort to the concepts of Jewish mysticism—to the eternal averting of divine countenance; or, as the Kabbala puts it: *Reisha delo yada* (the unattainable head).[86]

As Benson points out in *Graven Ideologies*, Derrida's concern is the totalizing (and hence potentially idolatrous) impulse behind all speaking and even not speaking about God. Both are engendered by the desire to image or manifest the Other.[87] Derrida is, of course, borrowing heavily from Levinas and uses the Levinasian term "trace" to highlight the inability of language to speak of anything as it really is; it can only point to a trace of the thing.[88] Though negative theology and deconstruction share common ground, fundamental differences exist. Benson explains that "What separates theology from deconstruction, at least on Derrida's account, is that the former is concerned with establishing God's 'hyperessentiality' beyond the realm of predication and being. Such is not the concern of *différance*, even if its logic is similar."[89]

Idel observes that Derrida finds in Rabbi Berditchev's tale a parabolic expression of a sort of textual atheism in its emphasis on the plurivocality of the text. As Derrida interprets the tale, it expresses a resistance to "a monosemic reading" and to the notion that God exists apart from the text.[90] In its so doing, it gives voice to foundational assertions of deconstruction. Umberto Eco also reads the tale through the lens of deconstructive critical theory, which allows him to conclude that the tale gives rise to an "atheistic"

85. Wolfson, "Assaulting the Border," 475–76; Idel, "White Letters," 182–83.
86. Ofrat, *Jewish Derrida*, 55.
87. Benson, *Graven Ideologies*, 110–19.
88. Benson, *Graven Ideologies*, 150–55. For a brief overview of the connections between Levinas and Buber, see the discussion in the footnote on immediacy in chapter 2. Again, for a very helpful analysis of similarities and differences between essential tenets of the two philosophers, see Atterton et al., *Levinas and Buber*. Also, for an excellent and rigorous analysis of the parallels between Levinas's and Dillard's conception of God, see Carroll, *Savage Side*.
89. Benson, *Graven Ideologies*, 151.
90. Idel, "White Letters," 183.

hermeneutical model, since "without a referential mode of designation . . . the white letters may appear as godless."[91] Eco asserts that Rabbi Levi Isaac's tale, in its affirmation of the "autonomy of the symbolic as the chain of the signifiers . . . has allowed the new and atheistic mystics of the godless drift, to rewrite indefinitely, at every reading, the new Torah."[92] Yet for the Jewish mystic, there is never a question of the ontological reality of God as the referent of the white spaces. As explained previously, within both Kabbalistic and Hasidic thought, the white blanks no matter how variously they were interpreted were always understood to be connected in some way to the Holy One of Israel. Whether that was anthropomorphically as the skin of God or symbolically as white and black letters that were mystically enjoined as divine lights, the ontic reality of God always lies behind or within the text. Idel is adamant on this point:

> The white spaces of the Torah scroll were not considered by the Hasidic teachers to be holes or gaps, negative features inherent in the canonical books to be filled with new sorts of content by the readers. On the contrary, they constitute the very divine presence found within the sacred scriptures.[93]

---

91. Idel, "White Letters," 182–84. It must be emphasized that Idel characterizes Derrida's understanding of *the text*, not Derrida's person or deconstruction, as atheistic. Furthermore, he notes that for Derrida, an atheistic hermeneutic connotes the plurivocal possibilities of the text, whereas for Eco, it connotes the dearth of possibilities engendered by "an indefinite sort of semiosis" (Idel, "White Letters," 184). For an illuminating argument for Derrida's hesitant openness to "religion without religion," see Caputo, *Prayers and Tears*. Caputo notes, "It is a serious misunderstanding, a little perverse, I would say, to think that there is something inherently atheistic about deconstruction, as if, lodged deep down inside *différance* or 'the trace' there were . . . some sort of negative ontological argument against God" (Caputo, *Prayers and Tears*, 4). Caputo acknowledges that although Derrida may correctly be labeled an atheist because he lacks belief in God in the traditional sense, the affinities between negative theology and deconstruction suggest that Derrida is open to, even desirous of, the absolute surprise of the absolutely other about which one cannot speak. Caputo observes, "That is why, with the passage of the years, Derrida's relationship with negative theology became more and more affirmative, more and more linked by the impossible. The difference is that in negative theology the *tout autre* goes under the name of God, and that which calls forth speech is called 'God,' whereas for Derrida every other is wholly other (*tout autre est tout autre*). But the name of God is not a bad name and we can love (and save) this name" (Caputo, *Prayers and Tears*, 3–4).

92. Idel, "White Letters," 183.

93. Idel, "White Letters," 185. Idel points out that interpreting the tale in light of modern sensibilities without regard for its historical and literary context results in the bizarre paradox that Rabbi Levi Isaac, a man known by his contemporaries as being extraordinarily "godfull," is now viewed as the inspiration behind modern "atheistic mystics of the godless drift" (Idel, "White Letters," 183, 185).

This seems to be Dillard's conviction as well. The "text" she contemplates expands, as it did for the Hasids, well beyond written words to the text of the world where the holy sparks of God's Shekinah remain hidden in things.[94] Although God may be incomprehensible, elusive, perhaps even unlikable at times, at no point does her bewilderment and anger lead to textual or spiritual agnosticism, let alone atheism. Epistemic uncertainty for Dillard, whether generated by texts or by life, is not synonymous with Godlessness. As the examples in this chapter illustrate, blanks, gaps, absences are "fertile ground."[95] The grammatical and structural gaps along with the stammering of her asyndetic style have, to borrow Idel's phrase, a "semantic pregnancy" that is risky *because* it can generate multiple readings. Readers can (and have) filled in the gaps erroneously or can get frustrated by them and walk away. Yet, as noted at the outset of this chapter, Dillard's conviction that "the gaps are the thing" compels her to take the risk. By moving readers into the spaces between unsettling grammatical and existential contradictions, she moves them into a white space of potential semantic and spiritual plenitude. As she observes in *For the Time Being*, "[God's] home is absence, and there he finds us."[96]

Neither does the epistemic uncertainty generated from the hiddenness or inscrutability of God in this world signify for Dillard such a radical absence of God that one might as well call it atheism. Elie Wiesel explains in his chapter on Levi-Isaac of Berditchev in *Souls on Fire* that "If other mystics maintained I-and-Thou relations with God, he, Levi-Yitzhak, threatened Him with breaking off these same relations. In this way, he wished to demonstrate that one may be Jewish with God, in God and even against God; but not without God."[97] Dillard's position seems to be the same. At the end of *Pilgrim at Tinker Creek*, she reinterprets the Old Testament sacrificial rite of the heave offering as humans' "violent, desperate way of catching God's eye. It is not inappropriate. We are people; we are

---

94. See Peterson, "Annie Dillard." Peterson calls her "an exegete of creation" who probes "the book of creation with the care and intensity of a skilled textual critic" (Peterson, "Annie Dillard," 178).

95. PTC, 27.

96. FTB, 139.

97. Wiesel, *Souls on Fire*, 109. In *Jewish Derrida*, Ofrat asks "Cannot it be justly claimed as well that rupture, the absence of God, the rift—are among the basic experiences of Judaism, whether ancient or modern?" He then quotes Martin Buber: "'What is it we refer to when we speak of the eclipse of the Divine light, that is in effect at this time? . . . We make the significant assumption that we can lift to God our "spiritual eye" . . . as we can lift to the sun our "corporeal eye"; and that something is liable to intervene between our own being and his being, as between earth and heaven'" (Ofrat, *Jewish Derrida*, 6–7).

permitted to have dealings with the creator and we must speak up for the creation. God *look* at what you've done to this creature, look at the sorrow, the cruelty, the long damned waste!"[98] It can be inferred therefore that when Dillard speaks of an affective absence, she is not speaking as Derrida is of "the wholly other that is neither a presence nor an absence"[99] but of a space charged with a potency that indwells every crevice like the shape of the air, that gives wordless intellectual structure to a word-filled text, and that surrounds black letters with white fire.[100]

To return to this chapter's beginnings, Dillard's habit of "minding the gaps" seems to be a thoroughly pervasive feature of her texts. It is evidenced through various oppositional motifs that she holds in tension—God as both present and absent, the twinned fiords of beauty and pain, shadow and light, presence and absence. Moreover, her texts enact the very oppositional tensions of which they speak. The stammering prose, ruptures in logic, and fractured narratives create an asyndetic style that potentially provokes in readers a "holy insecurity," a sense that in her texts as in life there are moments when one finds oneself free-falling in white spaces where logic fails, and there are

---

98. PTC, 269. See also Exodus: "And thou shalt sanctify the breast of the wave offering, and the shoulder of the heave offering, which is waved, and which is heaved up, of the ram of the consecration, even of that which is for Aaron, and of that which is for his sons" (Exod 29:27)

99. Wolfson, "Assaulting the Border," 476.

100. Idel has sharp criticism for contemporary theorists "using modern sensibilities to decode" a premodern text and for their interpreting the Hasidic notion of white spaces as if it were "pertinent for any text," all the while ignoring the fact that Rabbi Levi Isaac's thinking applied *only* to a sacred text, the Torah, and had an historical context vastly different from the modern one. As noted above, this has lead in his view to a radicalized version of Rabbi Levi Isaac as the progenitor of "the new and atheistic mystics of the godless drift" (Eco quoted in Idel, "White Letters" 183). He adds that although some of these postmodern theories may be interesting in their own right, they have lead to "universalistic assumptions" that "were undreamed of by the original author himself" (Idel, "White Letters" 185–86).

Do Idel's criticisms apply here? While Dillard's texts are certainly not sacred, they do embody a Judeo-Christian worldview and ontological assumptions about God underwriting the text of creation that, has been argued, are far closer to those of Rabbi Levi Isaac than those allegedly espoused by postmodern mystics of the "godless drift." Thus, applying the thought of Rabbi Levi Isaac to Dillard seems unlikely to radicalize him or his thought; in fact, Dillard's texts seem to reinforce and augment the power of his observations by illustrating how they are manifested in a modern text.

Even if such a reading could never have been dreamed of by the original author, it does not mean it cannot open up new dimensions of a text. If this were the case, one would have to do away with all literary criticism since very little if any critical analysis could be said to reflect an author's knowledge of and intention for his own text. Holding Dillard's texts and Hasidic texts side by side so that their converging themes can illuminate each other seems therefore a legitimate and fruitful interpretive exercise.

no grammatical or metaphysical bridges across them. Dillard, remarkably, is committed to locating herself and her readers in the gaps because she recognizes they are, indeed, "fertile ground."[101] Like the Hasidic master, Rabbi Levi Isaac, she recognizes the latent potency, the semantic and spiritual plenitude, of the white spaces in texts and in life. In her essay, "Write Till You Drop," Dillard claims, "The artist is willing to give all his or her strength and life to probing with blunt instruments those same secrets no one can describe any way but with the instrument's faint tracks."[102] Hence, it could be said that her literary work endeavors to fix readers' gaze on the absences and gaps circumscribed by her words' faint traces so that they might one day glimpse white fire blazing up within blank spaces.

---

101. PTC, 27.

102. Dillard, "Write Till You Drop."

CHAPTER 6

Tikkun: Redemption, Memory, and Mysticism Turned *Ethos*

> "The work is not yours to finish, Rabbi Tarfon said, but neither are you free to take no part in it."
>
> —Annie Dillard, *For the Time Being*

Introduction

To review briefly at the outset of this final chapter, the overarching structure of this book follows the arc of Dillard's tripartite concerns with the manifestation of God in the material creation; the presence of evil and suffering in it; and finally, redemption within rather than outside a creation bound by time and space. The aim has been to demonstrate how within these three seminal theological movements, typically used to frame a specifically Christian worldview, her work reveals the shaping influence of her life-long interest in Jewish thought, particularly that of Martin Buber and the persons and theological legacies of Isaac Luria and the Baal Shem Tov. At the heart of this analysis is the assertion that Dillard's work cannot be properly understood without examining ways in which she is a *Judeo*-Christian, not merely a Christian, thinker and writer.

This final chapter brings the theological arc of creation, evil, and redemption full circle by examining Dillard's adoption of the stance and voice of a poet-prophet in her literary works' calls to attentiveness, remembrance, and redemptive action. The chapter's first section, "The Prophetic Stance," will argue that Dillard adopts what Martin Buber, in his essay "Prophecy,

Apocalyptic, and the Historical Hour," identifies as a prophetic rather than apocalyptic stance. It will suggest that, in keeping with such a view, Dillard's texts quite literally eclipse through textual silence the apocalyptic ending of the Christian gospel story, namely Christ's resurrection and return. In doing so, Dillard adopts what Buber identifies as the prophetic attitude toward the historical hour in which the future can "establish itself ever anew," the antithesis of the apocalyptic view in which the end of the story is already determined, or to use Buber's phrase, "inescapably destined."[1] To do so, the discussion will return to the image of the eternally suspended Christ introduced in chapters 3 and 4 and argue that the suspension of an ending is an inherently ethical move that compels readers to endure, love, and work *within* the absurdities of life now. Thus, the context of faith and redemptive actions is, as her final book's title suggests, "for the time being." Dillard's prophetic stance and voice therefore urges readers to act redemptively on God's behalf now rather than project that redemption into a messianic future and thereby neglect their responsibility to think and act ethically in the present.

The chapter's second and third sections will suggest that Dillard actually summons the reader into a prophetic dialogue through her frequent use of the apostrophic voice through which she confronts the reader through second-person direct address. Like that of Israel's prophets, the "I" Dillard constructs in her narratives functions in two roles—first, as the visionary attempting to make sense of her encounters with God and, second, as the prophetic voice communicating those encounters to others. Unlike the Neoplatonic mystic whose experience is both consummation and illumination, an ineffable end in itself, Dillard-as-prophet seems compelled to follow the revelation with communication, acting as both receiver and instigator of a moral vision. As Heschel explains in *The Prophets*: "Prophecy points beyond itself. . . . The reception of the word must be followed by the proclamation of the word. The prophet's role is that of a mediator; neither the author nor the final addressee. . . . Prophecy is never complete in itself; it is a burden, a tension, a call."[2] Dillard's texts and public comments testify to the seriousness with which she undertakes the "call" as a poet-prophet both to communicate and provoke encounters with the divine through her work. This section of the chapter therefore explores how Dillard's apostrophic voice allows her to create a literary equivalent of the "*Shema*, Israel" and precipitate in readers a potentially ethical and redemptive theological moment.

This ethical move, it will be suggested in the chapter's final section, answers in part the frequent criticism that Dillard's work is irresponsibly

---

1. Buber, *On the Bible*, 173.
2. Heschel, *Prophets*, 361.

apolitical and that she is the only person of concern in her literary cosmos. The section will argue to the contrary that Dillard's work is profoundly ethical. However, its ethics are predicated not upon ideology but upon memory and that this is a distinctively Hebraic feature of her work. In "The Moral Necessity of Metaphor," Jewish writer Cynthia Ozick asserts that at the heart of the Pentateuch's ethos is the spiritual and intellectual discipline of remembering. This final chapter concludes by exploring ways that Dillard's work could be understood as embodying what Buber argues is one of Hasidism's most distinctive traits—its taking religious life out of the "seclusion of the ascetics" and bringing it into the fullness of communities.[3] In its doing so, "mysticism has become *ethos*."[4] This section examines closely various calls to remember found throughout Dillard's work and will suggest that her work is not *about* ethics but performs and provokes ethical reflection in its commitment to noticing others' suffering, to converting memory into the metaphors of art, and to urging readers through her prophetic voice to imagine "what it is to be someone else."[5]

The Prophetic Stance: A Suspended Christ, A Suspended Ending

Martin Buber's essay, "Prophecy, Apocalyptic, and the Historical Hour," sets forth two contrasting human attitudes to life's moments, particularly pivotal ones, that of necessity require a response. The first, identified as the prophetic stance, is that of the individual who, when confronted with a decision whose outcome has consequences not only for the current historical hour but also the future, affirms his power to choose and "cherishes the until-now-unsuspected certainty of thus being able to participate on the ground of becoming, in the factual decision that will be made about the make-up of the next hour, and thereby in some measure also about the make-up of future hours."[6] The second, or apocalyptic, attitude expressed in Jewish and Christian apocalyptic literature is that of the individual who suppresses the impulse to dare the impossible that answers the situation and instead, out of prudence (he thinks), resolves not to become embattled with those unseen and unconquerable historical forces which act upon him but upon which he cannot act. And so "he surrenders anew to the turmoil," resolving that

---

3. Buber, *Origin and Meaning*, 198–99.
4. Buber, *Origin and Meaning*, 198–99.
5. Ozick, *Metaphor and Memory*, 279.
6. Buber, "Prophecy, Apocalyptic," 172.

"everything is linked invincibly with everything else, and there is nowhere a break where he can take hold."[7]

Buber argues in this essay and elsewhere, most notably in *The Prophetic Faith*, that the prophetic view requires trust, or to call it by its "sacral name," faith, but this faith is not unprecedented.[8] One does not stand alone in exercising it. In fact, the Hebrew prophets and their sayings, Buber argues, exemplify this former attitude of belief in the power of humans to speak a divine summons and freely respond within the offered dialogical relationship to God, and thereby alter their own and the world's destiny. Both the prophetic and apocalyptic texts presuppose "faith in the one Lord of the past, present, and future history of all existing beings," and "both views are certain of His will to grant salvation to His creation. But how this will manifest itself in the pregnant moment" is where the two views differ.[9] Whereas the apocalyptic stance discloses the future as an already-determined event that in Buber's view truncates the human power of choice in shaping that eschatological future, the prophetic stance leaves the future open to be fashioned and refashioned as the dialogical relationship between heaven and earth continues. Drawing upon the metaphor of the potter and the clay found in Jeremiah 18, Buber insists that both God and man have a hand in shaping the historical hour and its future:

> Thus, the divine potter works on the historical shapes and destinies of human nations. But, in accordance with His will, this work of His can itself will, can itself either do or not do; with this doing and not-doing that it wills, it touches on the work of the Worker. From the beginning He has granted this freedom to them, and in all sovereignty of His fashioning and destroying, He still gives to them, just in so doing, the answer—fashioning and destroying.[10]

Even on the precipice of doom, Buber asserts, the "gate of grace still remains open" for the one who chooses to respond in the dialogue between God and man and "[turn] his whole being back to God."[11] Thus, there is no ending "set to the real working power of the dialogue between divinity and mankind."[12]

---

7. Buber, "Prophecy, Apocalyptic," 172.
8. Buber, "Prophecy, Apocalyptic," 173.
9. Buber, "Prophecy, Apocalyptic," 174.
10. Buber, "Prophecy, Apocalyptic," 176.
11. Buber, "Prophecy, Apocalyptic," 176.
12. Buber, "Prophecy, Apocalyptic," 176.

One of the most curious and conspicuous features of Dillard's literary non-fiction[13] is its suspension of the apocalyptic ending to the gospel narratives created by the absence of any macro- or micro-level intertextual reference[14] to the resurrection of Jesus Christ. Though there are brief and tenuous images that suggest the revitalizing work of the Holy Spirit in and through creation, nowhere in the canon of Dillard's major works of literary non-fiction can one find words, phrases, or sentences that call to mind the gospel account of Christ's triumph over the grave through bodily resurrection after his sacrificial death on the cross.[15] Given Dillard's public and well-documented extra-literary commitment to Christianity for most of her life, as well as her intellectual rigor and editorial fastidiousness, this omission could hardly be accidental. At the very least, it is the logical outcome of the kind of God and world she constructs within the body of her work, about which more shall be said shortly. No matter whether the omission is intentional or accidental, her textual silence about this essential Christian claim is one of the most theologically conspicuous gaps or omissions in her work and consequently one of its most theologically significant. To understand its theological import, it is necessary to return to perhaps Dillard's clearest and most emphatic symbolical argument for the sort of God she believes in, found at the end of chapter 6's section "Evil" in *For the Time Being*.

The section immediately follows a quotation of Hegel's strange description of God as the "oyster-like, gray or quite black Absolute" and begins

---

13. As noted in chapter 1, this is the genre term Dillard uses to describe works that include *Pilgrim at Tinker Creek*, *Holy the Firm*, *Teaching a Stone to Talk*, and *For the Time Being*. It is in these works, rather than in her novels, poetry, literary criticism, or autobiography, that the issues of creation, evil, and redemption of concern here most clearly emerge, so it is to these works primarily that this chapter's argument appeals.

14. See Genette, *Architext*. Genette identifies the macro- and micro-levels of "transtextuality," or "textual transcendence" as "everything that brings it into relation (manifest or hidden) with other texts" (Genette, *Architext*, 81). He includes under this umbrella heading the micro-levels of intertextuality such as quotation and allusion, as well as the macro-levels such as genre or commentary on a text, what he calls "metatext" (Genette, *Architext*, 82). I am indebted to Deanne Westbrook's textual analysis in *Wordsworth's Biblical Ghosts* for the critical framework suggested by macro- and micro-intertextual references.

15. In *Holy the Firm*, Dillard alludes to Christ's ascension but skips over the resurrection (HTF, 47). In *For the Time Being*, Dillard quotes Teilhard de Chardin's biographer who alludes to the stone being moved from Christ's grave (FTB, 163). Neither of these examples could be considered textual evidence for the resurrection. Colleen Warren suggests that an image in *Holy the Firm* depicting dormant vegetation stirring with internal light is a resurrection image (Warren, *Annie Dillard*, 118). However, the context is Christ's transfiguration, not his resurrection. Perhaps a more accurate interpretation, therefore, is that the objects are transfigured, not resurrected, by the indwelling presence of God.

with the question "Who is dead? The Newtonian God."[16] Clearly alluding to "God is dead" theology whose origin is in Hegelian thought,[17] Dillard goes on to describe this dead God as monarchical and exacting, "who with the strength of his arm dishes out human fates, in the form of cancer or cash, to 5.9 billion people—to teach, dazzle, rebuke, or try us."[18] To underscore the apparent primitiveness and possessiveness of this outmoded God, Dillard adds that Teilhard de Chardin called him "'the great Neolithic proprietor.'"[19] This is "the God of the old cosmos, who was not yet known as the soul of the world but as its image."[20] In the next sentence Dillard makes a crucial logical leap. She concludes, "History, then, was a fix. And God was a Lego lord."[21] The omniscient, omnipotent, and impassive "old God of the cosmos" is also a God who determines the end from the beginning and executes his will, says Rabbi Lawrence Kushner, "'without human agency.'"[22] In Buberian terms, this is the God of the apocalyptic view.

Dillard then provides a brief chronology of seven centuries of thinkers who questioned God's omnipotence, beginning with Aquinas, moving through Leibniz, Tillich, and ending with Alfred Whitehead.[23] The list is telling in that it simultaneously presents evidence for the argument that God is not omnipotent (hence the old God of the cosmos is indeed dead) and suggests that God is vulnerable to the exigencies of human choice, as she goes on to assert.[24] History therefore is *not* a fix, and Dillard finds it

16. FTB, 165.

17. Paul Fiddes points out that Hegel used the phrase "God is dead" before Nietzsche made it famous, albeit each meant different things by it (Fiddes, *Creative Suffering of God*, 188). Important to note is that "God is dead" theologians, as well as Dillard, certainly do not intend the phrase "God is dead" to mean that God does not objectively exist, but that the antiquated ("Newtonian," as Dillard calls it) God is dead. This can be understood to mean, Fiddes adds, that the world is such that no experience of that old God is possible any longer (Fiddes, *Creative Suffering of God*, 185). See Fiddes's helpful and thorough analysis of "God is dead" theology, its relationship to the idea of a suffering God, and its connection to process theology in Fiddes, *Creative Suffering of God*, 174–206.

18. FTB, 126.

19. FTB, 165.

20. FTB, 165.

21. FTB, 165.

22. FTB, 166.

23. FTB, 166.

24. It should be noted that Dillard is not entirely sympathetic to Whiteheadian process theology. She adds parenthetically the following critique: "Some theologians— Whitehead's school—rescue the old deductive idea of God by asserting that God possesses all good qualities to an absolute degree, therefore he must be absolutely sensitive, and so absolutely vulnerable. They could not have known then that this made God

not only untenable but also logically impossible to worship a "Lego lord" whose will and purposes fit together neatly in ready-made destinies. This refusal of the notion of fixed outcomes and of a God who by divine fiat works his will "without human agency" constitutes in part her prophetic stance. To put it in Buber's terms, she rejects an apocalyptic attitude that subtly encourages passive human conformity to divine will, and she adopts instead a prophetic view in which God, his creation, and his creatures are in dialogue to determine both human history and God's future. To return to Buber's assertion, "this work of His can itself will, can itself either do or not do; with this doing and not-doing that it wills, it touches on the work of the Worker."[25] Since God allows his creation and creatures "either to do or not do," human agency has a real effect on divine being, in the present historical hour, and thus on the future of creation.[26]

The section "Evil" ends with the image of the eternally incarnate, eternally crucified Christ. As discussed in chapters 2 and 3, the image synthesizes Jewish and Christian theology to suggest not only an eternally suspended Christ but thereby a suspended apocalyptic ending to human history that, as the final section of this chapter will suggest, has significant ethical ramifications. For ease of reference, the passage is quoted here again: "Nature works out its complexities. God suffers the world's necessities with us, and suffers our turning away, and joins us in exile. Christians might add that Christ hangs, as it were, on the cross forever, always incarnate, and always nailed."[27] Crucially, nowhere in the canon of Dillard's literary non-fiction does Christ come down from the cross. There is no apocalyptic in-breaking of resurrection power to redeem the world's fallenness in the narratives Dillard constructs. Thus, within her literary cosmos for both the Jew and the Christian, God is always incarnate but hidden and always immanent but bound, exiled from his own power within the world he has made.

The image has significant theological implications for understanding the notion of redemption in Dillard's work. As has been well established, the problem of evil and unjust suffering is central to Dillard's thinking and writing for the whole of her career. The final and apocalyptic Christian answer to the problem of evil and suffering is, first, Christ's triumph over death and sin through the resurrection, and, second, his return, or second

---

sound like a sensitive new-age guy. At any rate, subjecting our partial knowledge of God to the rigors of philosophical inquiry is, I think, an absurd, if well-meaning, exercise" (FTB, 166–67).

25. Buber, *On the Bible*, 176.

26. See chapter 3 for a full discussion of the kenotic-perichoretic God Dillard depicts within her works.

27. FTB, 169.

coming, to establish for all eternity his perfect rule and reign. Thus, the centrality of the resurrection for Christians to any prolonged meditation on the problem of evil seems indisputable, since the primary basis for Christian hope is that the resurrection demonstrates Christ's complete and irrevocable victory over death and thereby His unassailable power ultimately to right all wrongs. It is the orthodox Christian claim therefore that without the resurrection, the Christian gospel simply cannot be "good news" since the whole of the story depends upon the ending. If Christ was not raised, the world remains captive to sin and death, and his claim to be the promised messiah would seem to be invalidated. Yet it is precisely the resurrection ending that Dillard leaves out. Upon closer examination, however, this refusal of an ending—or at least this particular ending—seems entirely consistent with the whole of Dillard's thought about a kenotic God and could perhaps even be said to be a faithful literary rendering not only of the agonizing silence of the day between the cross and the resurrection but also of the theological space opened by the absent-yet-resurrected Christ portrayed in the New Testament.

First, it seems to be a logical and consistent outworking of Dillard's view of a kenotic God who elects to limit his omnipotence. If the gospel narrative ends on Holy Saturday, as it does in Dillard's texts, one's hope is suspended both literally and figuratively with the suspended Christ. Without the certainty of Christ's ultimate triumph over evil and death, which is the apocalyptic victory that the resurrection declares, one cannot make sweeping claims about God's omnipotence in the here and now. This is precisely what Dillard insists upon. As was discussed in chapter 4, Dillard adopts Teilhard de Chardin's view in asserting that "It is 'fatal'" to hang onto the old belief "that we suffer at the hands of an omnipotent God."[28] In fact, she adds, "it is fatal to reason" about evil in general. "It does not work."[29] Dillard holds that "the omnipotence of God makes no sense if it requires the all-causingness of God," noting that "even Aquinas dissolved the fatal problem of natural, physical evil by tinkering with God's omnipotence."[30] Consequently, the eclipsing of the gospel story's ending can be understood not as a denial of the possibility of the resurrection so much as a literary silence that allows Dillard to foreground the existential reality of the universal human condition as well as the kenotic nature of God. Unjust suffering goes unexplained, evil goes unchecked, natural calamities occur; therefore this kenotic God "suffers the world's necessities along with us, and suffers our

28. FTB, 84.
29. FTB, 84–85.
30. FTB, 85.

turning away, and joins us in exile"; Christ remains "on the cross forever."[31] Alan Lewis, in his theological meditation on Holy Saturday, completed just before his own untimely death from cancer, insists that the Christian church far too often forgets the staggering silence and finality of the day between Good Friday and Easter Sunday:

> It is supremely difficult—though actually supremely important—still to think of [Christ's] death in its own right, without or before his resurrection. . . . As the events of that climactic weekend occurred, and as the gospel story recounts them, this did not *begin* as a three-day happening, destined to end as a story of victory and life. Far from being the first day, the day of the cross is, in the logic of the narrative itself, actually the last day, the end of the story of Jesus. And the day that follows it is not an in-between day which simply waits for the morrow, but it is an empty void, a nothing, shapeless, meaningless, and anticlimactic: simply the day after the end. . . . These were anonymous, indefinite hours, filled with memories and assessments of what was finished and past; and there was no reason to imagine that an imminent triumph might render those judgments premature and incomplete. When today we ourselves fail to identify with the story of this *Shabbat*, refuse to ponder the death of Christ as seen from this vantage point where death is his only fate, and defeat the only verdict on his life, then do not faith and theology cease actually to hear the very narrative which the church lives?[32]

Lewis goes on to affirm that the narrative does, of course, proceed to its triumphant and apocalyptic conclusion which is the in-breaking event of the resurrection.[33] There is no reason to suppose that Dillard's extra-literary faith does not do the same. However, within the literary cosmos she constructs, the narrative stops prematurely, eclipses the gospel's triumphant ending, and leaves Christ hanging "as it were, on the cross forever."[34] In doing so, she refuses to allow readers to turn away from the horrific and often brutalizing images, facts, and events presented in her work and relocate themselves imaginatively in much more hospitable terrain where resurrection light transforms their seeing by softening the ragged edges of suffering with redemptive promise.

---

31. FTB, 169.

32. Lewis, *Between Cross and Resurrection*, 31–32.

33. Lewis, *Between Cross and Resurrection*, 32.

34. FTB, 169.

Furthermore, Dillard's synthesis of Jewish and Christian imagery in this passage seems to suggest that in many ways Christians and Jews must exercise the same faith in that both live within an epoch of not-yet-fulfilled messianic hopes. For the Christian, though the resurrection signals an eventual and final defeat of death and evil, life now, like that of the eternally incarnate, eternally crucified Christ, is subject to the inexplicable and unjust incursions of violence, suffering, and pain. And though the resurrection is Christ's decisive victory over evil, it is an event whose effects have yet to be made fully manifest. The Christian can apprehend imaginatively a new day when there will be no more death or suffering and when every tear shall be wiped away, but this day can be seen only through the eyes of faith since how or when such a state of being will be universal cannot be known precisely, and Dillard provides plenty of evidence within her canon to suggest that meanwhile evil has the upper hand. For the time being, as her book's title reminds readers, suffering is not abrogated by miracles but is hallowed by Christ's "suffering the world's necessities" alongside his creatures, his willingness to journey in exile with them. In so doing, Christ's being continues to intersect time and space in the suffering and (one must conclude) redemption of his creation as it responds in prophetic faith and participates in the "work of the Worker."[35] Dillard seems to suggest that God's being immanent is not supernatural intervention but sacramentalizing participation. She offers Paul Tillich's assertion that "God's activity" in the world is not "interference, but instead divine creativity—the ongoing creation of life with all its greatness and danger."[36] Consequently, because the image of the eternally crucified Christ also suspends the apocalyptic ending of the resurrection, it foregrounds human responsibility to act redemptively now on God's behalf and to envision the future not as predetermined by a "Lego lord" but open to be changed by those who engage creatively with a suffering and exiled God to redeem a broken world. This is, in short, the prophetic stance. The full ethical implications of the prophetic view will be explored through an analysis of Dillard's appeal to the Lurianic concept of *tikkun* later in this chapter.

Secondly, the image of the eternally suspended and suffering Christ seems richly suggestive of a theological space opened by the absent-yet-resurrected Christ portrayed in the New Testament, whose suffering has yet to be completed in human history through his body, the Church (Col 1:24).[37] The thinking of Paul Fiddes is particularly helpful here. In *The Cre-*

35. Buber, *On the Bible*, 178.
36. FTB, 169.
37. "Now I rejoice in what I am suffering for you, and I fill up in my flesh what is

ative Suffering of God, Fiddes argues that there are both active and passive dimensions of God's suffering. Christ suffers actively by choosing to experience the consequences of human sin and journey into the depths of utter alienation from God though he was innocent:

> Moreover, because God has committed himself to Christ as his agent of forgiving love, making himself one with him, we may conclude (with astonishment at the mercy of God) that the Father himself embarks upon this agonizing voyage of discovery. Far from simply forgetting about the sins of the world, he journeys deeply into the heart of man's condition.[38]

In other words, if, as Dillard maintains, Christ suffers the world's necessities along with it, the whole of the Trinity joins humans in pilgrimage on the "agonizing voyage"[39] through the wilderness of suffering, where the outcome can often look God-forsaken indeed. God in Christ suffers passively in his electing to become vulnerable to life's vicissitudes, including his own creation's rejection as well as utter meaninglessness evidenced in the cross's cry of dereliction. Fiddes maintains that in Christ's experience of God-forsakenness "there is a sheer vulnerability" to "a loss of meaning which befalls him whatever his deliberate, sacrificial intentions might have been to share the state of outcasts to the uttermost. *There is no such thing as programmed suffering in such an act of acceptance.*"[40] This vulnerability to the present and future choices of his creation seems exactly what Dillard suggests when she concludes that "[God] suffers our turning away."[41] If Christ is still on the cross, he too in some sense endures the suspension of an ending since his creation can and will turn away from him.[42] What the future will be simply cannot be known since what God's creation will or will not do potentially

---

still lacking in regard to Christ's afflictions, for the sake of his body, which is the church" (Col 1:24); "Now if we are children, then we are heirs—heirs of God and co-heirs with Christ, if indeed we share in his sufferings in order that we may also share in his glory" (Rom 8:17); "For just as we share abundantly in the sufferings of Christ, so also our comfort abounds through Christ" (2 Cor 1:5).

38. Fiddes, *Creative Suffering of God*, 162.
39. Fiddes, *Creative Suffering of God*, 162.
40. Fiddes, *Creative Suffering of God*, 163 (emphasis mine).
41. FTB, 169.
42. Of course, one could take issue with Dillard's position since it seems clear in the gospels that Christ knew of his impending death and his resurrection; he spoke of both repeatedly to his disciples. One could argue that Christ did, therefore, know the end of his own story. For example, see Matt 12:40; Mark 8:31; 9:31; John 2:19. However, the discussion here is not concerned with whether Dillard's images and narrative are theologically accurate but rather with the ways they suit her literary and theological purposes.

changes everything, including God himself.[43] Hence, the creative suffering of God means, in part, his making himself subject to and wholly participatory in the process of human choices and the unfolding of creation history. Fiddes affirms, "There can be no suffering love unless there is an element of the unknown which calls for trust. Suffering love abandons securities and goes out like Abraham into a desert journey."[44]

To conclude this section, a brief note of clarification is necessary about the historical resurrection of Christ, which, as noted above, orthodox Christianity claims is the apocalyptic ending to the gospel of Jesus's life on earth. In an extra-literary sense, the whole of Christianity hangs on the resurrection. So, it does matter. The present discussion of Dillard's omission of it should not be mistaken for claims about her Christian belief at the time, nor should this analysis be understood as a defense of a resurrection-less gospel. The passible and eternally suspended God Dillard constructs in her texts does not negate the necessity or validity of the bodily resurrection of Christ in an extra-literary, theological sense. Nor should the present discussion be interpreted theologically to suggest that outside the text God's final victory is somehow uncertain. As Fiddes[45] explains, "God, unlike us, knows all possibilities that can be known; at the same time he knows the power of his love to persuade and influence creation. So he has the certainty of perfect hope, where ours can only be partial and hope 'is the evidence of things not seen.' The divine certainty is not prediction, but confident hope."[46]

Nonetheless, what humans will choose or not choose, do or not do, and whether their choices will attain what was potentially possible, may not be entirely known by them. Fiddes posits that God is thus eternally creative and active in a dynamic relationship with the world in order to redeem it. He works with the endlessly new possibilities that emerge from the "interaction between Creator and creatures" and from the limitless possibilities that "God himself conceives spontaneously from his own creative imagination."[47] Buber seems to suggest the same in *I and Thou* when speak-

---

43. "God changes himself through suffering, out of his self-giving love for us which takes form in forgiveness" (Fiddes, *Creative Suffering of God*, 169). It should be noted Fiddes's views are open to challenge. His thinking on this matter, he readily admits, borrows heavily from process theology, a movement that has its outspoken critics, particularly of its arguments for God's passibility and mutability.

44. Fiddes, *Creative Suffering of God*, 103.

45. Fiddes, *Creative Suffering of God*, 105.

46. Fiddes, *Creative Suffering of God*, 102–3.

47. Fiddes, *Creative Suffering of God*, 95–96. Fiddes's argument as a whole maintains that for God truly to suffer, he must be passible. The image of the clay man with a hole in his side that occurs four times in the span of twenty-five years in Dillard's work suggests that all the world's suffering is held within the eternally crucified Christ. But

ing of the dialogical relation between God and humans that involves the creative coming into being both of God and of the world's destiny:

> You know always in your heart that you need God more than everything; but do you not know too that God needs you—in the fullness of His eternity needs you? How would man be, how would you be, if God did not need him, did not need you? You need God, in order to be—and God needs you, for the very meaning of your life. In instruction and in poems men are at pains to say more, and they say too much—what turgid and presumptuous talk that is about the "God who becomes"; but we know unshakably in our hearts that there is a becoming of the God that is. The world is not divine sport, it is divine destiny. There is divine meaning in the life of the world, of man, of human persons, of you and of me.[48]

To recast this in Martin Buber's description of the prophetic stance, there is no ending "set to the real working power of the dialogue between divinity and mankind."[49]

The Prophetic Vocation: A Literary *Nabi*

Dillard's texts summon readers into this dialogical relationship through a distinguishing stylistic feature—their remarkably frequent use of second-person narrative, directly addressing, challenging, and questioning the imagined but absent reader in an apostrophic voice. In doing so they presuppose and engage readers in dialogical relationship like the one Buber conceives as occurring between God and man in the prophetic address; and secondly, the narratives remain open-ended in that they lack arrival or closure since the apostrophic summons within them moves readers outside

---

whether its pain causes him pain or motivates him to intervene is questionable. Dillard describes the hole as one he fingers, yet rarely if ever heals (FTB, 168). In Dillard, "Expedition to the Pole," she asserts that God is not moved by human folly but requires his creatures to adapt to spiritual conditions. He sets the terms. This sounds in some respects like the Platonic ideal of a god who does *not* change or respond to the world's prayers or cries. However, Dillard's claims in *For the Time Being* that Christ suffers the world's necessities with it, must mean that he does suffer and therefore is passible, as chapter 3 argues. Whether the God of Dillard's literary cosmos does or does not suffer, the point here remains valid. The eschatological ending of human history—whether ultimately good but not known fully by God, known only as potential, or known as promise yet to be fulfilled—is an ending that is suspended both in Dillard's image of Christ eternally crucified and in her works' silence about the resurrection.

48. Buber, *I and Thou*, 82.
49. Buber, *On the Bible*, 176.

of diachronic time into a suspended "now" created by the vocative. Consequently, they function rhetorically in ways that are strongly suggestive of the prophetic voice and stance as Martin Buber conceives of them. In short, the use of second-person address causes the texts to *function* prophetically in several senses. As Jonathan Culler's notes in his seminal essay "Apostrophe," "invocation is a figure of vocation" that dramatizes the act of calling itself in order that the speaker might "summon images of its power so as to establish its identity as poetical and prophetic voice."[50] Further, apostrophic addresses unlike narrative sequences "where one thing leads to another," create "a timeless present" wherein the act of calling constitutes an event in and of itself; "its *now* is not a moment in a temporal sequence but a *now* of discourse, of writing."[51] It could be said therefore that Dillard's apostrophic voice functions prophetically by temporally locating readers in what Buber calls "the infinite ethos of the moment."[52] Such an address also moves readers from the role of an "overhearer" to that of the addressee of a prophetic call eliciting a response.

A few disclaimers are necessary at the outset. First, the notion of the poet-as-prophet (or prophet-as-poet) is ancient and hardly unique to Dillard. As James Kugel observes, "That poets and prophets have something in common with each other is an idea with a long history"; it traces its way back through Wordsworth, Blake, Milton, and Dante in Western literature to Israel and the Hebrew prophets themselves.[53] Robert Lowth's eighteenth-century discovery (or re-discovery)[54] of biblical parallelism and his *Lectures on the Sacred Poetry of the Hebrews* reintroduced the question, at least at the level of form, of whether the Hebrew prophets were poets, since many of the prophetic texts exhibit the "poetic" convention of parallelism.[55] The questions remain complex and their answers diverse.[56] The current argu-

50. Culler, *Pursuit of Signs*, 142.

51. Culler, *Pursuit of Signs*, 149–53.

52. Buber, *Origin and Meaning*, 117.

53. Kugel, *Poetry and Prophecy*, 1. See also Roston, *Prophet and Poet*, esp. 126–42; Balfour, *Rhetoric of Romantic Prophecy*, esp. 55–81.

54. Heschel makes the point that although Lowth is commonly credited as being the first to recognize parallelism in biblical prophecy, centuries before Lowth, Menahem ben Saruk, a tenth-century Hebrew philologist, was well aware this feature (Heschel, *Prophets*, 155).

55. Kugel, *Poetry and Prophecy*, 1–5.

56. See Heschel's argument for the essential differences between poetic inspiration and biblical prophecy in Heschel, *Prophets*, 2:147–69. In brief, they are that, first, whereas poetic inspiration seems to come from an unknown or ineffable source, the prophet knows exactly "Who confronts him" and is unequivocal about the source being YHWH (Heschel, *Prophets*, 168). Second, while the poet assumes a passive role under

ment, however, focuses on the literary artifacts Dillard has produced and the features that cause them to function in ways consistent with Martin Buber's conception of the prophetic role and stance. Therefore, the analysis will touch only briefly on Dillard's literary and extra-literary understanding of what might be called her vocation as a poet-prophet. Its primary focus is the rhetorical trope of apostrophe and the ways it functions theologically. Grammar is highly instructive, especially when a particular feature is all-pervasive as is the second-person apostrophic voice for Dillard.

A second disclaimer concerns the use of the terms "prophet" and "prophetic." The Hebrew prophets were not homogenous nor did they speak with one voice. As Kugel notes, "The pictures of prophecy found within the Bible are scarcely harmonious: prophecy in the north was different from prophecy in the south, and prophecy in its incipient stages was apparently quite different from what it became in the eighth and seventh and sixth centuries."[57] Thus, the terms "prophet" and "prophetic" as used here are not meant to gloss over crucial differences or minimize their uniqueness but are used as Buber uses them both in *The Prophetic Faith* and in "Prophecy, Apocalyptic, and the Historical Hour" to express the "prophetic *theologem*"[58]—a general outlook and participatory role available to every person of which the Hebrew prophets are the embodiment and highest expression.[59] Buber explains that "wherever a living historical dialogue of divine and human actions breaks through, there persists, visible or invisible, a bond with the prophecy of Israel."[60]

---

the influence of sudden and unexpected inspiration and simply brings forth unawares the creative artifact, the prophet is fully self-aware and "definitely knows what his utterance implies." He thereby is concerned primarily with the "message rather than the form" (Heschel, *Prophets*, 168). Third, the prophet unlike the poet is aware of a central historical and thematic unity and coherence in his message born out of the sameness of the Source, the God who has spoken to the prophets before him. Finally, and perhaps most importantly, while the poet's experience is that of an impersonal address by an unknown force, the prophet experiences a "staggering awareness" of having been addressed and impinged upon by "a personal Being, of another I; not an idea coming from nowhere or from a nameless source, but always a communication reaching him from the most powerful Subject of all" (Heschel, *Prophets*, 169). Therefore, the prophet, unlike the poet, can say "Thus says the Lord" (Heschel, *Prophets*, 169). The significance of the source of the prophet's inspiration cannot be overstated since it provides the prophet with the very "justification of what he is and for what he does" (Heschel, *Prophets*, 169).

57. Kugel, *Poetry and Prophecy*, 5.
58. Buber, *On the Bible*, 178.
59. Buber, *On the Bible*, 174, 176.
60. Buber, *On the Bible*, 181.

Two distinguishing features of the role and outlook of the *nabi*, as the prophets came to be known, are relevant here. One defining trait is that a primary role of the prophet is to declare, to be an intermediary voice bringing to his hearers what has been revealed through encounters with God and conversely bringing before God the petitions of earth.[61] The prophet's words are not an argument or proof but a witness to the reality of God; they do "unto others what God does unto him. In speaking, the prophet reveals God: . . . in his words, *the invisible God becomes audible.*"[62] Therefore, it is possible to speak of the literary persona Dillard constructs in her texts as functioning in the role of a literary *nabi*, by which it is meant that she is compelled by her vocation as a writer to declare and bear witness to her encounters with God through language that embodies and creates paradox, contradiction, and tension.

Although the primary focus here is on apostrophe and its theological functions rather than on Dillard as poet-prophet, it bears mentioning that not infrequently does Dillard quite literally write herself into the narratives of Hebrew scripture as one of its prophets, an Ezra or Ezekiel, for example. The most numerous and overt examples emerge in *Pilgrim at Tinker Creek*. In the chapter, "Fecundity," Dillard recounts in macabre detail the glut, cannibalism, and patricide of the insect world, ending the section with an account of the clothes moth's molting frenzy induced by starvation; it continues to molt until it sheds itself literally into oblivion, never satiating its hunger. In response, Dillard quotes from Ezra 9:3, crying out "I feel like Ezra: 'And when I heard this thing, I rent my garment and my mantle, and plucked off the hair of my head and of my beard, and sat down astonied.'"[63]

In the final pages of *Pilgrim at Tinker Creek*, Dillard returns to the imagery of Exodus 33, proclaiming that the gaps in the cleft where terror and glory pour down are the "spirit's one home"[64] and urges the readers to live boldly, resisting ferociously the temptation to fritter one's life away with "itsy-bitsy friends and meals and journeys for itsy-bitsy years on end."[65] "I won't have it," she declares.[66] She proceeds to quote from Ezekiel 13:5 in which Ezekiel denounces the false prophets as those who have refused to enter "the gaps" as intermediaries for Israel and then, once again, she begins

61. Buber, *Prophetic Faith*, 2.
62. Heschel, *Prophets*, 22.
63. PTC, 173.
64. PTC, 274.
65. PTC, 274.
66. PTC, 274.

to speak directly to the audience in the second person and imperative mood, uttering a brisk and unwavering series of commands:

> The gaps are the cliffs in the rock where you cower to see the back parts of God . . . Go up into the gaps. . . . Stalk the gaps. . . . Squeak into a gap in the soil, turn, and unlock—more than a maple—a universe. This is how you spend this afternoon, and tomorrow morning, and tomorrow afternoon. *Spend* the afternoon. You can't take it with you.[67]

Clearly, Dillard presents herself here as one of the true rather than false prophets who is not only willing to enter the gap herself but also is willing to declare right action in order to provoke a right response within her audience. The parallelism of the imperative mood verbs, the alliteration and rhyme within the sequence, not to mention the final italicized verb all convey Dillard's exalted prophetic pitch and fervency. Further, the "I" Dillard constructs in her narratives like that of the Hebrew prophet functions in two roles—first, as the recipient of revelation and second, as the prophetic voice compelled to follow the revelation with communication, acting as both receiver of the vision and instigator of one in the reader. In short, she understands her role as an artist to be an intermediary who presents her particular vision of God and the world to her audience, and she often speaks directly to that audience in second person, issuing a prophetic summons to respond.

Both her texts and public comments testify to the seriousness with which she undertakes the "call" as an artist-prophet both to communicate and provoke encounters with the divine through her work. Tellingly, Eudora Welty, in her review of *Pilgrim at Tinker Creek*, observes that Dillard "seems to live in order to declare."[68] In her 1978 interview with Michael Burnett, Dillard emphatically insists that the reader "not turn any attention to me whatsoever" but "turn[69] your attention to God. And if I can set

---

67. PTC, 274.

68. Welty, "Meditation on Seeing," 4. Welty goes on to criticize Dillard's narrative voice for being too other-worldly. She complains that Dillard "is trying to speak to me out of a cloud instead of from a sociable, even answerable, distance on our same earth."

69. The notion of "turning" is central to Buber's I-Thou address. When one is confronted by the address of a *Thou*, the response that leads away from the illusions holding captive an isolated "I" is what Buber describes as a "turning" toward the summoning voice, an act that begins the process of redemption. Buber suggests that when confronted, even the alienated "I," in a moment of naked reflection might really know "the direction of turning, leading through sacrifice" (Buber, *I and Thou*, 70). The final paragraphs of *I and Thou* repeatedly speak of the "movement of turning," the moment of choice that brings theophany ever nearer. From the world's side, this event is "called turning"; from God's side, it is called "redemption" (Buber, *I and Thou*, 120). As this

myself up as a patsy and make you believe it, and it will turn you to God, then I will have done my job, even if I'm wrecking my own damn life in the process."[70] Speaking with Maureen Abood, she explains her understanding of the dedicated artist in almost missiological terms, with the urgent message being for readers—particularly agnostics—to wake up: "I strive toward writing good books, and the aim of those books has always been to address the agnostic intellectual. I want to get him to consider once again that it's not only stupid people who are Christians."[71] In *Pilgrim at Tinker Creek*, she wryly describes her attempts to engage some unsuspecting person with entymological trivia as serious spiritual business: "I am not making chatter; I mean to change his life."[72]

Moreover, various critics and reviewers have with notable consistency likened her narrative stance to that of a zealous preacher[73] or prophet using modifiers such as "fierce," "merciless," "rough" and "relentless" to describe Dillard's tone. Many have made overt comparisons between the Hebrew scriptures and Dillard's concrete, poetical prose style. Heschel's description of the prophet's message and its linguistic features seems particularly apt: "the prophet's use of emotional and imaginative language, concrete in diction, rhythmical in movement, artistic in form, marks his style as poetic," yet it is far from tranquil or poised but "charged with agitation" and brimming with tension arising from the life or death stakes of his message.[74] "The language is luminous and explosive," emphasizes Heschel, "firm and contingent, harsh and compassionate, a fusion of contradictions."[75] Its "images must not shine, they must burn" with the aim of stripping its audience of pretense, excuse and illusion for the sake of salvific truth.[76] This sometimes requires words designed "to shock rather than to edify."[77]

Reviewers use language uncannily like Heschel's when describing Dillard's style and purpose. Mark Cladis calls Dillard a "stone-thrower with

---

chapter will seek to demonstrate, for both Dillard and Buber the second-person address can effect a turn within a hearer toward the summoning voice and precipitate a potentially redemptive moment.

70. Burnett, "Interview," 90.
71. Abood, "Natural Wonders," 32.
72. PTC, 134.
73. See Krauth, "Diving into Life." Krauth asserts that Dillard "preaches that you've got to live so fully that you feel constantly like you're standing under the rush of a freezing waterfall, every cell alive."
74. Heschel, *Prophets*, 6.
75. Heschel, *Prophets*, 7.
76. Heschel, *Prophets*, 7.
77. Heschel, *Prophets*, 7.

expert aim" who hurls images at the audience in order "to wake us up to the silence and hum and complexity that surround us."[78] Abood notes that Dillard's writing "demands something from the reader—to be woken up, challenged, and asked to look closely at something that might be repulsive."[79] Reviewer Michael Farrell identifies Dillard as an artist who "urges us not to turn away" from life's hard truths and who says "Here, let me show you. . . . Relentlessly."[80] Terri Brown-Davidson warns "She is fierce," calling Dillard "one of the most fearless writers I have ever read."[81] Peggy Rosenthal claims a distinguishing feature of Dillard's career is "finding just the right image to shock us"[82] and in her review of *For the Time Being* states, "I've never read anything, with the exception of parts of the Bible, that gives me more a sense of how earth and human life on it might look from the viewpoint of God."[83] Melvin Maddocks, reviewing *Pilgrim at Tinker Creek*, likewise draws comparisons between Dillard's work and the Hebrew Bible: "Miss Dillard mercilessly brings on bridge-battering floods and hemlock-bending whirlwinds. Here is not only a habitat of cruelty and 'the waste of pain' but the savage and magnificent world of the Old Testament presided over by a passionate Jehovah, with no Messiah in sight . . . a remarkable psalm of terror and celebration."[84] Virginia Stem Owens links Dillard's "fierce voice" to a prophet's calling: "Vocations are like that. Remember Moses? Remember Jeremiah?"[85] The language of her novels, too, possess the compressed urgency of a prophetic summons. Reviewer Adam Davis remarks in his review of *The Maytrees*: "[It] carries an imperative: Pay attention, be conscious. Readers of Dillard will be familiar with this imperative."[86]

The second distinguishing feature of the *nabi* and his message relevant to the present discussion is his relationship to time. In declaring

78. Cladis, "Stone-Throwers with Excellent Aim," 81.
79. Abood, "Natural Wonders," 30.
80. Farrell, "Annie Dillard Demands," 29.
81. Brown-Davidson, "Choosing the Given," 1.
82. Rosenthal, "God's Eye View," 30.
83. Rosenthal, "God's Eye View," 29.
84. Maddocks, "Terror and Celebration," 92.

85. Owens, "Truth through Testimony," 23. Dillard also uses and adopts the role of Levitical priest most notably in the final chapter of *Pilgrim at Tinker Creek* and the role of nun at the end of *Holy the Firm*. In all three functions—prophet, priest, and nun—Dillard casts herself as the intermediary or intercessor, a role she envisions for the dedicated artist. She explains to Karla Hammond, "I suppose I use priest and nun as a substitute for the figure of the artist. It's the dedicated life." See Hammond, "Drawing the Curtains."

86. Davis, "Sharing the Love," 56.

truths meant to provoke a wholly free response from its hearers, the *nabi* affirms that "the future is not fixed, for God wants man to come to Him with full freedom" and thus he affords humans a real say in shaping the future.[87] As Buber explains, though the current historical crisis directs the prophet's gaze to the future, "the connection between the *nabi* and the future is not that of one who predicts. To be a *nabi* means to set the audience, to whom the words are addressed, before the choice and decision, directly or indirectly. The future is not something already fixed in this present hour, it is dependent upon the real decision, that is to say the decision in which man takes part in this hour."[88] Buber is adamant that the hour for responding to the prophetic summons is now: "The time the prophetic voice calls us to take part in is the time of the actual decision."[89] This "now" feature is one of the most distinctive traits of the prophetic *theologem*. Although the prophetic summons within the Hebrew Bible arise from and are directed to the historical hour to which they first came, because that summons is recorded in a literary artifact, it continues to be a timeless invocation that calls out even yet.

Significantly, the apostrophic voice creates a timelessness or a "timeless present."[90] Jonathan Culler illustrates with the following example:

> If one brings together in a poem a boy, some birds, a few blessed creatures, and some mountains, meadows, hills and groves, one tends to place them in a narrative where one thing leads to another; the events which form ask to be temporally located; . . . But if one puts into a poem *thou shepherd boy, ye blessed creatures, ye birds,* they are immediately associated with what might be called a timeless present but is better seen as a temporality of writing. Even if the birds were only glimpsed once in the past, to apostrophize them as 'ye birds' is to locate them in the time of the apostrophe—a special temporality *which is the set of all moments at which writing can say 'now.'*[91]

Another significant aspect of the prophetic discourse of the Hebrew prophets is its emphasis on aural rather than visual perception. Because God's face is absent or averted, the "God of the prophets is not often the object of prosopopoeia."[92] This absence "throws all the more emphasis

87. Buber, *On the Bible*, 178.
88. Buber, *Prophetic Faith*, 2–3.
89. Buber, *On the Bible*, 180.
90. Culler, *Pursuit of Signs*, 149.
91. Culler, *Pursuit of Signs*, 149 (emphasis mine).
92. Balfour, *Rhetoric of Romantic Prophecy*, 67.

on the voice of God, as a sensible but invisible presence."[93] Obviously, all readers have in Dillard's case is her persona's voice, an invisible but conspicuous presence who makes itself impossible to forget because it directly addresses the reader.

The Prophetic Voice: An Apostrophic Summons

The contention here is that Dillard's literary voice achieves its prophetic edge in part through its all-pervasive, apostrophic voice. It is difficult to overstate Dillard's use of the vocative. The second-person address can be found on nearly every page of Dillard's corpus. A brief overview of works not featured in this chapter's analysis serves to illustrate the extensiveness of its use. In her collection of poems, *Tickets for a Prayer Wheel*, all but four of twenty-four poems include second-person addresses, most to an extradiegetic *you* as in this example from "The Man Who Wishes to Feed on Mahogany": "Is he sympathetic? Do you care? / And you, sir: perhaps you wish to feed / on your bright-eyed daughter, on your baseball glove / on your outboard motor's pattern in the water. / Some love weights your walking in the world; / some love molds you heavier than air."[94] In *Teaching A Stone to Talk*, only three of the fourteen essays do *not* include second person. In *Living By Fiction*, Dillard speaks to and even jokes directly with the reader: "As a reader, however, you may easily omit to worry about any of this [writers' concerns about internal, narrative structures] . . . You may enjoy the story in the light of its actual sense. (I trust you did not greatly enjoy my account of the sense alone.)"[95] In *The Writing Life*, Dillard calls readers to their unique vocation in the second person: "Why do you never find anything written about that idiosyncratic thought you advert to, about your fascination with something no one else understands? Because it is up to you."[96] Remarkably, even her autobiography, *An American Childhood*, slips frequently into second-person narration. For example, the chapter on rock collecting, written in part like a "how-to" manual, uses *you* in manifold rhetorical modes. Dillard's tone is especially energetic, and the referent for *you* is the intradiegetic young Annie Dillard ("You subjected your rocks to scratch tests"), as well as the adult Annie Dillard and the extradiegetic reader ("When you pry open the landscape, you find wonders").[97] Through

93. Balfour, *Rhetoric of Romantic Prophecy*, 67.
94. TST, 40–41.
95. LBF, 157.
96. TWL, 67.
97. AAC, 137, 143.

the second-person narrative stance Dillard directly addresses readers with the aim of pointing them both to God and to the world with the prophetic challenge to see and respond in the present hour.

Numerous modalities exist for the use of *you* in narrative non-fiction as well as in poetry and fiction. Bruce Morrissette's analysis, "Narrative 'You' in Contemporary Literature," provides a helpful historical survey and rough taxonomy of narrative and non-narrative uses of *you*, the nomenclature of which will be used throughout this discussion. These modalities include the implied *you* in the imperative mood; an oratorical *you* used in the direct address of an audience; a generalized *you* used when describing a "*typical* event or one so characteristic of a given situation that the reader can well imagine its appropriateness"[98]; conversational modalities of *you* that, like the editorial "we," are employed to avoid the excessive use of "I" and the potential egotism or self-indulgence its overuse might imply; and an editorial *you*, wherein the speaker directs his or her address to readers in order to involve the reader in the scene, "particularly when an evaluative judgment is to be provoked."[99]

In both non-narrative discourse (by which Morrissette means non-fiction and lyrical poetry) as well as in the novel or short story, *you* can have rhetorical overtones of "generalizing, moralizing, or axiomizing."[100] Well-known features of the rhetoric of prophecy are its moralizing and axiomizing tone and purpose. Heschel explains that the prophet's theme is often "exhortation, not prediction," and his message is inherently ethical: "Above all, the prophets remind us of the moral state of a people: Few are guilty, but all are responsible."[101] Dillard's apostrophic voice often functions in similar ways. As her extra-literary comments in interviews indicate, the life of the dedicated artist is a life of sacrifice, and her purpose is to obscure her own hand and direct the reader's gaze to God, his creatures, and creation. She attempts to involve readers in this inherently ethical endeavor by shaking them out of the lethargy of custom and awakening them to the summons of an eternal *Thou* through second-person direct address.

---

98. Morrissette, "Narrative 'You,'" 4.

99. Morrissette, "Narrative 'You,'" 6.

100. Morrissette, "Narrative 'You,'" 12. See, for example, Morrissette's analysis of Hemingway's use of *you* in *Farewell to Arms*. A shift to *you* in the midst of a first-person narrative "suddenly generalizes the situation and constitutes almost a maxim of behavior, guiding the reader to prepare, as it were, for an identical or similar event: '*I* went out swiftly, all of myself, and I knew *I* was dead and that it had all been a mistake to think *you* just died. Then *I* floated.'" (Morrissette, "Narrative 'You,'" 9).

101. Heschel, *Prophets*, 12, 16.

Two theoretical views are helpful for understanding how Dillard's use of the apostrophic voice engages readers in a prophetic dialogue. Jonathan Culler's well-known deconstructivist view provides useful theoretical tools to explain how the grammar of apostrophe functions. Richard Gerrig's speech-act theory proves useful for explaining readers' roles and experiences of apostrophe,[102] features that Culler mentions but does not explore. Furthermore, Culler and Gerrig share common ground in their conclusions about the fundamental features of apostrophe of concern here, namely that the apostrophe or second-person narration sets in motion complex relationships between a text and its readers, and these relationships are at the very least triadic, constructing connections between the speaker, the subject being addressed, and the reading audience.[103] Gerrig identifies these as speaker, addressee, and "side-participant."[104] The speaker is the persona making the address, the addressee is the intended subject of address, and the side-participant is the reader who is listening alongside but is an intended hearer, thus a participant in the communication event.[105] In second-person narration, the *you* who is the addressee can be intra-or extradiegetic, "existing" within the narrative world or outside it. What is remarkable about Dillard's style is how frequently she summons an *extra*diegetic *you*, namely the imagined reader, through direct address in various modalities. Brief examples from *Holy the Firm* and *For the Time Being* will suffice to illustrate the ways this narrative mode often functions prophetically.

The third and final section of *Holy the Firm* includes what might be called an artist's manifesto. Dillard begins the section asking, "How can people think that artists seek a name? A name, like a face, is something you have when you're not alone. There is no such thing as an artist: there is only the world, lit or unlit as the light allows."[106] In charged language reminiscent of prophetic discourse Dillard asserts, "But the world without light is

---

102. Gerrig does not call the trope "apostrophe" but uses several examples that reveal he includes it under the general heading of his "informative analysis of narrative utterances" (Gerrig, *Experiencing Narrative Worlds*, 110). He quotes examples of apostrophic addresses found in Keats, Milton, and Shakespeare to illustrate the ways readers are intentionally included as side-participants or excluded as overhearers of apostrophic addresses. See Gerrig, *Experiencing Narrative Worlds*, 111.

103. "The vocative posits a relationship between two subjects even if the sentence denies the animicity of what is addressed" (Culler, *Pursuit of Signs*, 141). Culler goes on to clarify that this dualistic structure fails to account for the fact that there is a third party—the audience of the text (Culler, *Pursuit of Signs*, 141).

104. Gerrig, *Experiencing Narrative Worlds*, 103–10.

105. Gerrig, *Experiencing Narrative Worlds*, 106.

106. HTF, 71–72.

wasteland and chaos, and a life without sacrifice is abomination."[107] What follows is a full paragraph of rhetorical questions making the point that artists, indeed all persons, are called to illuminate the "wasteland and chaos" of life's dark landscapes by offering sacrificially "the short string" of their own lives, "in flawed imitation of Christ."[108] Throughout this passage, the reader remains a side-hearer. Though Dillard asks questions, they are rhetorical and directed to no one in particular.

Immediately following erupts a paragraph of ecstatic praise. Midway through, though, Dillard turns abruptly to the readers:

> Ladies and gentlemen! You are given insects, and birdsong, and a replenishing series of clouds. The air is buoyant and wholly transparent, scoured by grasses. The earth struck through it is noisome, lighted, and salt. Who shall ascend into the hill of the Lord? Or who shall stand in his holy place? "Whom shall I send," heard the first Isaiah, "and who will go for us?" And poor Isaiah, who happened to be standing there—and there was no one else—burst out, "Here am I; send me."[109]

When read in light of the previous paragraphs' charge to offer oneself up sacrificially, the prophetic nature of this emphatic apostrophic address seems clear. Dillard has just declared that a life without sacrifice is an abomination and depicted how narrow and costly will be the path to giving the world light and meaning. Getting readers to understand this requires an abrupt wrench from their role as a side-hearer, listening askance to Dillard's rhetorical questions, to that of addressee suddenly being spoken to in an exclamatory, apostrophic address ("Ladies and gentlemen! You are given"). As Richardson notes, "Addresses to the reader carry a certain defamiliarizing charge not just because they expose a text's artificiality, but because they jostle readers out of their accustomed 'side-participant' position to become, momentarily, what Volosinov calls the 'heroes' of apostrophic invocations."[110] Dillard then immediately confronts readers with the terrifying apostrophic addresses in Psalm 24 and asked of the prophet Isaiah: Whom shall ascend? Whom shall I send?[111] Thus, the arresting prophetic

---

107. HTF, 72.
108. HTF, 72.
109. HTF, 73.
110. Richardson, "Apostrophe," 372.
111. Dillard is quoting Psalms and Isaiah: "Who shall ascend into the hill of the Lord? or who shall stand in his holy place?" (Ps 24:3); "Also I heard the voice of the Lord, saying, 'Whom shall I send, and who will go for us?' Then said I, 'Here am I; send me'" (Isa 6:8).

call from, what in Levinasian terms, might be described as the Other comes directly to the reader. As the context of Julie Norwich's inexplicable suffering is no doubt meant to prompt readers to ask, when *your* neighbor is suffering unspeakably will you answer "Here am I; send me"?

Because apostrophe posits what might be described as a social relationship in its triadic configuration of speaker, addressee, and side-participant, that relationship conceivably becomes much more potent when the positions of addressee and side-participant are conflated, as they are when Dillard moves abruptly into second-person narration, moving as it were into readers' personal space through an extradiegetic leap into their world outside the text. A radical shift in narrative perspective, as well as power, has now occurred, for as Matt DelConte notes, "second-person narrative by definition is a point of reception, not a point of seeing or speaking."[112] In this case, the point of reception is a flesh-and-blood reader external to the text who now has in his or her possession the power to answer a direct, inherently ethical question. The rhetorical overtones are unmistakably moralizing and axiomizing. Through an apostrophic address Dillard, like the Hebrew prophets, sets before the audience the choice between abomination and sacrifice.

In what ways could this passage be said to function prophetically and what might be the theological implications of its doing so? Dillard's move to address and present questions to an imagined but real reader external to the text means that these questions potentially move into what Buber calls the present hour, and their setting forth a choice means that, in Buber's terms, "the future is not something already fixed in this present hour, it is dependent upon the real decision, that is to say the decision in which man takes part in this hour."[113] Thus, Heschel's description of the relationship between the prophet and addressee is particularly apt in Dillard's case: "prophecy is never complete in itself; it is a burden, a tension, a call."[114] Because Dillard's invocation brings readers into a "timeless present," her calling is an open and conceivably endless rather than closed and finite endeavor that, moreover, invokes a response since it is directed to an extradiegetic reader. Thus, Dillard's apostrophization of the audience in the final pages of *Holy the Firm* generates unique rhetorical power by conflating the roles of addressee and side-hearer, and this allows moral questions to be put squarely before a reader. The asking itself, the urging toward gratitude and sacrifice, presupposes a future in which the readers' choices will make a difference. This is not to suggest Dillard is prophesying

---

112. DelConte, "Why *You* Can't Speak," 208.
113. Buber, *Prophetic Faith*, 2–3.
114. Heschel, *Prophets*, 361.

in the theological sense either as a poet or prophet; it is suggesting, however, that the second-person address causes the text to *function* prophetically in its imaginative anticipation of an open-ended future, its consequent suspension of an ending, and its shifting of power to the receiver, the addressee, to choose his or her path. In short, whether the "Ladies and Gentlemen!" Dillard addresses choose sacrifice or self-indulgence *is* a moral issue, and the outcome is up to the hearer alone.

Two final examples from *For the Time Being* are especially emphatic and rhetorically charged, as seems fitting in Dillard's most grim and fragmented work where questions about life and death, moral and physical evil seem particularly urgent. Ray Kelleher opens his review of *For the Time Being* by warning readers that Dillard begins *For the Time Being* "roughly by shoving our faces in . . . horrendous cruelty" and though there are graces in the book, they are "edgy graces," emerging tentatively from the rubble of heart-rending suffering.[115] This sense of Dillard's mercilessness toward the reader is the rhetorical effect not only of the grim subject matter with which the book begins (children born with birth defects), but it is also the effect of the concentrated presence of second-person, direct address of the reader that for the first four pages relentlessly confronts readers with a series of questions.

For the Time Being begins with a frank, unsentimental description of children identified as "bird-headed dwarfs" in *Smith's Recognizable Patterns of Human Malformation*. The reader immediately discovers he or she will be no casual overhearer of Dillard's narrative. In the first paragraph, Dillard moves into second-person direct address and confides to an extradiegtic reader that the book is a "volume to which, in conscience, I cannot recommend your prolonged attention."[116] Yet Dillard soon forces the reader to examine the pages of Smith's book with her. By the fifth paragraph the narrative shifts to an editorial *you* meant to compel the reader's inner eye to see what Dillard sees on the page:

> The stunning thing is the doctor's hand, which you notice at third glance: It shows the children in scale. The doctor's hand props the boy up by cupping his shoulders—both his shoulders—from behind. The six-year old's back, no longer than the doctor's open hand, is only slightly wider than a deck of cards. The children's faces are the length of the doctor's thumb.[117]

---

115. Kelleher, "In the Face of Brutality," 58.
116. FTB, 3.
117. FTB, 4–5.

Then follows a series of disturbing images and questions aimed at forcing readers to personalize an issue Dillard knows they would rather not:

> And [the bird-headed dwarfs are described as] friendly and pleasant, but easily distracted. There is a lot to be said for children who are friendly and pleasant. And you—are you easily distracted yourself, these days?
>
> If your child were a bird-headed dwarf, mentally deficient, you could carry him everywhere. The bird-headed dwarfs and all the babies in Smith's manual have souls, and they all can—and do—receive love and give love. If you gave birth to two bird-headed dwarfs, as these children's mother did—a boy and a girl—you could carry them both everywhere, all their lives, in your arms or in a basket, and they would never leave you, not even to go to college.[118]

This passage makes a number of sophisticated rhetorical moves with theological implications. Dillard's stark description of the physical deformities, mental capacities, and inconceivable smallness of the children is crafted to appall the reader and heighten a sense of their otherness. However, Dillard swiftly moves to humanize the children by including the heart-breaking fact that they are "friendly and pleasant but easily distracted."[119] When this is followed by the question aimed squarely at an apostrophized reader, "And you—are you easily distracted yourself, these days?", she forces the reader to consider the deformed children's apparent deficiencies in the light of his or her own human frailties. It is the rare reader who could claim not to be easily distracted these days. The first *you*, appearing in a clipped opening phrase, creates an abrupt, emphatic address of the reader: "And *you*—are *you* easily distracted *yourself*, these days?" The repetition of the pronoun *you* and the shift to the reflexive pronoun, *yourself*, reinforce the address, in case readers have any doubts as to whom Dillard is confronting. The interrogative sentence places before readers a question that requires them to turn inward and assess their own distractibility. The apostrophe is the very means, therefore, by which Dillard engages readers in self-reflection about their current state (as "these days" underscores), preparing them to reassess their initial responses to her description of the bird-headed dwarfs. Thus, through the second-person address Dillard precipitates an ethical internal shift in readers as they are forced to consider that these children are perhaps not so different from themselves after all. The differences, Dillard seems to suggest, are a matter not of kind but of degrees of physical and cognitive brokenness.

118. FTB, 4–5.
119. FTB, 5.

This is made even clearer by the following paragraph's moral claim that these children too have souls and are able to love and be loved.

The subsequent paragraph's use of apostrophic voice presses the issue even closer to home, making the bird-headed dwarf "your child" and putting the deformed child figuratively in the reader's arms ("you could carry him everywhere"). Furthermore, Dillard's augmentation of numbers in parallel sentences augments pity. The first sentence, "If your child were a bird-headed dwarf, . . . you could carry," appears nearly verbatim in the third sentence, but this time the reader is forced to imagine having two such children: "If you gave birth to two bird-headed dwarfs, . . . you could carry them both."[120] In the first sentence, the second person challenges the reader to imagine giving birth to and carrying *one* deformed child; the second asks her to imagine giving birth to *two*, as the mother of the boy and girl exhibited has done. In short, apostrophizing the audience has the rhetorical and theological effect of engaging the reader's sympathetic imagination, so they do not merely feel pity for an unfortunate other but momentarily *become* the one pitied—the tiny, easily distracted child, or the parent of such a child. In so doing, the text potentially engenders an inherently ethical imaginative act. The second-person narrative mode places the reader in the role of an addressee who is the receiver of a prophetic summons to look at life's inexplicable cruelties with the same intimacy as if one—or two—of these children were in his or her very arms.

As rough, and perhaps even coercive or emotionally manipulative, as the apostrophic voice may seem in this passage, it could be argued that the text's vocative call to enter in the present hour into another's suffering causes it to function prophetically. Buber, in the chapter "The God of the Sufferers," in *The Prophetic Faith* identifies in his analysis of Jeremiah a subtle but in many ways far more dangerous false god than Baal. It is the "wish-deity" humans construct and call God because they do not want to hear a hard truth that confounds human psychology and reason.[121] The true God "leaves to man the choice of opening his heart to the hard truth or of accepting the easy fraud as truth."[122] Yet it is this same God whose incomprehensibility "is mitigated and even compensated by His becoming the God of the sufferers and even by suffering becoming a door of approach to Him. . . . Between God and suffering a mysterious connection is opened."[123] In the same way, Dillard refuses to construct a "wish-deity" by trivializing life's cruelties.

120. FTB, 5.
121. Buber, *Prophetic Faith*, 179.
122. Buber, *Prophetic Faith*, 177.
123. Buber, *Prophetic Faith*, 183.

Instead, as Kelleher notes, she "uses the blackest turns of phrase to smash through our stubborn tendency to sentimentalize death and domesticate God."[124] The apostrophic voice challenges readers, in this case, to carry another person's suffering in his or her arms, and in so doing open themselves to a hard truth: God has endowed these bird-headed dwarfs with souls. Dillard's prophetic task is not to explain, only to bear witness—and to provoke readers to notice as well.

A second example from the "Numbers" sections found in chapters 2 and 4 of *For the Time Being* is especially illustrative of the ways *you* frequently axiomizes in Dillard's work. In chapter 2's section "Numbers," Dillard tells the reader that on April 30, 1991, in one afternoon 138,000 people drowned in Bangladesh when a tsunami made landfall.[125] She casually remarks at dinner to her seven-year old daughter how difficult it is to imagine so many people dying in one event. "No, it's easy," [her daughter] said. "Lots and lots of dots, in blue water."[126] Dillard goes on to recount staggering figures about the number of dead there are on earth, the larger point being how transient and brief human life is and how, despite all the rhetoric about the preciousness of a single human life, it is difficult to feel its value in the face of such numbers. Dillard returns to the narrative of the April 30, 1991, tsunami in chapter 4, also in "Numbers," this time with the reader in her sights. The six-paragraph section has a symmetrical structure, beginning and ending with paragraphs written in the second person.[127] The paragraphs apostrophizing the reader are book-ends to the sense and structure of the section:

> What were you doing on April 30, 1991, when a series of waves drowned 138,000 people? Where were you when you first heard the astounding, heart-breaking news? Who told you? What, seriatim, were your sensations? Who did you tell? Did your anguish last days or weeks? . . . It took only a few typhoon waves to drown 138,000 Bangladeshi on April 30, 1991. We see generations of waves rise from the sea that made them, billions of individuals at a time; we see them dwindle and vanish back. What will move you to pity?[128]

---

124. Kelleher, "In the Face of Brutality," 58.
125. FTB, 48.
126. FTB, 48.
127. The second and third paragraphs are in first person, the fourth and fifth paragraphs are in the third person, so the narrative point of view is sequenced symmetrically as second, first, first, third, third, second person.
128. FTB, 107–9.

The relentless series of *you* questions in the opening paragraph are literally an interrogation, a series of interrogatives in which the reader is the addressee and is being asked to give an account of who, where, when, and what was done and felt, "seriatim," which, interestingly, has legal connotations. The first paragraph's final question is leading in that it presupposes the reader felt anguish. If the reader even knew about the tsunami when it happened, anguish is an unlikely first response (as Dillard's daughter's response makes clear). In that case, the question exposes the fact that readers are guilty of indifference or at best compassion fatigue—a common effect, Dillard notes, of such numbers.[129] The final paragraph concludes with another loaded interrogative: "What will move you to pity?" The sentence begs the question in that it presupposes these numbers have *not* provoked pity, so Dillard can therefore ask the reader what in heaven's name *will*?[130] The clear rhetorical intent of the apostrophic *you* in the interrogative sentences throughout this section is to involve and perhaps even implicate the extradiegetic reader to moral effect. In so doing, the section adopts a prophetic stance from which simultaneously to ask and to axiomize. The interrogatives put before the reader open-ended questions requiring a response while also presupposing the axioms (anguish and pity) by which a response or lack thereof is implicitly being judged.

The prophetic stance explored in the preceding section and the prophetic voice, manifested as an apostrophic address most frequently of an imagined reader external to the text, work in concert to enable Dillard to function as what one might call a literary *nabi* who declares and bears witness to hard truths that often engender a potentially redemptive theological moment. The provocations serve to challenge, disturb, and exhort readers by removing them from the "side-participant" role and making them instead an addressee from whom a response is required in the "now" of apostrophic time. The shift of focus, and thereby of power, from speaker to recipient that is effected by second-person narration puts squarely before the hearer the creaturely freedom Buber identifies as central to the prophetic *theologem*:

129. "The paleontologist suffered, he said, the sense of being 'an atom lost in the universe.' Individuals blur. Journalists use the term 'compassion fatigue.' What Ernest Becker called the denial of death is a kind of reality fatigue. Do you suffer this? At what number do other individuals blur for me?" (FTB, 131)

130. Dillard's handwritten marginal notes in the publisher's proofs of this paragraph reveal she knows full well that the subject matter and relentless use of direct address is likely to provoke readers. Her editor at Alfred Knopf has corrected her grammar in the sentence, "Who did you tell?," changing "Who" to "Whom." Dillard fires back, "Of course I know it's whom. I decided this paragraph was already making the reader angry, slightly, and a 'whom' would push him all the way to rage" (Dillard, *Annie Dillard Papers*).

"This work of [God's] can itself will, can itself either do or not do; with this doing and not-doing that it wills, it touches on the work of the Worker."[131] Insofar as Dillard's apostrophic summons invite readers to be active participants in the theological and ethical work of the text by engaging them in a textual, dialogical relationship to which there is no fixed ending, they could be said to embody a prophetic stance and voice.

Tikkun, Memory, and Mysticism Turned *Ethos*

Lingering at the corners of this discussion is the question of the relationship of theology to ethics. Dillard gives voice to the question in the "Author's Note" at the beginning of *For the Time Being*: "Given things as they are, how should one individual live?"[132] In other words, if this is the way God is and the world is, what are the ethical implications? To frame the question in light of this chapter's examination of the eternally suspended Christ, if one's existential experience of God is not the resurrected but the eternally crucified Christ, what—and whose—power redeems a broken world? In terms of the prophetic voice, the question might be asked, to what kind of life is the prophetic summons calling its hearers? The answer to these questions is found in Dillard's appeals to the Jewish mystical notion of *tikkun* in which one finds a consummating doctrine for the ethical tenor of the whole of Dillard's work and thought.

In Jewish history, Luria's conception of "the *tikkun* represents the complete fusion between Jewish mysticism and Jewish ethics" in that Luria connected mundane life and the "seemingly endless demands" of Jewish law and ethics to the cosmic battle between good and evil; every faithful act or fulfilled commandment weakened the power of evil and hastened "the terrestrial redemption and the celestial correction."[133] Martin Buber's antipathy toward the cloistered gnosis and magicizing of Kabbalistic thought that attempted to "get 'behind' the problematic" rather than endure and sustain "life's contradictions," however, causes him to attribute the full flowering of mystical ethics to the Hasidim.[134] He, too, sees a fusion of mysticism and theology as occurring through a revitalization of an "old-new *principle*: the principle of the responsibility of man for God's fate in the world."[135] In Hasidism's sacralizing of the whole of life by seeing each moment as a potential

---

131. Buber, *On the Bible*, 176.
132. FTB, x.
133. Dan, *Jewish Mysticism and Jewish Ethics*, 98–99.
134. Buber, *Origin and Meaning*, 179.
135. Buber, *Origin and Meaning*, 117.

meeting between God and man, it removes theology and ethics from their narrowly defined religious domain and revitalizes them both.[136] In his essay, "Love of God and Love of Neighbor" in *Hasidism and Modern Man*, Buber explains ethics in Hasidic thought:

> The "ethical" is now no longer an affair between men authorized and sanctioned by the religious authority, but it is, no less than the religious in the narrower sense, an affair between man and God. . . . The isolated religious element has disappeared here even as the isolated ethical one. . . . One cannot, says Hasidism, have to do essentially with God if one does not have to do essentially with men.[137]

This leads Buber to conclude that "In Hasidism—and in it alone, so far as I can see, in the history of the human spirit—mysticism has become *ethos*."[138]

Although Dillard alludes to Hasidic and Lurianic notions of *tikkun* in her earliest works, in *For the Time Being* she appeals specifically to the idea to suggest that each individual is responsible to act redemptively *within* life's manifold absurdities rather than project their mending imaginatively into an apocalyptic future wherein all will be well. Dillard's apostrophic voice and body of work as a whole invites readers to participate in *tikkun's* radical summons whereby, as Scholem explains, "every Jew [is raised] to the rank of a protagonist in the great process of restitution."[139] In so doing, she creates what might be called a literary *shema*, calling readers to hallow and redeem the world by participating in what Buber calls the "infinite ethos of the moment."[140]

The doctrine of *tikkun* is introduced early in *For the Time Being*, first in the section "Israel" of chapter 2 and again in "Evil" of chapter 5.[141] Quoting

136. Buber, *Origin and Meaning*, 124–25.
137. Buber, *Hasidism and Modern Man*, 232–33.
138. Buber, *Origin and Meaning*, 198–99.
139. Scholem, *Major Trends*, 284. In *On the Kabbalah*, Scholem makes the fascinating observation that in Lurianic thought, "fundamentally every man and especially every Jew participates in the process of *tikkun*. This enables us to understand why in Kabbalistic myth the Messiah becomes a mere symbol. . . . To Luria the coming of the Messiah means no more than a signature *under a document that we ourselves write*" (Scholem, *On the Kabbalah*, 117 [emphasis mine]).
140. Buber, *Origin and Meaning*, 117.
141. Dillard introduces readers to the history of the expulsion of the Jews from Spain in 1492. Quoting Gershom Scholem, she explains the link in Jewish mystical thought between the historical exile of Israel and the exiled Shekinah of God: "Only redemption—restoration, *tikkun*—can return the sparks of light to their source in the primeval soul; only redemption can restore God's exiled presence to his being in eternity. Only redemption can reunite an exiled soul with its root. The holy person, however, can hasten redemption and help mend heaven and earth" (FTB, 51–52).

Hasidic Rabbi Yehuda Aryeh Leib Alter of Ger, Dillard identifies the task of redemption as "the specific mission of the Jew to free the entrapped holy sparks" through prayer and Torah study.[142] In the following section, "Now," she broadens the responsibility for *tikkun* to all of human kind by directly addressing the reader in the imperative mood: "This is the human task: to direct and channel the sparks' return. This is *tikkun*, restoration. Yours is a holy work on earth right now, [the Hasids] say, whatever that work is, if you tie your love and desire to God. You do not deny or flee the world, but redeem it, all of it—just as it is."[143]

The book's final chapter includes the most extensive treatment of the theme of redemption, and again Dillard expands the notion of *tikkun* to include the ethical responsibility every person, not just the Jew, has to mend the world's brokenness. In "Evil," Dillard speaks of *tikkun* within a context that suggests more fully its ethical and theological implications. After narrating the harrowing story of a lost Jewish girl, Suri Feldman, being safely found and returned to her parents after hundreds of Hasidic Jews and local emergency personnel searched through the night for her, Dillard quotes Rabbi Lawrence Kushner: "God does not have hands, we do. Our hands are God's. It is up to us, what God will see and hear, up to us, what God will do."[144] In the subsequent section, "Now," Dillard paraphrases Abraham Heschel's claim that if God is to be immanent, it is up to human beings to make him so: "God needs man; kenotically or not, he places himself in our hands."[145] The text then shifts into an apostrophic voice through which the reader moves from being a side-participant to an addressee of the ethical commission Dillard is about to deliver: "You cannot mend the chromosome,

142. FTB, 139.

143. FTB, 141. This passage synthesizes ideas from two of Buber's works and quotes from *Tales of the Hasidim*. Buber explains the Hasidic understanding of redemption: "It is incumbent upon man to do all that he does with his intention directed to the unification of the highest divine being with its Shekina [sic], which dwells in the world. But nowhere here, in contrast to all ascetic teaching that strives to surmount reality, is it intimated that the indwelling principle would draw itself out of the world; rather the unification of the separated means just the unification of God with the world, which continues to exist as world, only that it is now, just as world, redeemed" (Buber, *Origin and Meaning*, 85). Dillard's final phrase, "just as it is," comes from Buber's introduction to *Tales of the Hasidim*: "The world in which you live, just as it is and not otherwise, affords you that association with God, which will redeem you and whatever divine aspect of the world you have been entrusted with" (Buber, *Tales of the Hasidim*, 4).

144. FTB, 196.

145. FTB, 200. See Heschel's *Man is Not Alone*: "God is in need of man for the attainment of His ends, and religion, as Jewish tradition understands it, is a way of serving these ends, of which we are in need, even though we may not be aware of them, ends which we must learn to feel the need of" (Heschel, *Man is Not Alone*, 241).

quell the earthquake or stanch the flood. You cannot atone for dead tyrants' murders, and you alone cannot stop living tyrants."[146] "You cannot" is an emphatic, phonetically hard directive. By repeating it, Dillard unequivocally delimits the scope of human power. The miraculous is out of hand for humans, as well as, it seems, for God. If so, what is one to do in response to moral and physical evil? Dillard's calls upon Martin Buber to answer, quoting from *Tales of the Hasidim*:

> As Martin Buber saw it—writing at his best near the turn of the last century—the world of ordinary days "affords" us that precise association with God that redeems both us and our speck of world. God entrusts and allots to everyone an area to redeem: this creased and feeble life, "the world in which you live, just as it is and not otherwise."[147]

One hears echoes in this call to redemptive action of Buber's prophetic *theologem*; human history is not fixed. God entrusts each person with the responsibility to redeem and hallow life as it comes to him or her in each moment. This requires, asserts Buber, "faith in the *factual* character of human experience, as existence that factually meets transcendence," and so humans can be "a center of surprise in creation. Because and so long as man exists, factual change of direction can take place toward salvation as well as toward disaster, starting from the world in each hour, no matter how late."[148] To return to the question as to what kind of life the prophetic summons is calling its hearers, the answer is to a life that takes seriously the ennobling and terrible reality that a human can, in the decision of the present hour, move his or her world one step closer toward salvation or toward disaster.

With the doctrine of *tikkun* now in view, the ethical import of Dillard's choice to eclipse, and thereby suspend, the resurrection ending to the gospel of Christ takes on an added dimension. If Christ is "always incarnate, and always nailed" then God requires humans to be his hands and feet and entrusts the work of redemption to them.[149] The Christian's hope for redemption therefore cannot be exclusively in the future triumph of good over evil to which the resurrection points but must arise from and be for, as the book's title suggests, the time being. It could be argued, therefore, that

---

146. FTB, 201.

147. FTB, 201. Dillard is quoting for a second time the following lines from Buber's introduction: "The world in which you live, just as it is and not otherwise, affords you that association with God, which will redeem you and whatever divine aspect of the world you have been entrusted with" (Buber, *Tales of the Hasidim*, 4).

148. Buber, *On the Bible*, 178.

149. FTB, 169.

Dillard removes the resurrection from readers' view in order that their gaze might be focused on the present and on its summons to act redemptively in *this* historical hour on behalf of a suffering creation and its creatures. Edmund Fleg whom Dillard quotes in the final chapter of *For the Time Being*, explains that "'For the Jew the world is not completed; people must complete it.'"[150] The Christian might add, as Dillard indeed seems to, that the story of Christ's suffering and its redemption is not yet completed. God has left it up to humans to write in stammering voices redemptive endings to the world's broken narratives.

One final point remains. The allusive theological power of Dillard's work is engendered in part by its refusal to be about ethics and its commitment instead to enact the ethics of attentiveness to God and the world, as well as the spiritual discipline of remembering so central to the ethics of the Hebrew scripture. In short, *tikkun* in Dillard's work begins with noticing and remembering. Jewish writer Cynthia Ozick's essay, "Metaphor and Memory," explains powerfully the literary nature of memory and its ethical entailments. Ozick argues that central to the moral vision of Hebrew scripture is the injunction to remember, which necessitates converting memory into metaphors that furnish the imagination with the cognitive tools necessary for ethical living. Ozick explains that "metaphor relies on what has been experienced before; it transforms the strange into the familiar."[151] Consequently, "Four hundred years of bondage in Egypt, rendered as metaphoric memory, can be spoken in a moment; in a single sentence. What this sentence is, we know; we have built every idea of moral civilization on it. . . . 'Love thy neighbor as thyself.'"[152] Yet Ozick goes on to explain that as exquisitely beautiful in its moral simplicity and profundity as that one sentence is, it is not the pinnacle of metaphor's moral achievement in ancient Israel. Thirty-six times in the Pentateuch Israel is commanded to love the alien and stranger in its midst "for you were aliens in Egypt" (Lev 24:22):

> Bondage becomes a metaphor of pity for the outsider; Egypt becomes the great metaphor of reciprocity. "And a stranger shall you not oppress," says Exodus 23, verse 8, "for you know the heart of a stranger, seeing you were strangers in the land of Egypt." There stands the parable; there stands the sacred metaphor of belonging, one heart to another. Without the metaphor of memory and history, we cannot imagine the life of the Other. We cannot imagine what it is to be someone else. Metaphor is

---

150. FTB, 196.
151. Ozick, *Metaphor and Memory*, 280.
152. Ozick, *Metaphor and Memory*, 278.

the reciprocal agent, the universalizing force; it makes possible the power to envision the stranger's heart.[153]

Ozick concludes, "metaphor . . . is the herald of human pity."[154] One of the most transformative legacies of Hebrew scripture therefore is the conviction that the wellspring of ethical behavior is memory, specifically a metaphorical memory. As the etymology of "metaphor" suggests (*meta*—over or across + *phora*—to carry), an empathetic imagination awakened by the narratives, symbols, and images of the past can transmute memory into ethics that then bear one across to love of God and love of neighbor. Memory is at the heart of the most central prophetic declaration to Jewish faith—the *Shema*. The Mosaic command is found in Deuteronomy 6:4–9 and begins with an apostrophic summons, "Hear, O Israel: The Lord our God, the Lord is one. Love the Lord your God with all your heart and with all your soul and with all your strength." The declaration proceeds to command its hearers to "impress" these commands upon one's heart and one's children's hearts: "Talk about them when you walk along the road, when you lie down and when you get up. Tie them as symbols on your hands and bind them on your foreheads. Write them on the doorframes of your houses and on your gates" (Deut. 6: 5–9). As the *Shema* makes clear, maintaining love of God necessitates first remembering him. The *Shema*'s wisdom about the frailties of human psychology and memory is found in its very pragmatic instructions to "tie," "bind," "write." People do otherwise forget.

So, "write" is precisely what Dillard has done. The ethical dimension of Dillard's work is found not in its allegiance to any particular issue but in its fidelity to noticing and remembering another's suffering through the macro-metaphor that is a work of art. In an interview with Philip Yancey, Dillard identifies the failure to remember as a "pressing spiritual problem."[155] Dillard explains, "To me, the real question is, How in the world can we *remember* God?" She then recounts the story from 2 Kings 22 of King Josiah's rediscovery of the law after generations have passed:

> A whole nation simply forgot God. We think, how can we forget—we who have seen God? Is it right of God to insist we wear strings around our fingers to remember him? This notion of recollection is a pressing spiritual problem—not only how can we remember God, but why does he let us forget? I'm always forgetting God—always, always. That famous prayer "I will in the course of this day forget thee; forget thou not me" is sometimes

---

153. Ozick, *Metaphor and Memory*, 279.
154. Ozick, *Metaphor and Memory*, 274.
155. Yancey, "Face Aflame," 19.

> thought of as a warm Christian joke. I don't think it is so warm. I think that is a lot to ask.[156]

Dillard alludes here to the portion of the *Shema* in Deuteronomy 6:8 when the Israelites are commanded to tie to their hands and foreheads Moses' words as reminders to worship God alone. For Dillard, tying and binding occur through the crafting of narratives, symbols, and images that become her memorial stones, securing to pages fleeting glimpses of life's glory and suffering so that readers might be provoked through metaphor both to pity and praise.

The connection between attentiveness, memory, and ethics, as well as their roots in Hebrew scripture, is not a late-emerging or ancillary theme in Dillard's work. One finds the whole of it in her earliest works, *Tickets for a Prayer Wheel* and *Pilgrim at Tinker Creek*. In "Feast Days," appearing in *Tickets for a Prayer Wheel,* one finds clearly articulated the Christian incarnational analogue to Rabbi Kushner's notion that "God does not have hands, we do. Our hands are God's. It is up to us, what God will see and hear, up to us, what God will do."[157] In Part III of the poem, which begins with a quotation of God's apostrophic address to Joshua in Joshua 5:15, the narrator states, "God empties himself / into the earth like a cloud. / God takes the substance, contours / of a man, and keeps them, / dying, rising, walking, / and still walking / wherever there is motion."[158] The allusion to the pillar of cloud that accompanied the Israelites out of Egypt connects a symbol of God's incarnate presence from the Hebrew Bible to its New Testament counterpart in Christ's incarnation, described in the lines immediately following. Both taken together signify Dillard's conviction that God continues to incarnate himself in all that exists, indeed "wherever there is motion." As a man or woman rises, walks, and dies, so God rises, walks, and dies.[159] In *Pilgrim at Tinker Creek*'s chapter 5, "Untying the Knot," Dillard explains that "Hasidism has a tradition that one of man's purposes is to assist God in the work of redemption by 'hallowing' the things of creation. By a tremendous heave of his spirit the devout man frees the divine sparks trapped in the mute things of time. . . . Keeping the subsoil world under trees in mind, in intelligence, is the *least* I can do."[160] This singleness of mind

---

156. Yancey, "Face Aflame," 19.

157. FTB, 196.

158. TPW, 33–35.

159. Another vivid example is Dillard's parallel declarations in *For the Time Being*: "We are the earth's organs and limbs; we are syllables God utters from his mouth" (FTB, 133).

160. PTC, 96.

holds one's spirit open to incursions of the divine and to claims made upon it by one's neighbors. Hence Dillard identifies it as "part of what Buber calls 'the infinite ethos of the moment.'"[161] She clearly perceives that "keeping" the wonders of creation "in mind" is the most elemental of redemptive actions, and therefore attentiveness is at the heart of ethical living. Holding the world, as it presents itself in the moment, at the center of one's intelligence can become the means of hallowing it.

Remembering is foundational not only for love of God but also love of neighbor.[162] When Christ responds to the question "Of all the commandments, which is the most important?," he quotes from the *Shema*, Deuteronomy 6:4–5 and Leviticus 19:18: "'Hear, O Israel, the Lord our God, the Lord is one. Love the Lord your God with all your heart and with all your soul and with all your mind and with all your strength.' The second is this: 'Love your neighbor as yourself.' There is no commandment greater than these" (Mark 19:29–31). The New Testament's expression of love of neighbor derives from Hebrew scripture's guiding metaphor, "as thyself."[163]

161. PTC, 96. Dillard quotes Buber's *Origin and Meaning of Hasidism*. The context of the phrase clarifies its relationship to the prophetic stance and the ethical choice to act in response to circumstances presented by the current moment. Buber asserts: "Of highest importance [in Hasidism] is not what has been from of old but what again and again happens; and again, not what befalls a man but what he does; and not the extraordinary that he does but the ordinary; and more still than what he does, how he does it. Among all the movements of this type probably none has proclaimed as clearly as Hasidism the infinite ethos of the moment" (Buber, *Origin and Meaning*, 116–17). Thus, every moment of life has latent ethical significance insofar as the choices of ordinary people in ordinary circumstances really do affect the being of God and the outcome of human history. Human responsibility—"not in a conditioned, moral, but in an unconditioned, transcendent sense"—is an ancient idea in Judaism (Buber, *Origin and Meaning*, 117).

162. In Judaism a revolutionary shift merging mystical theology and ethics occurred in Safed in the sixteenth century following the devastating exile of Jews from Spain. Joseph Dan explains that prior to this seismic shift, ethics had been "directed toward the Jewish public as a whole, while mysticism was an esoteric subject, the domain of a close circle of the initiated" (Dan, *Jewish Mysticism and Jewish Ethics*, 76, 79). The most influential mystic in Safed before Isaac Luria, Rabbi Moses Cordovero, formulated perhaps one of the most lucid responses to the question in Jewish ethics not of *what* should one do, but *why*: "Ethical behavior should be adopted and followed not only because God says so, but because God is so; one should conform not only to the divine laws, but to the divine nature. The righteous, thus, is not only an obedient servant of God but an imitator of His essence and therefore a part of the divine system as a whole. Mystical ethics and everyday ethics are fused into one, and the highest achievement of communion with God is attained by following the most mundane and elementary demands of social ethics" (Dan, *Jewish Mysticism and Jewish Ethics*, 86–87). Subsequently, all the esoteric knowledge of the Kabbalah could be employed in the most practical social ethics (Dan, *Jewish Mysticism and Jewish Ethics*, 87).

163. Ozick, *Metaphor and Memory*, 279. What is perhaps more important, Ozick

Because Dillard's work largely recounts her solitary experiences of God and the world, it would be easy to dismiss her work, as several critics have, as irresponsibly self-absorbed, especially given that Dillard has publicly admitted to being uninterested in writing *about* ethics. In response to Yancey's observation during an interview that she does not write "much about ethics," Dillard's rejoinder is "I don't write at all about ethics. . . . There are lots of us here. Everybody is writing about politics and social concerns. I don't."[164] Eudora Welty complained in her review of *Pilgrim at Tinker Creek* that Dillard "is trying to speak to me out of a cloud instead of from a sociable, even answerable, distance on our same earth."[165] Hayden Carruth calls *Pilgrim* a "dangerous, literally a subversive book," because of its nostalgia "for an abstract past" and its myopic focus on self and nature "with little reference to life on this planet at this moment, its hazards and misdirection."[166] Why doesn't Dillard consider, Carruth suggests, that there might be bull-dozer operators just as focused and destructive as the aphids at Tinker Creek? Pamela Smith labels Dillard's work "ambivalent" and complains, "what seems puzzling is her policy of nonintervention. There is never a hint that she is moved to save whales, contribute to the World Wildlife Fund, protest oil spills, campaign against the destruction of rain forests, push legislation against refrigerants that might expand the ozone hole, or do any other of a sundry of ecologically minded things."[167] Though their points are well taken, such critics mistakenly assume that for a work to be ethical it has to be *about* ethics and therefore take on issues rather than *embody* an ethos of attentiveness to God and others that turns memory into metaphors. In her interview with Yancey shortly after the publication of *Pilgrim at Tinker Creek*, Dillard explained that this was indeed her position:

> As I wrote *Pilgrim*, I kept before me the image of people who were suffering. They were right there in the room as I wrote the book. I could not write a cheerful nature book, or a new version of the argument from design—not with a leukemia patient next

---

notes, is metaphor's capacity for engendering imaginative reciprocity that can compel one to have pity and show mercy when none is warranted. Logic can find no basis for loving one's enemies, but the memory of Egypt's tyrannical cruelty can translate "concrete memory into a universalizing metaphor of reciprocity" and "convert imagination into a serious moral instrument" (Ozick, *Metaphor and Memory*, 278).

164. Yancey, "Face Aflame," 16.
165. Welty, "Meditation on Seeing."
166. Carruth, "Attractions and Dangers of Nostalgia," 637–40.
167. Smith, "Ecotheology of Annie Dillard," 350.

to me. I had to write for people who are dying or grieving—and that's everybody. I can't just write from any fat position.[168]

Memory welcomed the apparitions of those who suffer into Dillard's writing process and offered hospitality to their pain and sorrow.

Dillard's essay "The Deer at Providencia" provides another compelling example of the *ethos* of memory. In the piece, Dillard recounts savoring a lunch of stewed deer meat while she and three fellow North Americans in an Ecuadorian village watch a living version of the deer struggle violently against a rope noose, just yards away from them, tearing and bruising its own flesh in the attempt to free itself. Her male, North American counterparts are surprised by Dillard's silent acceptance of the deer's suffering. Dillard asks them rhetorically (in yet another apostrophe), "Gentlemen of the city, what surprises you? That there is suffering here, or that I know it?"[169] The narrative shifts abruptly from past to present tense, and from Ecuador to Dillard's bedroom, where each morning she combs her hair in a mirror on which she has taped a newspaper clipping. It includes a photograph of the "blackened face of a burnt man," a stranger named Alan McDonald.[170] Dillard states, "I read the whole clipping again every morning."[171] It begins with McDonald's own cry of dereliction: "Why does God hate me?"[172] The reader learns that McDonald spent most of his youth undergoing reconstructive surgery for severe burns he survived as a child. Now he is badly burnt once again.

Dillard's choice to face quite literally McDonald's question and image every morning embodies the ethic of remembering. How does Dillard know there is suffering in the idyllic Ecuadorian jungle? Because she has cultivated the habit of remembering. Daily she reminds herself that there is suffering that defies reason and dogma and that there is no theologically satisfactory answer to Alan McDonald's question of why he should suffer twice what she has never suffered. By holding Alan McDonald in her memory—binding him to her brain like a phylactery, not with leather or string but with tape on the mirror—she has created a metaphor for all the world's inexplicable cruelties, including those suffered by the deer at Providencia. It restrains her, in the end, from stripping McDonald and the deer of their dignity by making issues of what she calls mysteries.[173] There

168. Yancey, "Face Aflame," 17.
169. TST, 82.
170. TST, 82.
171. TST, 83.
172. TST, 82.
173. TST, 83.

are no easy answers, and the anguished cry of confused pain can be heard in the rain forest as loudly as it can be heard in the burn ward. "This is the Big Time here, every minute of it," Dillard concludes. "Will someone please explain to Alan McDonald in his dignity, to the deer at Providencia in his dignity, what is going on? And mail me the carbon."[174]

In summation, memory is a form of attentiveness. To hold or call something to mind is to practice what Simone Weil reminds readers in *Waiting for God* is the spiritual discipline at the heart of love of God and love of neighbor: "Not only does the love of God have attention for its substance; the love of our neighbor, which we know to be the same love, is made of this same substance."[175] Literary works, in their concretization of experience, can paradoxically transform the strangeness and isolation of an individual's experience into shared universals. Consequently, Dillard's texts are not only memorial stones carefully erected by an attentive and inquisitive mind but, as works of art, they are also a literary *shema* through which Dillard summons the reader to become in Scholem's words a "protagonist in the great process of restitution"[176] who is called to help mend the world's brokenness by, at the very least, keeping it in mind. The works invoke readers in apostrophic voice to cultivate the spiritual discipline of attentiveness and the ethical habit of remembering. It could be said therefore that, through Dillard's texts' prophetic appeals to be attentive to God and to remember another's suffering, "mysticism has become *ethos*."[177]

---

174. TST, 83–84.
175. Weil, *Waiting for God*, 114.
176. Scholem, *Major Trends*, 284.
177. Buber, *Origin and Meaning*, 117.

Conclusion

"Who will teach me to write? a reader wanted to know. The page, the page, that eternal blankness, the blankness of eternity"

—Annie Dillard, *The Writing Life*

From Annie Dillard's first writing notebook, dated "Summer 1970" to her research log nearly thirty years later for *For the Time Being*, from her earliest published poetry in 1974's *Tickets for a Prayer Wheel* to her final novel, *The Maytrees*, ample evidence exists for the enduring influence of Jewish mysticism on her literary vision and voice. As this book's analysis has sought to demonstrate in its movement through the overarching themes of creation, evil, and redemption, the symbols and theology of Kabbalistic and Hasidic traditions have profoundly influenced the shape of Dillard's cosmos-spanning meta-narratives. She asks and keeps on asking enormous and difficult questions: what is the relation of Creator to creation, why is there evil and unjust suffering, and who is responsible for redeeming the world's brokenness? In the ecstatic joy of the Hasids who discern beyond the material husk of creation the manifest presence of God's Shekinah, she finds a glorious and robust symbolic rendering of a pansacramental view of God's relation to creation. Shekinah glory can, and does, emerge from debasement. In "the gloomy Luria," whose brilliant and baroque theosophical imagination forged in exilic fires new understandings of *tsimtsum* and *shevirat ha-kelim*, Dillard finds an existential realism and theological elegance that expresses her own convictions about God's exiled presence within a creation whose cruelties continue to stun and perplex her. In the Hasidic mystical tradition of hallowing the "white spaces" of the Torah, one finds striking parallels to

Dillard's passionate theological and aesthetic assertion that gaps, blanks, and silence, both lived and literary, are "the thing." They are the "fertile ground" from which revelation, if and when it comes, will spring. Perhaps most importantly, the Hasidic and Lurianic notion of *tikkun* becomes in Dillard's texts a prophetic summons to mend the world's brokenness now rather than project its mending into a messianic future when "all shall be well." In summation, there seems to be compelling evidence for the claim that Dillard is a *Judeo*-Christian thinker and writer.

In keeping with the spirit of Buber's Hasidism, the mysticism found throughout Dillard's canon is steadfastly rooted in and focused on the grittiness and glory of the corporeal world. Because Dillard is a writer, her tenacious outward and earthly focus on human and creaturely life seems fitting. If she should close her eyes to the world or abandon hope of its ever mediating meaning, what in the world would she write about? Her work of literary theory, *Living by Fiction*, seems to bear this out. Literature, she argues, is the one form of high art that simply cannot transcend or escape referring to the world, in the way much of modern painting, sculpture, and music can, by being about its own surface. "Language is weighted with referents," Dillard insists, and "as soon as [the author] writes the least noun, the whole world starts pouring onto his page."[1] To illustrate the point, she demonstrates that even the most self-referential of modernist fiction, like Vladimir Nabokov's novel *Pale Fire*, lands one squarely back into the world with the first word: "To read *Pale Fire* you need English, you need the world evoked by the English, and you need, especially, the mental dictionary composed entirely of interdefined elements of *Pale Fire*."[2]

More importantly, language is a tool Dillard uses to probe the most challenging metaphysical and existential questions one endures in life. As Dillard explains, the literary arts open "up new and hitherto inaccessible regions."[3] She asserts:

> [Art is] a cognitive instrument, and with religion the only instrument, for probing certain materials and questions. Art and religion probe the mysteries in those difficult areas where blurred and powerful symbols are the only possible speech and their arrangement into coherent religions and works of art the only grammar. . . . If art objects quit the bounds of the known

---

1. LBF, 50.
2. LBF, 51–52.
3. LBF, 167.

and make blurry feints at the unknown, can they truly add to knowledge or understanding? I think they can.[4]

Significantly, the knowledge and understanding such works of art discover are mediated through words and the world, and they are *for* this world. To return to Dillard's rhetorical question asked in *Pilgrim at Tinker Creek*, "What use has eternity for light?"[5] Her answer seems to be "none." Similarly, *Holy the Firm* expresses her conviction that the physical world is the only place where ethics and art mean anything. It is this world that needs the artist's light.

Dillard's affirmation of the cognitive and spiritual power of works of art to illuminate difficult existential and theological issues suggests the arts have a significant role in revitalizing theological discussions. Mark McIntosh's analysis of the historical split between mysticism and theology, in *Mystical Theology*, argues compellingly that if theology is to be revitalized and relevant, it must become reconnected to and grow from authentic experiences with God, not merely discourse about God.[6] Using Buber's terminology found in "The Man of Today and the Jewish Bible,"[7] McIntosh suggests that such spirituality should be conceived of as "encounter with God" and argues that this is "the common ground of spirituality and theology: spirituality being the impression that this encounter makes in the transforming life of people, and theology being the expression that this encounter calls forth as people attempt to understand and speak of the encounter."[8] Theology is indeed one of the grammars at one's disposal for articulating and making sense of those encounters. Art is another. Yet works of art, Dillard seems to suggest, go beyond articulating one's experiences with God and the world; they actually add to them, probing and discovering the unknown.

Moreover, Dillard like McIntosh believes that Western culture has lost (or cast aside) crucial epistemological tools for exploring aspects of life that matter most—love, death, suffering, mystery. Assessing the current cultural landscape in *Living by Fiction*, she concludes that philosophy has abandoned the "wilderness regions" of the human soul "about which we care so much and know so little," and that science's tools simply "do not fit" these "hazardous terrains."[9] Only religion and art remain. Through their use of symbol, "or the structuring of symbols," they may just "render

4. LBF, 164, 166–67.
5. PTC, 81.
6. McIntosh, *Mystical Theology*, 6.
7. Buber, *On the Bible*, 11.
8. McIntosh, *Mystical Theology*, 6.
9. LBF, 170.

intelligible—or at least visible, at least discussible" those hinterlands along "the rim of knowledge where language falters."[10]

Dillard's literary and, one has to assume, moral courage to approach again and again the edge of that rim, as well as her refusal to close theodicean and epistemic spaces with totalizing narratives that present a coherent and ordered world, is perhaps her work's most remarkable achievement. A final example illustrates the point. In Dillard's journal marked "Notebook Ten, May–July 1972," Dillard explains to herself why her poems are "so skinny." She loves the sound "the empty space makes at the end of the line."[11] Both aesthetically and theologically, Dillard valued at an astonishingly early stage of her life and career (she was only twenty-seven) not just the linguistic signification of words but also their power to etch faint traces around a "nothing" that might really be a "something." For Dillard, white space is as pleasing and potent as black letters. By insisting for the duration of her career on the latent potential of theological, epistemic, and textual spaces, she has offered readers not the "wish-deity" Buber warns of but a God who, though personal, remains shattering and wholly Other. The literary *shema* sounded throughout the canon of Dillard's work is a call to prostrate oneself before a terrifying and stunningly magnificent God in holy insecurity. In its doing so, it could be said that her work resists idolatry so that it might engender doxology. She has refused to fashion God after an image constructed from human reason alone; the God of Dillard's literary world therefore remains one worthy of worship. Indeed, her works demonstrate that the "blankness of eternity" tutors willing pilgrims how to praise.

---

10. LBF, 170.
11. Dillard, *Annie Dillard Papers*.

Bibliography

Abood, Maureen. "Natural Wonders." Interview with Annie Dillard. *US Catholic* 64.11 (1999) 30–33.
Atterton, Peter, et al., eds. *Levinas and Buber: Dialogue and Difference*. Pittsburgh: Duquesne University Press, 2004.
Baillie, John. *Our Knowledge of God*. New York: Scribner's Sons, 1959.
Balfour, Ian. *The Rhetoric of Romantic Prophecy*. Stanford: Stanford University Press, 2002.
Bauerschmidt, Frederick C. "The Wounds of Christ." *Journal of Literature & Theology* 5.1 (1991) 83–100.
Benson, Bruce Ellis. *Graven Ideologies: Nietzsche, Derrida, and Marion on Modern Idolatry*. Downers Grove, IL: InterVarsity Academic, 2002.
Bergman, Hugo. "Martin Buber and Mysticism." In *The Philosophy of Martin Buber*, 297–318. Library of Living Philosophers 12. Edited by Paul Arthur Schilpp and Maurice Friedman. La Salle: Open Court, 1967.
Bloom, Harold. *Kabbalah and Criticism*. London: Continuum, 2005.
Brierley, Michael. "Naming a Quiet Revolution: The Panentheistic Turn in Modern Theology." In *In Whom We Live and Move and Have Our Being: Panentheistic Reflections on God's Presence in a Scientific World*, edited by Philip Clayton and Arthur Peacocke, 1–15. Grand Rapids: Eerdmans, 2004.
Brown, David. *Divine Humanity: Kenosis Explored and Defended*. London: SCM, 2011.
Brown-Davidson, Terri. "'Choosing the Given with a Fierce and Pointed Will': Annie Dillard and Risk-Taking in Contemporary Literature." *The Hollins Critic* 30.2 (1993) 1–9.
Buber, Martin. *Eclipse of God: Studies in the Relation Between Religion and Philosophy*. Atlantic Highlands, NJ: Humanities, 1952.
———. *Hasidism and Modern Man*. Translated and edited by Maurice Friedman. New York: Harper Torchbooks, 1958.
———. *I and Thou*. Translated by Ronald Gregor Smith. 2nd ed. New York: Scribner's Sons, 1958.
———. *The Legend of the Baal-Shem*. New York: Schocken, 1955.
———. *On the Bible: Eighteen Studies by Martin Buber*. Edited by Nahum N. Glatzer. New York: Schocken, 1982.

———. *The Origin and Meaning of Hasidism*. Edited and translated by Maurice Friedman. New York: Harper Torchbooks, 1960.

———. *Pointing the Way: Collected Essays by Martin Buber*. Edited and translated by Maurice Friedman. New York: Harper Torchbooks, 1957.

———. *The Prophetic Faith*. New York: Harper & Row, 1949.

———. *Tales of the Hasidim*. New York: Schocken, 1991.

Buechner, Frederick. "Island Journal: Review of *Holy the Firm*, by Annie Dillard." *New York Times Book Review*, September 25, 1977, 12.

Burnett, Michael. "An Interview with Annie Dillard." Interview with Annie Dillard. *Fairhaven Review* (1987) 87–102.

Caputo, John D. *The Prayers and Tears of Jacques Derrida: Religion without Religion*. Bloomington: Indiana University Press, 1997.

Carroll, B. Jill. *The Savage Side: Reclaiming Violent Models of God*. Lanham: Rowman & Littlefield, 2001.

Carruth, Hayden. "Attractions and Dangers of Nostalgia." *Virginia Quarterly Review* 50.4 (1974) 637–40.

Cheney, Jim. "'The Waters of Separation': Myth and Ritual in Annie Dillard's *Pilgrim at Tinker Creek*" *Journal of Feminist Studies in Religion* 6.1 (1990) 41–63. http://www.jstor.org/stable/25002122.

Cladis, Mark. "Stone-Throwers with Excellent Aim: Waking-up to an Environmental Democratic Vision." *Religion and Literature* 40.1 (2008) 81–108.

Clayton, Philip, and Arthur Peacocke, eds. *In Whom We Live and Move and Have Our Being*. Grand Rapids: Eerdmans, 2004.

Coakley, Sarah. "Kenosis: Theological Meanings and Gender Connotations." In *The Work of Love*, edited by John Polkinghorne, 192–210. Grand Rapids: Eerdmans, 2001.

Cobb, John B., and Christopher Ives, eds. *The Emptying God: A Buddhist-Jewish-Christian Conversation*. Maryknoll, NY: Orbis, 1991.

Conway Morris, Roderick. "De Chirico: Painting Landscapes of the Mind." *The New York Times*, February 9, 2007. http://www.nytimes.com/2007/02/09/arts/09iht-conway.4533707.html?pagewanted=all&_r=0.

Cooper, John W. *Panentheism: The Other God of the Philosophers*. Grand Rapids: Baker Academic, 2006.

Copan, Paul, and William Lane Craig. *Creation Out of Nothing: A Biblical, Philosophical, and Scientific Exploration*. Grand Rapids: Baker Academic, 2004.

Culler, Jonathan. *The Pursuit of Signs: Semiotics, Literature, Deconstruction*. Ithaca: Cornell University Press, 1981.

Cunningham, Lawrence S. "Revisiting Tinker Creek: Review of *Pilgrim at Tinker Creek*, by Annie Dillard." *Christian Century* 3 (1975) 768–69.

Dan, Joseph. *Jewish Mysticism and Jewish Ethics*. Northvale: Jason Aronson, 1996.

———. *The Kabbalah: A Very Short Introduction*. Oxford: Oxford University Press, 2006.

———. *The Teachings of Hasidism*. West Orange: Behrman House, 1983.

Davis, Adam. "Sharing the Love," *The Common Review* 6.3 (2008) 56–57.

Davis, Stephen T. "Is Kenosis Orthodox?" In *Exploring Kenotic Christology: The Self-Emptying of God*, edited by C. Stephen Evans, 112–38. Oxford: Oxford University Press, 2006.

DelConte, Matt. "Why *You* Can't Speak: Second-Person Narration, Voice, and a New Model for Understanding Narrative." *Style* 37.2 (2003) 204–19.
DeRoller, Joseph. "Recommended: Annie Dillard." *English Journal* (1983) 89–90.
Dillard, Annie. *An American Childhood*. New York: HarperPerennial, 1987.
———. *Annie Dillard Papers*. Yale Collection of American Literature, Beinecke Rare Book & Manuscript Library, New Haven, CT.
———. *For the Time Being*. New York: Alfred Knopf, 1999.
———. *Holy the Firm*. New York: Harper & Row, 1977.
———. *Living By Fiction*. New York: Harper & Row, 1982.
———. "Official Website." http://www.anniedillard.com.
———. *Pilgrim at Tinker Creek*. New York: Perennial Classics, 1999.
———. *Teaching a Stone to Talk*. New York: Harper & Row, 1982.
———. *Tickets for a Prayer Wheel*. New York: Harper & Row, 1974.
———. "Write Till You Drop." *New York Times*, May 28, 1989. http://www.nytimes.com/books/99/03/28/specials/dillard-drop.html.
———. *The Writing Life*. New York: Harper Perennial, 1989.
Dunn, Robert Paul. "The Artist as Nun: Theme, Tone and Vision in the Writings of Annie Dillard." *Studia Mystica* 1.4 (1978) 17–31.
Elshtain, Jean Bethke. "Review of 'For the Time Being.'" *The Journal of Religion* 80.30 (2000) 541.
Evans, C. Stephen, ed. *Exploring Kenotic Christology: The Self-Emptying of God*. Oxford: Oxford University Press, 2006.
———. "Kenotic Christology and the Nature of God." In *Exploring Kenotic Christology: The Self-Emptying of God*, edited by C. Stephen Evans, 190–217. Oxford: Oxford University Press, 2006.
Farrell, Michael J. "Annie Dillard Demands that We Look Life in the Eye." *National Catholic Reporter* 7 (1999) 29–31.
Feldman, Susan L. "If I Could Tell You." *Northwest Review* 39.1 (2001) 134–39.
Fiddes, Paul. *The Creative Suffering of God*. Oxford: Clarendon, 1988.
Fitzgerald, Karen. "The Good Books: Writers' Choices." *Ms. Magazine* 14 (1985) 80.
Friedman, Maurice S. *Martin Buber: The Life of Dialogue*. New York: Harper Torchbooks, 1955.
Fritzell, Peter A. *Nature Writing and America: Essays upon a Cultural Type*. Ames: Iowa State University Press, 1990.
Genette, Gérard. *The Architext*. Translated by Jane E. Lewin. Berkeley: University of California Press, 1979.
Gerrig, Richard J. *Experiencing Narrative Worlds: On the Psychological Activities of Reading*. New Haven: Yale University Press, 1993.
Goldman, Stan. "Sacrifices to the Hidden God: Annie Dillard's *Pilgrim at Tinker Creek* and Leviticus." *Surroundings* 74.1–2 (1991) 195–213.
Gregersen, Niels Henrik. "Three Varieties of Panentheism." In *In Whom We Live and Move and Have Our Being: Panentheistic Reflections on God's Presence in a Scientific World*, edited by Philip Clayton and Arthur Peacocke, 19–35. Grand Rapids: Eerdmans, 2004.
Hammond, Karla M. "Drawing the Curtains: An Interview with Annie Dillard." Interview with Annie Dillard. *Bennington Review* 10 (1981) 30–38.
Hart, Kevin. *The Trespass of the Sign: Deconstruction, Theology and Philosophy*. 2nd ed. New York: Fordham University Press, 2000.

Heffern, Rich. "The Real Miracle: to Walk on Earth." *National Catholic Reporter*, December 7, 2001, 37–40.

Heschel, Abraham Joshua. *Man is Not Alone: A Philosophy of Religion*. New York: FSG, 1951.

———. *The Mystical Element in Judaism*. Skokie: Varda, 2017.

———. *The Prophets*. Peabody: Hendrickson, 2010.

Idel, Moshe. *Absorbing Perfections: Kabbalah and Interpretation*. New Haven: Yale University Press, 2002.

———. *Hasidism: Between Ecstasy and Magic*. New York: State University of New York Press, 1995.

———. "White Letters: From R. Levi Isaac of Berditchev's Views to Postmodern Hermeneutics." *Modern Judaism* 26.2 (2006) 169–92.

Johnson, Sandra Humble. *The Space Between: Literary Epiphany in the Work of Annie Dillard*. Kent: Kent State University Press, 1992.

Kelleher, Ray. "In the Face of Brutality: Annie Dillard's Unsentimental View of God in the World." Review of *For the Time Being*, by Annie Dillard. *Sojourners Magazine* September 1, 1999. https://sojo.net/magazine/september-october-1999/face-brutality.

Kelley, Andrew. "Reciprocity and the Height of God: A Defense of Buber Against Levinas." In *Levinas and Buber: Dialogue and Difference*, edited by Peter Atterton, Matthew Calarco, and Maurice Friedman, 226–32. Pittsburgh: Duquesne University Press, 2004.

Krauth, Laurie. "Diving into Life with Annie Dillard." Interview with Annie Dillard. *Toledo Blade*, February 14, 1988, F1–2.

Kugel, James L, ed. *Poetry and Prophecy: The Beginnings of a Literary Tradition*. Ithaca: Cornell University Press, 1990.

———. "Poets and Prophets: An Overview." In *Poetry and Prophecy: The Beginnings of a Literary Tradition*, edited by James L. Kugel, 1–25. Ithaca: Cornell University Press, 1990.

Lavery, David L. "Noticer: The Visionary Art of Annie Dillard." *Massachusetts Review* 21.2 (1980) 255–70.

Levenson, Jon D. *Creation and the Persistence of Evil: The Jewish Drama of Divine Omnipotence*. Princeton: Princeton University Press, 1988.

Lewis, Alan. *Between Cross and Resurrection: A Theology of Holy Saturday*. Grand Rapids: Eerdmans. 2001.

Louth, Andrew. *The Origins of the Christian Mystical Tradition from Plato to Denys*. Oxford: Clarendon, 1981.

Maddocks, Melvin. "Terror and Celebration." *Time*, March 18, 1974, 92.

May, Gerhard. *Creatio Ex Nihilo: The Doctrine of 'Creation out of Nothing' in Early Christian Thought*. Translated by A. S. Worrall. Edinburgh: T. & T. Clark, 1994.

McFadden-Gerber, Margaret. "The I in Nature." *American Notes and Queries* 16.1 (1977) 3–5.

McGinn, Bernard. *The Foundations of Mysticism: Origins to the Fifth Century*. Vol. 1 of *The Presence of God: A History of Western Christian Mysticism*. New York: Crossroad, 2000.

McIntosh, Mark A. *Mystical Theology: The Integrity of Spirituality and Theology*. Malden, MA: Blackwell, 1998.

Mendes-Flohr, Paul. Introduction to *Ecstatic Confessions*, by Martin Buber. San Francisco: Harper & Row, 1985.

Moltmann, Jürgen. *God in Creation: An Ecological Doctrine of Creation.* Translated by Margaret Kohl. London: SCM, 1985.

———. "God's Kenosis in the Creation and Consummation of the World." In *The Work of Love: Creation as Kenosis*, edited by John Polkinghorne, 137–51. Grand Rapids: Eerdmans, 2001.

Morrissette, Bruce. "Narrative 'You' in Contemporary Literature." *Comparative Literature Studies* 2.1 (1965) 1–24. http://www.jstor.org/stable/40245692.

Ofrat, Gideon. *The Jewish Derrida.* Translated by Peretz Kidron. Syracuse: Syracuse University Press, 2001.

Owens, Virginia Stem. "Truth through Testimony." *Reformed Journal* 33 (1983) 23–25.

Ozick, Cynthia. *Metaphor and Memory.* New York: Alfred Knopf, 1989.

Peterson, Eugene H. "Annie Dillard: With Her Eyes Open." *Theology Today* 43.2 (1986–87) 178–81.

Pickstock, Catherine. *After Writing: On the Liturgical Consummation of Philosophy.* Oxford: Blackwell, 1998.

Plotinus. *The Enneads.* Translated by Stephen MacKenna and B. S. Page. Grand Rapids: Christian Classics Ethereal Library, 2009.

Polkinghorne, John. "Kenotic Creation and Divine Action." In *The Work of Love: Creation as Kenosis*, edited by John Polkinghorne, 90–106. Grand Rapids: Eerdmans, 2001.

———, ed. *The Work of Love: Creation as Kenosis.* Grand Rapids: Eerdmans, 2001.

Potok, Chaim. Foreword to *Tales of the Hasidim*, by Martin Buber, vii–xv. New York: Schocken, 1991.

Reimer, Margaret Loewen. "The Dialectical Vision of Annie Dillard's Pilgrim at Tinker Creek." *Critique: Studies in Contemporary Fiction* 24.3 (1983) 182–91.

Richardson, Alan. "Apostrophe in Life and in Romantic Art: Everyday Discourse, Overhearing, and Poetic Address." *Style* 36.3 (2002) 363–85.

Robinette, Brian D. "The Difference Nothing Makes: CREATIO EX NIHILO, Resurrection, and Divine Gratuity." *Theological Studies* 72 (2011) 525–57.

Rosenthal, Peggy. "A God's Eye View: Review of *For the Time Being*, by Annie Dillard." *Commonweal* 10 (1999) 28–30.

Rosenzweig, Franz. *The Star of Redemption.* Translated by Barbara E. Galli. Madison: University of Wisconsin Press, 2005.

Roston, Murray. *Poet and Prophet: The Bible and the Growth of Romanticism.* Evanston, IL: Northwestern University Press, 1965.

Scanzoni, Letha Dawson. "Review of *Teaching a Stone to Talk: Expeditions and Encounters*, by Annie Dillard." *Christian Century*, January 5, 1983, 23–24.

Schatz-Uffenheimer, Rivkah. "Man's Relation to God and World in Buber's Rendering of the Hasidic Teaching." In *The Philosophy of Martin Buber*, 403–34. Library of Living Philosophers, edited by Paul Arthur Schilpp and Maurice Friedman, vol. 12. La Salle: Open Court, 1967.

Scheick, William J. "Annie Dillard: Narrative Fringe." In *Contemporary American Women Writers: Narrative Strategies*, edited by Catherine Rainwater and William J. Scheick, 51–63. Lexington: University Press of Kentucky, 1985.

Scholem, Gershom. *Kabbalah: A Definitive History of the Evolution, Ideas, Leading Figures, and Extraordinary Influence of Jewish Mysticism.* New York: Meridian, 1978.

———. *Major Trends in Jewish Mysticism.* New York: Schocken, 1967.

———. "Martin Buber's Interpretation of Hasidism." In *The Messianic Idea in Judaism and Other Essays on Jewish Spirituality*, 227–50. New York: Schocken, 1971.

———. *The Messianic Idea in Judaism and Other Essays on Jewish Spirituality*. New York: Schocken, 1971.

———. *On the Kabbalah and Its Symbolism*. Translated by Ralph Manheim. New York: Schocken, 1996.

Shakespeare, William. *Hamlet*. The Plays of Shakespeare. London: Heineman, 1904.

Smith, Colleen. "Annie Dillard: Tinker Creek's Pilgrim Catholic." Interview with Annie Dillard. *Our Sunday Visitor* 83 (1995) 10–11.

Smith, Linda L. *Annie Dillard*. Twayne's US Authors Series. New York: Twayne, 1991.

Smith, Pamela A. "The Ecotheology of Annie Dillard: A Study in Ambivalence." *Cross Currents* 45.3 (1995) 341–58.

Strasser, Stephan. "Buber and Levinas: Philosophical Reflections on an Opposition." In *Levinas and Buber: Dialogue and Difference*, edited by Peter Atterton, Matthew Calarco, and Maurice Friedman, 37–48. Pittsburgh: Duquesne University Press, 2004.

Stroumsa, Guy. *Hidden Wisdom: Esoteric Traditions and the Roots of Christian Mysticism*. Leiden: Brill Academic, 2005.

Thompson, Thomas R. "Nineteenth-Century Kenotic Christology: The Waxing, Waning, and Weighing of a Quest for a Coherent Orthodoxy." In *Exploring Kenotic Christology: The Self-Emptying of God*, edited by C. Stephen Evans, 74–111. Oxford: Oxford University Press, 2006.

Toohey, Peter G., and Kathleen Toohey. "Giorgio de Chirico, Time, Odysseus, Melancholy, and Intestinal Disorder." Appendix to *Melancholy, Love, and Time: Boundaries of the Self in Ancient Literature*, by Peter G. Toohey, 283–94. Ann Arbor: University of Michigan Press, 2004.

Underhill, Evelyn. *The Essentials of Mysticism and Other Essays*. London: J. M. Dent, 1920.

———. *Mysticism*. 16th ed. New York: E. P. Dutton, 1948.

Vanhoozer, Kevin J. *Remythologizing Theology: Divine Action, Passion, and Authorship*. Cambridge: Cambridge University Press, 2010.

Vanstone, William Hubert. *Love's Endeavor, Love's Expense: A Response of Being to the Love of God*. London: Darton, Longman, and Todd, 1977.

Ward, Graham. *Barth, Derrida, and the Language of Theology*. Cambridge: Cambridge University Press, 1995.

Ward, Keith. "Cosmos and Kenosis." In *The Work of Love: Creation as Kenosis*, edited by John Polkinghorne, 152–66. Grand Rapids: Eerdmans, 2001.

Ward, Koral. *Augenblick: The Concept of the 'Decisive Moment' in Nineteenth and Twentieth-Century Western Philosophy*. Ashgate New Critical Thinking in Philosophy. Farnham: Ashgate, 2009.

Warren, Colleen. *Annie Dillard and the Word Made Flesh: An Incarnational Theory of Language*. Bethlehem: Lehigh University Press, 2010.

Weil, Simone. *Waiting for God*. Translated by Emma Craufurd. New York: Harper & Row, 1951.

Welty, Eudora. "Meditation on Seeing." *New York Times Book Review*, March 24, 1974. http://www.nytimes.com/books/99/03/28/specials/dillard-tinker.html.

Westbrook, Deanne. *Wordsworth's Biblical Ghosts*. New York: Palgrave, 2001.

Wiesel, Elie. *Souls on Fire*. Translated by Marion Wiesel. New York: Random House, 1972.
Wilde, Dana. "Annie Dillard's 'A Field of Silence': The Contemplative Tradition in the Modern Age." *Mystics Quarterly* 26.1 (2000) 31–45.
———. "Mystical Experience in Annie Dillard's 'Total Eclipse' and 'Lenses.'" *Studies in the Humanities* 28.1–2 (2001) 48–83.
Wolfson, Elliot R. "Assaulting the Border: Kabbalistic Traces in the Margins of Derrida." *Journal of the American Academy of Religion* 70.3 (2002) 475–514.
Wroe, Nicholas. "Rachel Whiteread: A Life in Art." *The Guardian*, April 5, 2013. http://www.theguardian.com/artanddesign/2013/apr/06/rachel-whiteread-life-in-art.
Wymard, Eleanor B. "A New Existential Voice." *Commonweal* 24 (1975) 495–96.
Yancey, Philip. "A Face Aflame: An Interview with Annie Dillard." Interview with Annie Dillard. *Christianity Today*, May 5, 1978, 14–19.
Yore, Sue. *The Mystic Way in Postmodernity: Transcending Theological Boundaries in the Writings of Iris Murdoch, Denise Levertov, and Annie Dillard*. Religions and Discourse 43. Edited by James M. M. Francis. Oxford: Peter Lang, 2009.

Index

Aaron, 3n6
Abood, Maureen, 5, 5n12, 7–8, 8nn24–25, 27n1, 38n40, 46n88, 84, 84n1, 87, 87n18, 155–56, 155n71, 156n79, 183
Abraham, 3, 3n6, 99, 149
absence(s), affective. *See* affective absence(s)
Abundance, The, 2n3
Adam, 21, 35, 40–42, 101–2, 104, 104n92. *See also* fall (in Genesis)
affective absence(s), xii, 93, 98, 112, 114–18, 120, 123–24, 126, 128–29, 132, 136
Akiva, 3
Alter, Yehuda Aryeh Leib, of Ger, 107n111, 170
American Childhood, An (*AAC*), 158, 158n97, 185
Amos, book of, 3n6
Angela of Foglio, 31
Annie Dillard Papers, 1–2, 2nn1–2, 13n45, 117n10, 126n45, 167n130, 182n11, 185
apocalypticism, xii, 139–47, 149, 169. *See also* prophet/prophetic voice
apophatic theology. *See* negative theology
apostrophe (literary device), ix, xii, 139, 150–53, 157–62, 160n102, 164–70, 173–74, 177–78
Aquinas, Thomas, 143, 145

Aristotle, 9nn26–27, 12, 70
Aryeh, Yehuda, 3
ascent, xi, 12, 20, 29, 31, 31n15, 37–38, 40–43, 40n50, 45, 47–48, 57–60, 72, 77, 113n135, 142n15, 161, 161n111. *See also* descent
asyndetic style, xi–xii, 60, 83, 84–86, 92, 92n39, 94, 94n48, 110, 114–15, 117, 120, 136
Atterton, Peter, 90n33, 133n88, 183, 186, 188
Augustine, 31

Baer, Dov, 3
Baillie, John, 46, 46n86, 183
Balfour, Ian, 151n53, 157n92, 158n93, 183
Bauerschmidt, Frederick C., 73n41, 111–13, 111nn125, 127, 112nn128–29, 113, 113n134, 183
Becker, Ernest, 3, 56, 167n129
Benson, Bruce Ellis, 133, 133nn87–89, 183
Bergman, Hugo, 30n12, 183
Bethlehem, 3, 57, 59
Blake, William, 151
Bloom, Harold, 11n36, 132, 132n81, 183
Brierley, Michael, 66nn4–5, 69n15, 183
Brown-Davidson, Terri, 156, 156n81, 183

Brown, David W., 68nn7, 9, 11, 75, 75n48, 183
Buber, Martin
   and apocalyptic, xii, xiin4, 143–44, 144n25
   creation, 95, 95nn53–54, 175
   devekuth, 21–25
   Eclipse of God, 89, 89nn24, 26, 91n37, 92n38, 107n110, 112n131, 183
   Hasidism, 3, 6, 8, 10, 13–14n50, 15n61, 21–22, 21n92, 22n102, 25, 32, 32n19, 34, 39, 44, 49, 49–50n105, 51, 51n114, 53–57, 53n126, 54nn132, 139, 56n141, 57n148, 61–63, 88, 88nn20–21, 123n30, 126, 126n44, 130n65, 168–71, 168nn134–35, 169nn136–38, 140, 170n143, 171n147, 175n161
   Hasidism and Modern Man, 19nn82–83, 21n92, 22n105, 25n123, 49nn103–4, 51n114, 53n126, 55nn132, 139, 56n141, 61, 169, 169n137, 183
   "holy insecurity," 86, 88–89, 91–92, 94–95, 98, 106, 114, 128, 136, 182
   I and Thou, 1, 6, 36, 36n33, 61–63, 90–91n33, 107, 107nn107–9, 123n30, 131n70, 135, 149, 150n48, 154n69, 183
   Kabbalism, 2–3, 7, 12n44, 25, 32, 37, 44, 88–89, 123n30, 128–30, 128n56, 168
   Legend of Baal-Shem, The, 15, 15n60, 95n53, 183
   Levinas, Emmanuel, relationship to, 63, 90–91n33, 133n88
   mediation, 12, 61–63
   mysticism, xi, xiii, xiiin5, 1, 15, 15n60, 25, 25n123, 29–30n11, 30, 49–51, 49nn103–4, 49–50n105, 54n130, 55–58, 55nn132, 139, 56n141, 57n148, 60–63, 60n163, 123, 123n30, 128–30, 128n56, 130n65, 131n70, 180–81
   On the Origin and Meaning of Hasidism, xiiin5, 1, 22n102, 25, 25n119, 30, 30n13, 37n37, 41n61, 44nn72–79, 49n105, 88, 88nn20–21, 89n23, 94nn49–50, 98n72, 107n106, 140nn3–4, 151n52, 168nn134–35, 169nn136, 138, 140, 170n143, 175n161, 178n177, 184
   panentheism, xi, 19, 53
   pansacramentalism, xi, 19, 30–32, 30n13, 37, 37n37, 54–55, 55n139, 60–63, 72
   prophecy, xii, xiin4, 130n65, 138–44, 139n1, 140nn3–4, 6, 141nn7–12, 144n25, 150–52, 150nn48–49, 151n52, 152nn58–60, 153n61, 157, 157nn87–89, 165, 165nn121–23, 167, 171, 171n148, 178, 178n177
   shevirat ha-kelim, 21n92, 37
   Prophetic Faith, The, 141, 152, 153n61, 157n88, 162n113, 165, 165nn121–23, 184
   Tales of the Hasidim, 1–2, 15n61, 34, 35n30, 57n148, 126, 126n44, 128, 128n56, 129n57, 170n143, 171, 171n147, 184
   tikkun, 22, 22nn102
Buechner, Frederick, 87, 87n16, 184
Buddhism, 4, 70
Burnett, Michael, 38n40, 46n87, 86–87, 87n12, 92, 92n41, 93n42, 154–55, 155n70, 184

Calarco, Matthew, 90n33, 186, 188
Caputo, John, 132, 132n79, 134n91, 184
Carroll, B. Jill, 4–5, 5n8, 7, 90, 91n34, 133n88, 184
Carruth, Hayden, 176, 176n166, 184
cataphatic theology, 37, 42
Catholicism. *See* Roman Catholicism
Chagall, Marc, 3, 56
Cheney, Jim, 85, 85n6, 184
Chirico, Giorgio de, 99, 99n74
Christ. *See* Jesus
Cladis, Mark, 155, 156n78, 184

clay, 4, 41, 52, 78, 86, 102, 105, 108–10, 108n112, 109n118, 119, 119n21, 125, 141, 149n47
Clayton, Philip, 66, 69n15, 183–85
Coakley, Sarah, 68, 68nn8, 10, 12–14, 73n39, 184
Cobb, John B., 66, 70, 70n21, 184
Colossians, book of, 148n37
Conway Morris, Roderick, 99n74, 184
Cooper, John W., 66n5, 184
Copan, Paul, 103n90, 184
Cordovero, Moses, 11, 175n162
Corinthians, Second book of, 148n37
Craig, William Lane, 103n90, 184
Crauford, Emma, 188
creation, xi, 5–6, 8, 15–20, 26, 42, 84, 86, 102–5, 103n91, 104n92, 105n99, 138, 142n13, 149, 159, 179
　creatio ex nihilo, 102–3, 112n130
　Genesis creation account, 40, 95, 103–4, 103n91, 103–4n92, 106
　Kabbalism and, 11, 15–21, 29, 32–34, 32–33n21, 37, 47–52, 53, 71–72, 79, 96–97, 104–6, 105n99, 110, 112n130, 119–20, 127
　presence of God in, 6, 26, 29, 31–32, 32n20, 37, 138, 179 (*see also* panentheism)
　wonder of, 120, 175
　See also Buber, Martin: creation; evil; Genesis, book of; *shevirat ha-kelim* ("breaking of the vessels"); theodicy
Culler, Jonathan, 151, 151nn50–51, 157, 157nn90–91, 160, 160n103, 184
Cunningham, Lawrence S., 6, 6n15, 184

Dan, Joseph, 9, 9n27, 11n32–33, 13nn47–48, 14n53, 16nn63, 65, 17n69, 19nn79–80, 20nn85, 87–88, 21, 21n98, 22nn100–101, 23, 23nn111–12, 47n91, 55n134, 71n28, 72nn32–33, 104n95, 168n133, 175n162, 184
Dante, 151
David, 3n6
Davis, Adam, 156, 156n86, 184

Davis, Stephen T., 68n11, 184
DelConte, Matt, 162, 162n112, 184
DeRoller, Joseph, 85, 85n7, 184
Dent, J. M., 188
Derrida, Jacques, 63, 90n33, 132–33, 134n91, 135n97, 136
descent, xi, 13, 16, 27–28, 31–32, 31n15, 37, 40–43, 45, 48, 56–57, 59, 64, 71, 77. *See also* ascent
Deuteronomy, book of, 89, 91, 98, 173–75. See also *shema*
devekuth ("devotion" or "fervent clinging" to God), 3, 16, 21–26, 50
Dillard, Annie
　Catholicism of, 1, 5, 7
　criticisms of, 115, 136n100, 139–40, 154n68, 176
　ethical considerations in, xii–xiii, 4, 139–40, 144, 159, 162, 164–65, 168–78
　faith of, 1, 4–5, 142, 146
　imagery in, 18, 31–33, 41n62, 42, 48–49, 58–59, 64, 99n76, 100, 105, 109–10, 119–20n21, 148n42, 149–50n47, 164
　holiness in, 30, 53 (*see also* holiness)
　humor in, 125, 158
　life of, x–xi, 46, 65, 87n13, 92n41, 142, 146, 166–67, 173 (*see also* Annie Dillard Papers)
　Martin Buber's influence on, 1–4, 6–8, 6–7n21, 39, 50n105, 61–63, 86, 126, 126n44, 129n62, 138–39
　mysticism in her work, x–xi, 1–2, 5–9, 13, 27–32, 27n2, 38, 42n63, 45, 66, 78, 130, 179–81 (*see also* Hasidism; Luria, Isaac; Kabbalah/Kabbalism; mysticism; Neoplatonism; Plotinus)
　Papers. *See* Annie Dillard Papers
　reading interests, ix–x, 2–6, 3n6, 6–7n21, 33, 65, 89n28, 96–97n63, 126n44
　scholarship on, 6–7, 29–30n11, 154n68, 176

194 INDEX

Dillard, Annie *(continued)*
  style. *See* apostrophe (literary device); asyndetic style
  theology of. *See* kenotic theology; negative theology; panentheism; pansacramentalism
  works of. *See specific titles*
  writing process, x, 1, 87n13, 116n10, 167n130
Dunn, Robert Paul, 85, 85n10, 185

Eckhart, Meister, 7, 43
Eco, Umberto, 132–34, 134n91, 136n100
Eisenberg, Robert, 3, 56
Eliezer, Israel ben. *See* Tov, Baal Shem (or Besht)
Elijah, 3n6, 96n63
Elisha, 3n6
Elshtain, Jean Bethke, 6n17, 185
Emerson, Ralph Waldo, 4, 7, 126n44
En Sof, 16, 21, 55, 72, 104, 105n98
epistemic space(s), 67, 87, 108n112, 115, 117, 182
epistemology, 5, 64, 87, 92, 94, 115, 117–23, 126, 130, 181–82
Eskimo, 4, 92
Eucharist, 46–47, 66n5, 75, 78
Evans, C. Stephen, 68n11, 184, 185, 188
evil, xi–xii, 5, 8, 15–18, 26, 40n58, 61, 65, 71, 79, 83, 84–85, 92n41, 93, 103n91, 104, 104n92, 105nn98–99, 106–7, 107n111, 108n112, 110, 112, 114, 138, 142–47, 170, 179. *See also* pain; suffering; theodicy
exile, 15–17, 19–20, 32, 33n21, 36, 55, 71–72, 77–80, 83, 86, 118, 142n13, 146, 169n141, 179
Exodus, book of, 3, 56, 136n98, 153, 172
Ezekiel, book of, 3, 3n6, 56, 58, 153
Ezra, book of, 3, 56, 153

fall (in Genesis 3), xi, 11, 40–42, 46, 84, 92n41, 96, 101–4, 103–4n92, 108–11, 118, 124, 144. *See also* Adam

Farrell, Michael J., 6, 6n19, 156, 156n80, 185
Feldman, Susan L., 6, 6n20, 185
Festugière, Père A.-J., 31
Fiddes, Paul, 143n17, 147–49, 148nn38–40, 149nn43–47, 185
Fitzgerald, Karen, 126n44, 185
Fleg, Edmund, 3–4, 56, 172
For the Time Being (*FTB*), x, 2–3, 2n4, 3n5, 4, 6, 6n18, 7n22, 12, 22n103, 28–29, 28n8, 29n10, 32, 33n21, 34n29, 52, 52nn124–25, 56–61, 56n140, 57nn142–147, 58nn152–53, 155, 59nn156–61, 60, 60nn162, 164–65, 64–65, 70, 71nn25–26, 78–79, 79nn64–69, 80nn71, 73–74, 81, 81nn75–76, 79–80, 82, 82nn81–82, 84–87, 84–88, 85n5, 88nn19, 22, 91n35, 92n41, 93, 93n44, 94n47, 97n63, 107n111, 108–11, 108n114, 109n118, 110nn119–23, 111n124, 112n132, 115, 115n1, 116n10, 126, 135, 135n96, 138, 142, 142nn13, 15, 143nn16, 18–23, 144n24, 27, 145nn28–30, 146nn31, 34, 147n36, 148n41, 150n47, 156, 160, 163, 163nn116–17, 164nn118–19, 165n120, 166nn125–28, 167n120, 168–69, 168n132, 169n141, 170nn142–45, 171nn146–47, 149, 174nn157, 159, 179, 185
Francis, James M. M., 189
Friedman, Maurice S., 15n62, 18, 18nn77–78, 19nn82, 84, 22nn104, 106–7, 23nn108–9, 24, 24nn113–14, 30n14, 53, 53n127, 54n130, 90n33, 183, 184, 185, 186, 187, 188
Fritzell, Peter, 87, 87n15, 185

Galileo, 125–26
Galli, Barbara E., 187
Genesis, book of, 3, 40, 40n50, 56, 95, 102–4, 103nn91, 92, 106. *See also* creation; fall

Genette, Gérard, 142n14
Gerrig, Richard J., 160, 160nn102, 104–5, 185
Glatzer, Nahum N., 183
gnosticism, 12, 12n44, 20, 29–30, 32, 33n21, 34–37, 44, 72, 76, 102, 103n91, 168
Goldman, Stan, 6n17, 84–85, 85nn2–3, 185
Goldsmith, Joel, 3
Gregersen, Niels Henrik, 109n118, 185
Griffin, David Ray, 66

Halevi, Abraham, 3
Halevy, Judah, 3
Hammond, Karla M., 5, 5n10, 156n85, 185
Harris, Lis, 3
Hart, Kevin, 132, 132n80
Hartshorne, Charles, 66
Hasidism, xi, xiii, 1–3, 6–11, 13, 13n49, 13–14n50, 15–16, 18–19, 22–25, 29nn9, 11, 32n20, 34n29, 39, 41, 44, 48, 50, 53–61, 54n130, 71–72, 75, 88, 89n28, 94, 96n63, 107n111, 109n118, 117 123n30, 126–27, 132, 134–35, 136n100, 137, 140, 153n62, 168–70, 170n143, 174, 175n161, 179–80. *See also* Buber, Martin: Hasidism; Heschel, Abraham Joshua; Idel, Moshe; Kabbalah/Kabbalism; *nizonot* ("sparks"); pansacramentalism; Scholem, Gershom; Tov, Baal Shem
Hebrews, book of, 113
Hechasid, Yehudah, 3
Heffern, Rich, 6n17, 186
Hegel, Georg Wilhelm Friedrich, 107, 142–43, 143n17
Heidegger, Martin, 63
Hemingway, Ernest, 159n100
Heraclitus, 4
hermeticism, 9n26
Heschel, Abraham Joshua, 2–4, 6, 10, 13, 13n46, 15n61, 32, 56, 79, 80n70, 126n44, 139, 139n2, 151nn54, 56, 153n62, 155, 155nn74–77, 159, 159n101, 162, 162n114, 170, 170n145, 186
holiness, 15, 19–23, 28, 30, 32, 35, 35n30, 37, 39–41, 41n62, 43–44, 46–51, 50n105, 53–56, 53n126, 58–61, 64, 72, 78, 86, 88–89, 91, 94–95, 96n62, 98, 106, 114, 127–28, 130, 134–36, 142, 161, 169n141, 170, 182.
"holy insecurity." *See* Buber, Martin: "holy insecurity"
Holy the Firm (*HTF*), 3, 7n22, 38n43, 46–55, 47nn89–90, 92–93, 48nn94–97, 49nn100–2, 50n112, 51n113, 115–19, 52nn120–23, 53n128, 54nn129, 131, 55nn133, 136–39, 64–65, 67n6, 76nn54–55, 77–78, 77nn57–60, 78nn62–63, 87, 92, 92n41, 93n44, 94n51, 99n76, 106, 106nn104–5, 116n8, 123, 131, 131nn69–72, 142n13, 142n15, 156n85, 160, 160n106, 161nn107–9, 162, 181, 185

I and Thou. *See* Buber, Martin: *I and Thou*
Idel, Moshe, 2, 2n2, 9n27, 10, 10nn28–30, 12n44, 14n50, 15n61, 24, 24n116, 126, 126n43, 127–30, 127nn46–52, 128nn53–54, 56, 129nn58–62, 130nn63–67, 131n68, 73, 132–35, 132nn74, 76, 82, 84, 133nn85, 90, 134nn91–93, 136n100, 186
immutability, 70, 79
impassibility, 70, 75–76, 79, 143
Irenaeus, 102, 103n91
Isaac, Levi, of Berditchev, xii, 126–31, 129n62, 131n68, 132–34, 134n93, 136n100, 137
Isaiah, book of, 3, 3n6, 56, 75, 103n91, 128, 161, 161n111
Ishmael, 99
Islam, 4
Ives, Christopher, 70, 70n21, 184

Jacob, 3n6, 40
Jacopone da Todi, 31
Jeremiah, book of, 3, 3n6, 56, 141, 156, 165
Jesus, 3–4, 20, 31, 35, 41n62, 43, 46–51, 57, 59, 65, 68, 70, 74–80, 82–83, 86, 109–13, 114, 116n8, 119, 120n21, 131, 139–40, 142, 142n15, 144–48, 148n42, 149, 150n47, 161, 168, 171–72, 174, 175. *See also* kenotic theology; Logos; resurrection of Jesus Christ
Job, 3n6, 101
Joel, book of, 3n6
John, Gospel of, 112, 148n42
John of Ruysbroeck, 7
Johnson, Sandra Humble, 6, 92n40, 122, 122n27, 186
Jordan River, 3, 98
Joseph, 53
Joshua, book of, 174
Judges, book of, 3, 56
Julian of Norwich, 7, 46

Kabbalah/Kabbalism, history of, 9–13, 9n27, 11n36, 12n44, 13–14n50
Lurianic Kabbalism, xi, 2–3, 7–10, 17–19, 23–25, 26n124, 29, 44, 54n130, 64, 112n130, 117, 123n30, 126–27, 130, 132, 175n162, 179
pre-Lurianic Kabbalism, 9nn26–27, 11–12, 15
See also Luria, Isaac
Kaplan, Aryeh, 3–4, 56
Keats, John, 160n102
Kelleher, Ray, 6n17, 87, 87n17, 163, 163n115, 166, 166n124, 186
Kelley, Andrew, 91n33, 186
kenosis. *See* kenotic theology.
kenotic theology, xi, 20, 64–78, 68nn7, 14, 72n36, 80–83, 84–85, 96, 104n92, 107–12, 116n8, 120n21, 144n26, 145, 170. *See also* Jesus
Kidron, Peretz, 187
Kierkegaard, Søren, 100
Kings, Second book of, 173
Krauth, Laurie, 155n73, 186

Kugel, James L., 151, 151nn53, 55, 152n57, 186
Kushner, Lawrence, 2–4, 56, 143, 170, 174

Lavery, David L., 6n17, 85, 85n8, 186
Leibniz, Gottfried Wilhelm, 143
Levenson, Jon D., 103n91, 186
Levinas, Emmanuel, 7, 63, 90, 90–91n33, 133, 133n88, 162
Leviticus, book of, 3, 56, 172, 175
Lewin, Jane E., 185
Lewis, Alan, 146, 146nn32–33, 186
Living, The, 65
Living by Fiction (LBF), 5n14, 93, 93nn43–46, 115, 115nn2, 4, 116nn6–9, 158, 158n95, 180–81, 180nn1–3, 181nn4, 9, 182n10, 185
Logos, 11, 74–75, 78, 111–12, 133. *See also* Jesus
Louth, Andrew, 28n7, 31, 31n17, 37n39, 38n42, 42n64, 48, 48n98, 74n46, 186
Lowth, Robert, 151, 151n54
Luria, Isaac, xi, 2, 8–13, 9n27, 14n50, 15–23, 15n61, 26n124, 28–30, 32, 32n20, 32–33n21, 34, 36, 40–41, 52, 53n126, 54, 67, 71–74, 79, 82–83, 85, 96–97, 97n63, 101, 104–11, 105nn98–99, 118, 120–21, 126, 138, 147, 168–69, 169n139, 175n162, 179–80. *See also* Kabbalah/Kabbalism
Lurianic Kabbalism. *See* Kabbalah/Kabbalism; Luria, Isaac

MacKenna, Stephen, 187
Maddocks, Melvin, 156, 156n84, 186
magic, 23, 30, 44, 89, 168
Maimonides, 3, 56
Manheim, Ralph, 188
Marcel, Gabriel, 90n33
Mark, Gospel of, 35, 148n42, 175
Matthew, Gospel of, 116n8, 148n42
Maximus the Confessor, 42n63
May, Gerhard, 103nn88–90, 186
Maytrees, The, 65, 156, 179
McFadden-Gerber, Margaret, 6n17, 186

McGinn, Bernard, 29–30n11, 186
McIntosh, Mark A., 42n63, 181, 181nn6, 8, 186
mediation, 12, 42, 45–47, 59–63, 64, 181
memory, xii–xiii, 75, 101, 138, 140, 172–74, 176–78, 176n163
Mendel, Menahem, 3, 34–36, 35n30, 59
Mendes-Flohr, Paul, 50n106, 186
Merkabah, 31n15, 57–58
Midrash, 3, 56
Milton, John, 151, 160n102
Mishnah, 3, 56
Moltmann, Jürgen, 66, 66n5, 68–70, 69n17, 70nn22–24, 72–75, 73nn38–40, 74nn42–45, 75n47, 81–82, 81n77, 82n83, 103n90, 187
Morrissette, Bruce, 159, 159nn98–100, 187
Moses, 3, 3n6, 89n25, 98, 128, 156, 174
Moses de Leon, 9
mysticism, ix–xiii, 1–3, 5, 7, 13–16, 18, 21, 23–25, 27–29, 29–30n11, 31–34, 37–38, 41, 42n63, 43, 45–51, 53n126, 54n130, 55–58, 60–61, 64, 66–67, 71, 78–79, 85, 114, 123, 123n30, 127–30, 129n62, 131n70, 132–35, 134n93, 136n100, 139–40, 168–69, 169n141, 175n162, 178–81. *See also* Dillard, Annie: mysticism in her work; Hasidism; Luria, Isaac; Kabbalah/Kabbalism; Neoplatonism; Plotinus
myth, 7, 12

nabi. See prophet/prophetic voice
Nabokov, Vladimir, 180
Nachman of Bratslav, 3, 57–58, 60
Nahum, Menachem, of Chernobyl, 3, 52
Nathan of Nemirov, 3, 58
naturalism, 7. *See also* Emerson, Ralph Waldo; Thoreau, Henry David; Transcendentalism
Nazareth, 3
negative theology, 37–39, 41–42, 92n41, 108n112, 127, 133, 134n91

Nehemiah, book of, 3, 3n6, 56
Neoplatonism, xi, 4, 7–9, 9nn26–27, 12–13, 16, 28–29, 28n7, 31, 33, 37–38, 42–46, 48–49, 60, 114, 139. *See also* Plato; Plotinus
Newton, Isaac, 143, 143n17
Nietzsche, Friedrich, 143n17
nizonot ("sparks"), 14, 15n61, 19–22, 19n81, 30, 32–33n21, 37, 39, 41, 47–49, 52–55, 53n126, 61, 64, 72, 79, 104, 107n111, 118, 135, 169n141, 170, 174
Noah, 3

Ofrat, Gideon, 132–33, 132n83, 133n86, 135n97, 187
omnipotence, xi, 20, 61, 64–67, 69–70, 74, 77, 79–83, 84, 96, 103n91, 106–7, 108n112, 110, 143, 145
omnipresence, xi, 65, 69–70, 74
omniscience, xi, 61, 64–66, 69–70, 77, 143
Owens, Virginia Stem, 156, 156n85, 187
Ozick, Cynthia, xiiin6, 3, 140, 140n5, 172, 172nn151–52, 175–76n163, 187

Page, B. S., 187
pain, ix, 38, 65, 76–77, 80, 82, 122–23, 136, 147, 150n47, 156, 177–78. *See also* suffering; violence
panentheism, xi, 19, 52–53, 60, 65–66, 66nn4–5, 69, 69n15, 71, 82, 109n118
pansacramentalism, xi, 4, 26, 32n20, 33, 37, 41, 45–46, 49, 55, 60–64, 78, 109n118, 179
pantheism, 18–19
Papers of Annie Dillard. *See* Annie Dillard Papers
parousia. See return of Jesus Christ
Peacocke, Arthur, 66, 183, 184, 185
Peterson, Eugene H., 135n94, 187
Philippians, book of, 20, 68, 70, 73
Pickstock, Catherine, 94n48, 187
Pilgrim at Tinker Creek (*PTC*), ix–x, 1–3, 6–7, 7n22, 18n74, 28, 32–46, 33nn22–27, 34nn28–29,

Pilgrim at Tinker Creek (PTC) (continued), 35nn31–32, 36n34, 37nn35–36, 38, 38nn41, 43, 39nn46–49, 40nn51–57, 41nn59–60, 62, 42nn65–67, 43nn68–71, 46n85, 49n99, 65, 65n1, 85, 85n4, 86n11, 87, 90, 90nn30–32, 91, 91n36, 92n41, 95, 95nn55–58, 96nn59–61, 63, 97, 97nn65–67, 98nn68–71, 99nn73, 75–76, 100–103, 100nn77–80, 101n84, 102nn85–87, 103–104n92, 105n99, 106nn101, 103, 107–9, 107n111, 108nn112–13, 109n118, 111, 111n126, 113–14, 113nn135–36, 117–19, 117nn11–12, 118nn15–16, 119nn17–20, 121nn23–25, 122–25, 122n28, 123nn29–30, 124nn31–37, 125nn38–42, 128, 128n55, 131n68, 132n77, 135, 135n95, 136n98, 137n101, 142n13, 153–56, 153nn63–66, 154n67, 155n72, 156n85, 174, 174n160, 175n161, 176, 181, 181n5, 185
Pinhas, 3
Plato, 4, 28n7, 31, 48, 74n46, 76, 103n91, 150n47. *See also* Neoplatonism
Plotinus, xi, 7, 11n36, 27, 28–29, 28n7, 31, 38–39, 38n44, 39n45, 43, 45, 187
Polkinghorne, John, 68–69, 68n14, 69nn18–19, 77, 77n61, 81, 81n78, 184, 187, 188
Potok, Chaim, 14n51, 15n61, 20n91, 72n35, 187
Presbyterianism, 5
process theology, 4, 66, 143nn17, 24
Proclus, 37
prophet/prophetic voice, xii–xiii, 1, 3n6, 4–5, 113, 130n65, 138–41, 144, 147, 150–57, 151n54, 151–52n56, 156n85, 159, 162, 167
Proverbs, book of, 3
Psalms, book of, 3, 3n6, 56, 103n91, 161, 161n111

Pseudo-Dionysius, 7, 31, 37–38, 42, 45

qelipot, 22, 32, 34, 104–5, 105n99

Rainwater, Catherine, 187
redemption, xi, 5, 15, 22–24, 26, 32, 46, 67, 80n72, 104, 114, 138, 142n13, 169n141, 170n143, 172, 174, 179
Reimer, Margaret Loewen, 28, 28nn5–6, 85, 85n9, 187
remembering. *See* memory
resurrection of Jesus Christ, xii, 8, 80n72, 139, 142, 142n15, 144–49, 148n42, 171
return of Jesus Christ, xii, 67, 80n72, 144–45
Revelation, book of, 74
Richard of St. Victor, 31
Richardson, Alan, 161, 161n110, 187
ritual, 7, 15n61, 103n91
Robinette, Brian D., 103n91, 187
Roman Catholicism, 1, 5, 7
Romans, book of, 148n37
Romanticism, 4
Rosenthal, Peggy, 6n17, 156, 156nn82–83, 187
Rosenzweig, Franz, 17, 17n68, 90n33, 187
Roston, Murray, 151n53, 187
Rubin, Louis, 92n41

Sachs, Nelly, 3
sacramentalism, xi. *See also* Eucharist; pansacramentalism
Safed (place), 3, 11–12, 15, 175n162
Saruk, Menahem ben, 151n54
Scanzoni, Letha Dawn, 6, 6n16, 187
Schatz-Uffenheimer, Rivkah, 32, 32n19, 49–50n105, 187
Scheick, William J., 92n40, 187
Schilpp, Paul Arthur, 183, 187
Scholem, Gershom, 2–3, 9–14, 9n26, 10n31, 11nn34–36, 12nn37–44, 13n49, 14nn50, 53, 58–59, 15n61, 16–18, 16nn64–65, 17nn66–67, 69–73, 18nn75–76, 19n81, 20, 20nn86, 88–90,

21nn93–97, 99, 23n110, 24–25,
  24n115, 25nn117–18, 120–22,
  29n9, 31n15, 32, 32n19,
  44, 44n80, 49–50n105, 50,
  50nn106–11, 53n126, 54n130,
  55n135, 56, 58n154, 71,
  71nn27–29, 72nn30–31, 34,
  73n37, 97n64, 104, 104nn93–97,
  105nn98–100, 106n102,
  112n130, 121, 121n26, 127n48,
  128n56, 129, 129nn58–59, 62,
  132nn75–76, 169, 169nn139,
  141, 178, 178n176, 187–88
science, 7, 70, 92
Sea of Galilee, 3
Second Coming. *See* return of Jesus
  Christ
Senden, Marius von, 33
Shabbateanism. *See* Zevi, Shabbetai
Shakespeare, William, 124n37, 160n102,
  188
Shalev, Meir, 3
Shekinah, 14, 15n61, 18–19, 21, 32, 34,
  37, 47, 53–55, 61, 71–72, 74–75,
  78–79, 104, 118, 132n76, 135,
  169n141, 179
shema, xii, 95–96, 98, 139, 169, 173–75,
  178, 182. *See also* Deuteronomy,
  book of
shevirat ha-kelim ("breaking of the
  vessels"), xi, 3, 16, 20–21, 26, 30,
  34, 37, 47, 66–67, 71–72, 75–76,
  78, 83, 85, 96, 104–6, 105n99,
  118–19, 121, 132n76, 179. *See
  also* Buber, Martin; creation;
  Luria, Isaac
Singer, Israel Joshua (I. J.), 3
Smith, Colleen, 5, 5n11, 188
Smith, Linda L., 4n7, 6, 188
Smith, Pamela A., 176, 176n167, 188
Smith, Ronald Gregor, 183
sparks. *See nizonot* ("sparks")
stammer, 59–60, 86, 92–95, 98,
  108n112, 110–11, 116–17, 124,
  135, 136, 172. *See also* asyndetic
  style
Steiner, George, 132
Strasser, Stephan, 90–91n33, 188

Stroumsa, Guy, 31nn15–16, 188
suffering, xi–xii, 4, 8, 15n61, 17–18, 26,
  40n58, 61, 65, 71, 77, 79–80, 85,
  96, 107–8, 111, 114, 122, 145,
  148–49, 149nn43, 47, 162, 165,
  181. *See also* evil; pain; theodicy

Tabor, Mount, 4
Talmud, 3, 44, 56, 60
Tarfon, 3–4, 56
Teaching a Stone to Talk (*TST*), 3, 6,
  7n22, 58n150, 65, 89–90, 89n27,
  90n29, 96n62, 116n5, 142n13,
  158, 158n94, 177nn169–73,
  178n174, 185
Teilhard de Chardin, Pierre, 4, 60,
  80n74, 82, 142n15, 143, 145
theodicy, 64–65, 67, 69–70, 76–78,
  80n72, 108, 111–12, 115,
  123n30. *See also* pain; suffering;
  theodicean space(s)
theodicean space(s), xi–xii, 67, 83,
  84–86, 108n112, 111, 114–15,
  182. *See also* theodicy
Thompson, Thomas R., 68n11, 69n20,
  188
Thoreau, Henry David, 7
Tickets for a Prayer Wheel (*TPW*), x, 2,
  32n20, 75, 75nn49–50, 76nn51–
  53, 108, 109nn115–17, 118,
  118nn13–14, 158, 174, 174n158,
  179, 185
tikkun ("mending" or "restoration"), xii,
  3, 16, 21–26, 30, 55–56, 138,
  147, 168–72, 169n139, 180
Tillich, Paul, 81, 143, 147
Toohey, Kathleen, 99n74, 188
Toohey, Peter G., 99n74, 188
Torah, xii, 2, 6, 15n61, 16, 23–25, 60,
  117, 126–32, 134, 136n100, 170,
  179
Torahnic white space(s). *See* white
  space(s)
Tov, Baal Shem (Besht), xi, 2–4, 6,
  13–14, 15n61, 20–21, 25, 28,
  49, 52, 56–57, 61, 72, 79, 85, 88,
  107n111, 138
Tracy, David, 52

Transcendentalism, 4, 53. *See also* Emerson, Ralph Waldo; naturalism; Thoreau, Henry David
tsimtsum ("withdrawal"), xi–xii, 3, 16–20, 19n81, 26, 34, 44, 53n126, 66–67, 71–76, 79, 83, 84–85, 96, 104, 105n99, 106, 109–11, 118–19, 132n76, 179
tzaddik, 10, 24–25, 58

Underhill, Evelyn, 31, 31n18, 45–46, 45nn81–83, 46n85, 188

Vanhoozer, Kevin J., 65, 65n3, 66n5, 68, 73n39, 74n45, 188
Vanstone, William Hubert, 77n56, 188
via negativa. *See* negative theology
via positiva. *See* cataphatic theology
violence, 80, 87, 90, 93n44, 111–12, 135, 147, 177. *See also* pain; suffering
Volosinov, Valentin, 161

Ward, Graham, 63
Ward, Keith, 69n16
Ward, Koral, 100, 100nn81–83, 188
Ware, Kallistos, 66
Warren, Colleen, 6, 142n15, 188
Weil, Simone, 80n73, 82, 110, 126n44, 178, 178n175, 188
Welty, Eudora, 154, 154n68, 176, 176n165, 188

Westbrook, Deanne, 142n14, 188
Whitehead, Alfred, 4, 66, 143, 143n24
Whiteread, Rachel, 120n22
white space(s), xii, 93, 117, 126–32, 134–37, 136n100, 182
Wiesel, Elie, 2, 14, 14nn52, 54–57, 57n148, 58nn149, 151, 135, 135n97, 189
Wilde, Dana, 27–28, 28nn3–4, 189
Wolfson, Elliot R., 132, 132n78, 133n85, 136n99, 189
Wordsworth, William, 151
Worrall, A. S., 186
Writing Life (TWL), The, 87n13, 89, 89n28, 96–97n63, 158, 158n96, 179, 185
"Write Till You Drop," 137, 137n102, 185
Wroe, Nicholas, 120n22, 189
Wymard, Eleanor B., 7, 7n23, 189

Yancey, Phillip, 5, 5n9, 38n43, 46n87, 65n2, 87, 87n14, 173, 173n155, 174n156, 176–77, 176n164, 177n168, 189
Yore, Sue, 6, 6–7n21, 27n2, 189

zaddik. *See tzaddik*
Zechariah, book of, 3, 3n6, 56
Zevi, Shabbetai, 15
zimzum. *See tsimtsum* ("withdrawal")
Zohar, 3, 15, 18, 32, 53n126, 56

www.ingramcontent.com/pod-product-compliance
Lightning Source LLC
Chambersburg PA
CBHW070324230426
43663CB00011B/2207